WOMEN AT WORK IN INDIA

WOMEN AT WORK IN INDIA

A Bibliography

Compiled by

Suchitra Anant
S V Ramani Rao
Kabita Kapoor

Institute of Social Studies Trust

Sponsored by Ministry of Labour, Government of India

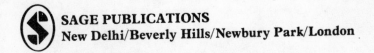

SAGE PUBLICATIONS
New Delhi/Beverly Hills/Newbury Park/London

First published in 1986 by

Sage Publications India Pvt Ltd
M-32 Greater Kailash Market I
New Delhi 110 048

Sage Publications Inc
275 South Beverly Drive
Beverly Hills, California 90212

Sage Publications Ltd
28 Banner Street
London EC1Y 8QE

Published by Tejeshwar Singh for Sage Publications India Pvt Ltd, phototypeset at A K Phototypesetters and printed at Taj Press.

ISBN 0-8039-9512-1 (U.S.)
    81-7036-030-7 (India)

Contents

Section 1

Scope and Coverage of the Bibliography   10
Preface   11
Acknowledgements   14
List of Abbreviations   15
Introduction by **Devaki Jain**   17
Methodology and Arrangement   33

Section II

	Entry No.	
1. Employment Situation	1-121	39
2. Employment Statistics	122-196	54
3. Women Workers : General Studies	197-241	65
4. Women in Industries : General Studies	242-274	71
5. Women in the Informal Sector : General Studies	275-314	76
6. Women Workers : Studies by Occupation/ Industry		82
1. Agarbatti Making	315-316	82
2. Agriculture	317-391	82
3. Armed and Civil Services	392-410	91
4. Banks	411-413	93
5. Beedi Rolling	414-427	94
6. Block Printing	428-429	96
7. Brick Kilns	430	96
8. Cashew Industry	431-432	96

9. Chikan Embroidery 433-434 96
10. Coir Industry 435-437 97
11. Construction Work 438-444 97
12. Dairying 445-454 98
13. Development Work 455-466 100
14. Domestic Work 467-481 101
15. Electronics Industry 482-485 103
16. Firewood Collection 486-487 104
17. Fishing 488-490 104
18. Food Processing Industry 491-495 105
19. Forestry 496-506 105
20. Garment Making 507-513 107
21. Handloom and Handicrafts 514-524 109
22. Hotel Industry 525 110
23. Jute Industry 526-527 111
24. Lace Making 528-532 111
25. Law 533-535 112
26. Leather Industry 536 112
27. Librarianship 537-539 112
28. Literature 540-542 113
29. Management 543-552 113
30. Match Box Making 553 114
31. Medicine 554-572 114
32. Mining 573-578 116
33. Paper Bag Making 579 117
34. Pappad Rolling 580-581 117
35. Pharmaceutical Industry 582-583 117
36. Plantations 584-591 118
37. Rag Picking 592 119
38. Sales Promotion 593-594 119
39. Sanitation Work 595-600 119
40. Science and Technology 601-607 120
41. Sports 608-609 121
42. Stone Quarrying 610-611 121
43. Street Vending 612-615 122
44. Teaching 616-622 122
45. Textiles 623-639 123
46. Transportation 640 125
47. Zari 641 125

7. Women and Political Participation   642-655   126
8. Welfare Schemes for the Economic
    Participation of Women   656-705   129
9. Women and Labour Welfare   706-727   137
10. Women and Labour Legislation   728-743   141
11. Women Workers and Automation   744-778   143
12. Women : Organisation and Unionisation   779-839   149
13. Education and Training of Women   840-886   157
14. Women : Attitudes to Work   887-908   163
15. Women and Multiple Roles   909-1044   166
16. Women and the Household   1045-1073   182
17. Women and Prostitution   1074-1077   187

Section III

Appendix 1 : List of Participating Organisations   191
Appendix 2 : List of Periodicals Indexed in the
    Bibliography   200
Appendix 3 : Select List of Periodicals and Newsletters
    on Women's Studies Published in India   204
Appendix 4 : List of Feminist Book Publishing Houses in
    India   206
Appendix 5 : An Update'   207
Author Index   215
Subject Index   226
Geographical Index   234

SECTION I

Scope and Coverage of the Bibliography

The bibliography covers selected books, periodicals, doctoral theses, research monographs, discussion and seminar papers (both published and unpublished) produced during the post-independence period on Indian women up to December 1985. Chapters in books have not been included. An attempt has been made to include as many unpublished articles and monographs as possible particularly in the unorganised sector. Women's studies journals like *Manushi* and *Samya Shakti* have been indexed in depth for the first time. The bibliography has tried to document literature on new emerging areas of research such as time allocation, debate on women's work, value of household work, enumeration of women in statistical sources, and female-headed households.

Preface

The Institute of Social Studies Trust has been concentrating on investigating the condition of workers in general and women workers in particular, in order to provide more information both to the non-governmental organisations which constitute the women's movement, as also to the Government in its attempts to plan and develop programmes to benefit this section of our society.

In this quest, the Institute has collected data through surveys, and also taken the initiative to organise several types of conferences ranging from purely academic ones, which discuss the findings of reports and the methods by which workers are enumerated, to those on the condition of workers in collaboration with the Government, trade unions and social institutions.

In this process, the Institute collected published and unpublished material on this subject. We received many enquiries from the Government, academic institutions and activists on this issue, its constraints and its possibilities. This led us to develop the idea of preparing a reference work on the working life of poor women. Starting from our own core collection we have tried to include the collection of many other institutions in the country.

Looking at a cross-section of this collection it becomes apparent that women, especially from the poorer classes — but not exclusively the poor — are central, both to the social aspirations of India as also to its economic aspirations. Their contribution in agriculture, industry and services is critical; and the neglect of this identification in employment planning, in designing of technological or social inputs has been one of the prime reasons for the failure in economic achievement.

Similarly, while women play central roles in shaping society and providing the most ethical inputs, this contribution has neither been recognised nor strengthened through social and economic strategies, which, in turn, has brought in another crisis in the Indian social fabric — namely, violence and a break down of moral values.

The condition of poor women has been a major preoccupation of both researchers and activists in India. In looking at this condition, one fact that stands out is the work burden of poor women. The hours of labour that they contribute hardly gets any support either in terms of social inputs like health, education, civic amenities or reduction of the burden of household work; or support in terms of economic inputs like credit, access to raw materials or in education and training programmes. Thus, one has a perception of a poor woman worker in India, compulsively providing cheap labour to the detriment of her health, her family well-being as well as the struggles of the working class. Yet she persists in providing this labour because of an overriding sense of responsibility for the survival sometimes of her family, sometimes of her 'new' family or perhaps even of society.

Thus, a review of literature in this field, however inadequate, would provide the important missing link to those who are concerned about some of the problems of Indian economy and Indian society. A review will also help to identify areas for future research apart from avoiding duplication of research.

Due to the unevenness of the information — its dispersal and sometimes its unavailability for perusal — the format may seem incomplete. However, we are offering this volume as a first step and hope that with participation and response of users, we will be able to bring out a more professionally complete second edition. We also hope that this will encourage communication among those who are interested in the field of women's work.

While classifying the items, we faced certain difficulties which were posed by the very lively debates on the standard definitions and classification used by economists and statisticians. For example, many of us who have worked closely with, or studied, women workers such as beedi rollers, vegetable vendors, and head loaders, would not agree that they belong to either the 'informal sector' or the 'unorganised sector'.

There are extremely formal rules that operate in all these occupations if formality is defined or denoted as the method by which labour is linked to the employer.

The women's movement is trying to press for the recognition of various types of workers, such as home-based workers, as full-fledged workers deserving labour legislation. In other words, the women's movement is trying to bring the theoretical and legislative system closer to reality in a socio-economy like ours.

Thus in presenting this bibliography we have not used the categorisation that we would like to challenge but have used the categorisation that we would like to recommend. This classification may create some difficulties for those who are used to the conventional categories but we think it is necessary to establish the reality.

January 1986

Suchitra Anant
S V Ramani Rao
Kabita Kapoor

Acknowledgements

We gratefully acknowledge the contribution of many friends and colleagues who have helped us in the preparation of this bibliography. Our special thanks are due to H C Jain, Librarian, South Campus, Delhi University, for his technical advice and Shikha Goel, Malini Chand Sheth, Mridula Udaygiri, Sudha Rao, Kalpana Kannabiran and Pushpa Rani for their assistance in compilation. We would like to mention the support, cooperation and guidance we received from the researchers—Vina Mazumdar, Bina Agarwal, Maithreyi Krishnaraj, Anila Dholakia, S Bharat, U Kalpagam, Gita Sen, Rajammal Devdas, Asghari Mohiuddin, Nirmala Banerjee, Zarina Bhatty, Viji Srinivasan and Madhu Kishwar; the librarians—Mani Subrahmanyan, Kalpana Das Gupta, S P Agarwal and S P Kulshresht; and officials at the Labour Ministry—Anil Bordia, Girija Eswaran and Meena Gupta. Our thanks are also due to Rekha Bezboruah and Vimala Sethi for editing the text. The typing for this bibliography was unending as it was composed in spurts. Our gratitude to Madhu Garg and Neeru Bala for their efforts. Above all, we thank the Labour Ministry for sponsoring the compilation of this bibliography.

List of Abbreviations

AERC	Agro-Economic Research Centre, Andhra University
AILS	Ambekar Institute of Labour Studies
AIWC	All India Women's Conference
ALHSCW	Avinasilingam Home Science College for Women
AUL	Andhra University Library
BUL	Bombay University Library
CDS	Centre for Development Studies
CED	Centre for Education and Documentation
CIRTPC	Central Institute of Research and Training in Public Cooperation
CSE	Centre for Science and Environment
CSSS	Centre for Studies in Social Sciences
CRL, DU	Central Reference Library, Delhi University
CWDS	Centre for Women's Development Studies
DSSW	Delhi School of Social Work
DST	Department of Science and Technology
GIDS	Giri Institute of Development Studies
GUL	Gujarat University Library
IAMR	Institute of Applied Manpower Research
ICSSR	Indian Council for Social Science Research
IEG	Institute of Economic Growth
IIM	Indian Institute of Management
IIPA	Indian Institute of Public Administration
ILO	International Labour Organisation
ISI	Indian Statistical Institute
ISST	Institute of Social Studies Trust
JL	Jayakar Library, Poona University

JNU	Jawaharlal Nehru University
LICL	Lady Irwin College Library
LML	Labour Ministry Library
LU	Lucknow University Library
MIDS	Madras Institute of Development Studies
MSSW	Madras School of Social Work
MUL	Madras University Library
NCAER	National Council for Applied Economic Research
NIEPA	National Institute of Educational Planning and Administration
NIPCCD	National Institute of Public Co-operation and Child Development
NIRD	National Institute of Rural Development
NISTADS	National Institute of Science, Technology and Development Studies
NL	National Library
NLI	National Labour Institute
NML	Nehru Memorial Library
NN	Nirmala Niketan
PC	Planning Commission
PU	Punjab University
RDAS	Rural Development Advisory Services
RTL	Ratan Tata Library
RUWS	Research Unit on Women's Studies, SNDT Women's University
SEWA	Self Employed Women's Association
SIDA	Swedish International Development Authority
SISI	Small Industries Services Institute
SNDTU	Shreemathi Nathibhai Damodar Thackersay University
SOWSTUD	Society for Women's Studies and Development
SPIESC	Sardar Patel Institute of Economic and Social Change
SSDC	Social Science Documentation Centre
TISS	Tata Institute of Social Sciences
WL	Women's Library
WWF	Working Women's Forum

Introduction

Purpose of Bibliography

Bibliographies are usually prepared to fill an academic need — and are especially useful for libraries. But this bibliography has been initiated and compiled for a different reason — to fill the enormous information gap on the nature of the work of women, the centrality of their economic contribution and the crisis in their lives.

Myth and ignorance cloud and confound the profile of women everywhere, including India. The myth is difficult to deal with but the ignorance can be tackled. In compiling this bibliography we found that there is, in fact, a great deal of information both macro and micro, qualitative and quantitative. However, it has not been put together in forms and formats that are useful for those who would like to undo the ignorance and present the reality to contradict the myth.

For example, unpublished dissertations can provide a wide base of information on women workers in the unorganised sector. Similarly, if all the micro studies of women workers in poverty households are brought together under different categories they may provide an alternative, more accurate macro picture of the situation of women workers and their employment. The categories under which such presentation of data can be made are, for example, impact of development; wage and working hours; differentials in health, education; energy expenditures and inputs and so forth. Such mapping of the data is necessary as there is a strong conviction among those who are working in the field of women's studies that the macro data does not reveal the real quantities in relation to women not only because of failure of the methodology of investigation but also because of the respondent's self perception.

This bibliography could provide the resource base, the data bank for facilitating those who would like to attempt such exercises. The bibliography could provide a short cut and there is a need for a short cut. Those who have been studying the condition of women especially amongst the very poor in India, feel a sense of urgency as they perceive the survival crises in the lives of these women. They see that these women are losing their place in the job market. They are often nutritionally deprived — and they are not yet sufficiently organised to make a noise about their condition.

It is a good sign that there are many users for this knowledge in India — women themselves, belonging to activist organisations as well as social and development delivery organisations; government agencies as well as policy-makers which includes social scientists.

The bibliography has been presented under different headings— even though they may not be entirely satisfactory categories. For example — the use of the term 'informal sector' is rejected by us as studies now reveal that the employer-employee relations in this sector are as formal as in the so-called 'formal sector'. The dynamics of the organisation of production and exchange are structured with well established procedures. Using the term 'informal sector' has tended to distract those interested in providing appropriate legal and other management cover for this sector. Yet we have had to use the term informal sector because it is 'current language' and, therefore, a medium of communication.

In other cases, the classifications may overlap but yet have to be used. We hope that researchers will go beyond this classificatory system and through this bibliography develop a more meaningful classification of the situation of women workers and women's employment.

The Employment Situation

Most studies indicate that the majority of Indian women work — i.e., they are engaged in some regular economic activity — and yet they form the majority of those who are seekers of work. This paradox can be explained if we look at the issue as a crisis in the lives of poor women. The majority of these women are acutely underemployed

—their wages are low, the work is not adequate and yet they must work in order to bring in some real or monetary income every day. These women are often the sole supporters or primary bread winners in their family. It is their income which provides the survival for the family. Since they are in low skilled, low paid jobs, they are the first to be disengaged from employment as soon as 'modernisation' takes place. They are silent not only in statistics but also in terms of their voices. They are not yet in a position to reveal their conditions and its implications. They are not organised. They are the most nutritionally deprived. One of the most important objectives of an employment policy for women in India would have to be how to safeguard and strengthen their existing work sources or employment sources.

In analysing employment, whether it is women's employment or the general subject of employment, it is customary to classify or categorise it, even for policy purposes, in the following ways :

Rural/Urban
Sectoral — primary, secondary, tertiary, i.e., agriculture, industry, transport and services
Organised/Unorganised — similar to formal/informal
Public/Private sector
Large/Small-scale

It is also customary in each case to look at trend differentials in male and female participation rates, and wage differentials. A whole area of concern is skill and training for employment and so on.

However, there is another categorisation which is more appropriate for looking at broad-based policies with special reference to women's employment and also to provide an umbrella to the categories listed above. These are (*a*) safeguarding and strengthening existing employment and (*b*) promoting new durable employment.

The implications of this analysis for policy, for example, if the aim is to safeguard women's employment, could be listed as :

1. A new view would have to be taken of technical research and technical management. Wavs and means have to be found of safeguarding women's existing employment without necessarily forfeiting technical progress.
2. New forms of organisations of women workers have to be

evolved which assist them both to preserve their employment and also in absorbing new trends.

3. New concepts in economic theory would have to be developed to resolve the so-called conflict between women's employment needs and, say, export needs, i.e., foreign exchange needs or growth and productivity goals. Thus both government and research and development institutions need to do exercises which would be helpful in appraising investments and technical changes in such a way that the cost of women losing jobs is properly evaluated against what are considered national budgetary gains.

4. Similarly new types of programmes and projects need to be designed which take up specific categories of women workers, review their existing conditions, anticipate the impact of new development or technology strategies, and resolve conflicts through interventions where neither goal is sacrificed, i.e., neither women's livelihood nor national output.

If the other aim is to promote new employment, then another list of possible policies would be :

1. In terms of new employment avenues in agriculture, post harvest storage and distribution of foodgrains offers massive employment potential especially because of the new *grain* surplus in India.

2. Agro-based industries—food production/processing and sale—specially new foods such as health foods, processed foods and vegetables, have potential for development. Similarly forest-based industrial products such as trays, baskets should be developed.

3. Non-farm employment such as handloom and handicraft need enormous attention both for safeguarding existing employment as well as developing organisation and training for strengthening the employment.

4. In construction, the greatest need is infrastructure, namely, food, child care, water facilities on sites. In other words, a basic need input in order to make the women workers healthy and productive.

Statistics

The NSSO continues to be the sole agency to produce (at all India and state/union territory level) comprehensive and detailed data on employment and unemployment levels and related variables such as wage/salary income, and consumption levels, through its quinquennial series of surveys on labour force beginning from 1972–73. The unorganised sector is covered in this series of surveys as well as in ad hoc sectoral surveys. The 32nd Round Survey (1977–78) has collected some useful information relating to the attitude of household women towards work and assistance needed. A special coverage of rural labour households (Labour Bureau's earlier series of Rural Labour Enquiries) is a new feature of the labour force survey series from the 32nd Round.

The decennial population census is another valuable source for providing certain basic socio-economic data down to the village level. The available results of the 1981 Census indicate stability in the measurement of main workers and a satisfactory coverage of marginal workers.

The DGE and T and the Labour Bureau under the Ministry of Labour continue to function as the data bank in respect of statistics relating to the organised sector and various labour laws respectively. They also conduct ad hoc field studies on selected topics.

The Annual Survey of Industries (CSO) also provides sex-wise employment and emoluments data in respect of large factories at three digit industry level. The economic census, 1977 and 1980, can also furnish disaggregated data on female employment in the sectors covered.

Some organisations under state governments, autonomous research institutions and individual research workers have been conducting micro studies concerning the socio-economic characteristics of workers in various context. The NCAER with the concurrence of the Steering Committee on Women's Employment set up by the Planning Commission in 1982 is currently carrying out a study on a sub-sample of NSS sample households for the 38th Round Survey on employment and unemployment to effectively measure the economically gainful activities in which women might be engaged in a regular or sporadic manner adopting the time allocation methodology.

Employment in the Organised Sector

Trend analysis of Indian data in employment suffers both from definitional change as well as the deeper problem of netting non-monetised as well as other forms of invisible work. There is an indication that the proportion of women engaged in service/occupation is much higher compared to the proportion of males in urban areas. The increase is primarily due to women working as nurses and teachers. The bulk of the labour force is in the unorganised sector with a preponderance of self-employment since the absorptive capacity of the organised sector is extremely low. Only about 12 per cent of the increase in the labour force is absorbed in the organised sector.

During the period 1977–82 the public sector accounted for 74 per cent and 70 per cent of the total increase in women's employment. The bulk of the increase was in the service sector. Manufacturing, transport and communication recorded only a fair amount of increase. A disturbing trend in women's participation in agriculture during the last decade is the progressive shift from the cultivator to the labourer status. The rise in the ranks of women agricultural labourers from less than one-third of the female work force in 1951 to more than half in 1971 points to the shrinking employment opportunities in family forms and the growing pressure on women to resort to wage labour often under exploitative conditions.

The trend in the employment of women in the public sector and organised private sector since 1971 indicates that the percentage of women employed in the private sector has been higher than that in the public sector; but the growth of employment in the private sector has been tardy. The average annual growth rate in the employment of women during 1971–82 was 5.7 per cent in the public sector and 2.0 per cent in the private sector. Corresponding rates in the total employment of the entire organised sector have been growing at an annual rate of 2.8 per cent and women's employment at 3.8 per cent.

The available comparable results from the 1971 and 1981 Censuses have classified the main workers as cultivators, agricultural labour, household industry workers and others. The main work participation rate in case of rural females had shown a marked rise in the 1981 Census as compared to the previous one.

Unemployment

Some statistics on unemployment and underemployment among women are contained in the results of the NSS 27th Round (1972–73) Survey. Though the 32nd Round (1977–78) Survey results are now available these cannot be utilised to obtain a reliable idea of the changes in the unemployment situation during the five year interval because of changes in the definition of usual status and in the classification of activities.

Some additional information collected in the NSS 32nd Round on the basis of probing questions included in the survey for the first time illustrates the pattern of work acceptable to women usually engaged in household duties and connected marginal activities.

In the present socio-economic situation a majority of women have little to choose but to stay outside the regular labour force and keep confined to household duties. The economically weaker sections among them are forced to take to very low productive activities to minimise the burden of livelihood. These and others engaged in household enterprises keep on shifting from one status to another in terms of standard classification : work status, unemployment status and outside labour force status — often two statuses overlapping at a time. The line of demarcation between household work and economically gainful activity is often too thin to be discerned through usual field enquiries. Hence the measurement of work in respect of a large majority of women continue to distort the results of field surveys.

The current concepts of marginal/subsidiary workers adopted by the NSSO and the Census is based on a time criterion applied to a long reference period like one year. Within this concept, there could be wide variation in the economic nature and content of the work done as well as the duration of such work. Similarly, even the main worker engaged in certain unorganised activities could be variously interpreted. The stability of these concepts is perhaps still to be tested.

Women in Industries

As far as the research areas are concerned, women in the organised sector especially in industries have been studied by quite a few researchers. There are a series of studies conducted by the Labour Bureau of Simla and Chandigarh highlighting the role played by women in many industries both in the organised and unorganised sectors. The surveys have also highlighted the kind of exploitation women have to undergo in both these sectors, and the fact that women perform unorganised roles even in the organised industry. The inadequacy of labour laws to provide protection and support services has been an issue of concern. Two studies of women workers in the free trade zones reveal that women are the dominant percentage of the workers in these zones.

Several micro studies reveal that there is a systematic difference in male and female earners. Operations that fetch higher wages are considered male preserves, and those in which women constitute a higher proportion of the work force bring lower wages to women. This is revealed in small-scale industries as well. Women are assigned unskilled work and are paid less even amongst the educated classes. In the organised sector, studies reveal that professional and skilled workers report lower remuneration for equal work as being one of the main problems faced by them. 90 per cent of the women are employed in unskilled and semi-skilled jobs. In the urban informal sector some of the lowest paid occupations have a disproportionately high percentage of women. Due to the prevalence of certain attitudes, female labour often respond differently from male labour, not only to offers of employment, but also to various other institutional arrangements. When women perceive their work as less valuable than men they cannot insist on the exercise of their right both to have to work as well as to earn an equal wage.

Women in the 'Informal Sector'

Earlier literature surveys highlighted the gap in data on the unorganised sector. This is now being filled by several in depth as well as extensive studies done by researchers, activists and the Labour Bureau. Since some of the Labour Bureau surveys are not women specific they have not been included in this bibliography. The informal sector, as revealed by the studies, is characterised by discrimination in wages, exploitation and harassment by middlemen, inadequacy of market links and lack of organisation. The emergence of middle class women entrepreneurs has been a recent phenomenon. These women are usually educated and organised and hence are able to get a better deal than their sisters in the informal sector. A majority of the studies in the informal sector are on women in agriculture. Almost all the rice and wheat cultivating areas of India have been studied extensively.

Case studies of women workers in milk production underline the physical burden faced by women workers and the lack of attention paid to the needs for easier access to water, fuel, child care and health facilities. The emergence of dairy cooperatives has been an important phenomenon noticed in quite a few states in India. These have been formed as a result of the spontaneous desire of women to organise to get better value for their products.

Studies done of beedi workers, stone crushers, cart pullers, as well as those specifically of occupational hazards reveal the arduous nature of women's work. The variation within the household in economic and social roles between men and women and its implication of receiving and giving to development by them has been documented by many studies.

Political Participation

Women's participation in the freedom movement and in public life has been documented by political activists and some researchers. Research studies are relatively few and most of them focus on the voting behaviour of women.

Welfare Schemes for the Economic Participation of Women

Evaluation of many of the economic schemes have revealed that the provision of small micro opportunities for women, which are usually classified as income generating projects, can make only a marginal dent on the strong and widespread need of women for gainful employment. Thus it is in mainstream agriculture, non-farm rural employment, including construction, and in the industry and services sector, specially as self-employed, that women have the basic opportunity for income earning. The lack of perception of women as a separate category of labour is most common in the poverty eradication programmes not only in India but elsewhere too. It is based on the assumption that labour especially from unskilled destitute classes can be treated as homogenous for analysis planning. It is more common to classify labour as under-employed, unemployed, below poverty line, seasonally employed, etc. Within these categories it is not considered necessary to underline the basic difference in terms of sex.

Labour Welfare

Most of the studies have indicated the lack of support services for women when they go out of their homes to work. Employers shirk from employing women on a regular basis because of the benefits/support services that they are supposed to provide under the Factories Act. This has led to women remaining as ad hoc and unorganised workers. Studies have also highlighted the health hazards faced by women in certain industries and the total apathy of the employers to provide safety measures.

There is an increasing recognition that hostels have to be constructed for working women, especially single women. A few studies have evaluated the working of such hostels and have provided an overview of the kind of problems that are involved in running them.

Studies conducted on access to credit facilities for low income earning women highlight a central problem faced by them — that they have no security to offer. The problems faced in extending credit to women are socio-economic. Attitudes to women do not allow them to take up independent economic ventures. Further, women are largely unaware of existing credit facilities, or physically unable to reach banks, particularly in rural areas. Where banking institutions exist, women, again especially in rural areas, are reluctant to approach them because they are unfamiliar with their policies and cumbersome procedures. Another obstacle, which is now sought to be changed, is the tendency of banks to finance large enterprises rather than small ones. This is a disadvantage to women as they tend to be involved in small enterprises.

Legislation

Studies on labour legislation reveal that though new laws are being formulated to improve the situation of women workers, there is a need to look into the existing laws and ensure effective implementation. Slackness in implementation of labour laws has led to exploitation of women workers especially in fish processing industries, agriculture, etc.

Women Workers and Automation

An issue that is causing concern in India is that the opportunities for women in the labour market are declining instead of increasing. Marginal improvements in sectors like electronics have been more than negatively compensated by the decline in other sectors. Yet from the data available, it is obvious that women are not only in need of employment but are going to any length to bring home a subsistence earning.

The impact of mechanisation on women's lives in Punjab has been studied in great detail and an attempt has been made to explain the low participation of women in agriculture. The issue of mechanisation has been taken up by many women's organisations who find that women are being displaced by the introduction of machines, for example, tobacco workers of Nipani.

Women: Organisation and Unionisation

Most of the studies on the issue of women's employment have pin-pointed the importance of organising women workers. Trade unions, usually dominated by men, have not taken as much interest in the unionisation of women workers. Yet those who have successfully organised women workers have found that this has not only strengthened and increased women's income through wage struggles and by the provision of backward and forward linkages, but has also provided forums for opinion formation. These forums have been effective on many issues such as :

1. Resistance against changes in technology which could create loss of employment.
2. Appeals for improving legal services to safeguard women's rights.

3. Reduction of occupational and health hazards.

Thus organisation of women workers built around occupational and other entry points is a critical need.

Education and Training of Women

If women have to be a part of the mainstream of future development, new avenues would have to be thrown open to them. There would have to be an upgradation of skills. Technical, financial and marketing supports would have to be extended to them. There would not only have to be a large investment in their training but training itself would have to be far more innovative and diverse in character. For instance, women who now migrate long distances in search of earning opportunities need to be trained in work which they could get nearer home. Thus the demand pull sectors of production would have to be identified and training organised.

Further, women in rural areas participating in agriculture, such as growing crops, need to be trained not only in new technologies but also in related fields such as fertiliser feeding into the fields, spraying of pesticides, treatment of seeds, and repair of pumpsets. Training of farm women in prevention of grain loss and food processing is useful but not necessarily an income earning activity. In the non-farm sector there are many new demands in rural areas in the field of extension which provides another area for training. Rural industry is dominated by women in the cottage sector. Yet training institutions do not have the facilities to absorb women as it is not a part of the overall design of rural industrialisation. Vocational training institutes tend to concentrate their curriculum for women in activities such as cutting and sewing, secretarial services and beauty care. Organisations working with the poorest women have pointed out how the majority of rural and urban women prefer to be trained in more demand-oriented skills like watch repair, plumbing and light engineering.

Women and Multiple Roles

The multiple roles performed by women have been much studied and many of the doctoral theses are on the familial problems of working women, performance of dual roles, rearing of children, decision-making, etc. Studies on how women cope with stress and use their leisure time has been investigated by some researchers. The change that new technology has brought into women's lives and the way it has affected their work at home and the different tasks performed by them has been examined. Many studies have emphasised women's participation in various economic activities especially in rural areas. The issue of women being nutritionally deprived even though they work as much as men, because they do not get an equal share of food has been pointed out by many studies on nutrition. Role conflict and the problems of single working women such as accommodation, transport, and marriage have also been subjects of research in many universities. One of the main issues in women's studies has been female-headed households. Census data usually gives the percentage of female-headed households as 10 per cent and the primary cause for their occurrence as widowhood. Available data shows that there are more female-headed households among the poorest and the reasons are not only widowhood, but also male migration and abandonment. It has been found that female-headed households have not been able to utilise the development benefits and in most cases they end up as destitutes.

Women : Attitudes to Work

Opinion surveys of working women point to the fact that working women have been losers both at home and at the place of work. Most of the middle class working mothers live with a guilt feeling that they are not able to provide enough care and security to their children. Studies on working mothers highlight this problem. Studies of attitudes of educated women indicate that they prefer white-collar jobs and would prefer to work as teachers.

Women in the Household

Providing infrastructure becomes important once the role of the household is recognised as a 'releaser' and 'inhibitor' of female labour supply. The household contains within it characteristics that provide much of the impetus or inhibition towards female labour participation or to the emergence of women in the labour force. Those policies which unlock the household would automatically provide the key to female entry into the labour market.

While the demand pulls expressed in employment opportunities, training and raising of awareness are vital factors, they are not in themselves sufficient to bring about the kind of responses from female labour that is noticed among male labour. Yet poverty presses them into *unaccounted productive work*, free-collection of goods for themselves or wage employment — which is irregular, underpaid and physically strenuous. With deforestation collection of fuel for home consumption has become a difficult task. Studies on the allocation of time reveal that women spend very long hours fetching fuel and water which, though strenuous, is not recognised even as work. The debate on house work has reached an interesting stage where researchers have tried to quantify house work and have also assessed its contribution to the gross national product.

Women in Prostitution

Many studies indicate that economic necessity and employment have driven women, especially tribal women, into prostitution. Though most of the studies included in this bibliography pertain to tribal and hill women, it can be said to be partly true for women belonging to other classes and groups as well. Studies and action programmes with tribal women reveal the special problems linked to culture. They usually hold forest-based occupation and deforestation and forest use by industrialists as well as forest preservation by axe have all added to their economic stress.

Review

It is extremely important that the implications of the differential impact of development on the basis of gender and age be analysed in greater detail. This differential impact not only causes problems in our attempts at achieving the goals of equality but it also creates structural imbalances due to the invisibility of certain economic transactions. This invisibility often presents a barrier to those who are committed to social justice and to the eradication of poverty.

Unfortunately, sufficient data which can provide some sharp indicators to policy-makers is not yet available. Some hypotheses that require statistical analysis are given below. They could be diagnostic studies:

1. That fast growing agricultural areas or areas with fast growing agricultural output tend to accentuate certain types of inequality. For example, an increase in the percentage of landless labourers has been noticed in a study of six of the granary districts of Andhra Pradesh.
2. That provision of social infrastructure to the poor, such as that provided by the basic needs basket constitutes the minimum conditions for the utilisation of the economic poverty programmes by the poverty households. In other words, inputs such as health, education, fuel and water, provide the critical mass to the poor especially to women and children if they are to benefit by the economic progress. This input will increase the value of human capital.

Apart from such macro hypotheses which can only be tested through careful presentation of available data, another area which is being discussed is the impact of technological change on employment (for example, mechanisation of tobacco, textile, and so on). What is needed is not merely the numbers lost and gained but an exercise to see the implications of loss of wage work against the gains in productivity or quality exports. In other words, new concepts, new indices for calculating benefit costs of the introduction of new technologies in an employment surplus labour market. Such diagnostic representation of existing information of building new conceptual frameworks is still to be done and can be done with existing information.

The perception of women especially poor women in the overall economy of India has to change from being only targets of health and social welfare programmes to being beneficiaries of investment and developmental programmes. Policy-makers believe that women have to be given a greater share of development benefits. However, women are already playing central roles in production and distribution and what they need is strengthening of these roles. Data and analysis are needed to legitimise as critical, and as high priority, the provision of support services to these workers and to perceive them as not only marginal and supplementary but as central. The aggregation of documents in this bibliography, we hope, will provide proof of this centrality of women in the economic profile of India.

DEVAKI JAIN

Methodology and Arrangement

Initially this bibliography was thought of as a listing of documents but during the course of compilation it was decided to add brief annotations. Annotations have been added to entries with fanciful titles, titles which are not very explicit and to unpublished documents which are not easily accessible. Annotations have not been provided for those that were not readily available for consultation. The annotations are purely descriptive for purposes of classification and categorisation. The location of documents available in specific libraries and institutions has been provided.

During the first phase of the compilation of the bibliography several letters were sent to various institutions, university libraries and women's organisations. While some libraries sent us detailed lists, including doctoral theses, some of the women's organisations invited us to visit their institutions. One of the compilers visited various institutions and women's organisations in twelve major cities in India and with local help was able to cover all the cities in approximately two months.

Coverage

The bibliography covers selected books, periodicals, doctoral theses, research monographs, discussion papers and seminar papers (both published and unpublished) produced during the post-independence period on Indian women up to December 1985. Chapters in books have not been included. An attempt has been made to include as many unpublished articles and monographs as possible, especially in the unorganised sector. Women's studies journals like *Manushi* and *Samya Shakti* have been indexed in depth for the first time. The bibliography has tried to document literature on new emerging areas of research such as time allocation, debate on women's work, value of household work, enumeration of women in the statistical sources, and female-headed households.

Chapter Headings

No standard classification system or a thesaurus has been used for classifying and arranging the documents. The ILO thesaurus for labour, employment and training has been very useful in selecting terms for the subject index. The chapter headings have been chosen arbitrarily but an attempt has been made to stick to the terms used by the ILO as far as possible. Under the subject heading 'Employment Statistics' emphasis has been given to entries contributing to the debate on the enumeration of women workers in the statistical sources. Entries dealing with statistics on women in a particular sector have been put under the concerned industry/occupation. The chapter on women workers contains entries which describe women workers in general or women working in three or four industries, professions/occupations. The various professions and occupations in the formal and informal sectors have been listed in alphabetical sequence because most of the researchers are of the opinion that women perform unorganised roles even in the organised sector. Agriculture and plantation have been considered as two separate sectors for the sake of convenience and also recognising the fact that plantation workers are covered separately by legislation.

A special emphasis has been given to the welfare schemes initiated for the economic development of women during the past few years. The entries under 'Women and Economic Participation' would give an idea of the various socio-economic projects undertaken by governmental and non-governmental agencies, which are mostly through income generation projects. Under 'Labour Welfare' entries pertaining to the welfare of women workers have been included even though we broadly agree that women have a right to some of the basic facilities. An attempt has been made to highlight the impact of technological change on women and how this has affected the work and home life of women. Of late, there has been a great deal of effort to organise women workers specially those belonging to the 'informal sector'. Experiences of such attempts to organise women to form cooperatives and trade unions have been documented by activists. We have tried to bring together some of these attempts in this bibliography. There are a number of articles on the multiple roles performed by women and how this has affected the lives of women. They have been clubbed under the general category 'Women and Multiple Roles'. Articles and studies relating to decision-making and female-headed households have also been included in this chapter. The chapter 'Women and the Household' includes entries on the debate relating to women's work, paid and unpaid labour, time allocation, work in the household and the value of household labour. To enable researchers to identify gaps in literature, single entries have been included under some sub-headings.

Indexes

Author, subject and geographical indexes have been provided. It is suggested that when one is looking for something specific they should first consult the index.

Appendices

Appendix 1 lists organisations which responded to our initial letter requesting for documents on women's studies available with them. Appendix 2 gives the list of periodicals indexed in the bibliography. Appendix 3 lists periodicals and newsletters on women's studies published in India. Since some of these periodicals have limited circulation, their addresses have been given to enable researchers to write to the editors of these periodicals for articles. Some of the feminist book publishing houses are listed under Appendix 4, while Appendix 5 lists some of the documents acquired by ISST in the latter half of 1985.

Sample Entry

1. **Jain** (Devaki) : Women's employment, possibilities for relevant

research. Copenhagen, Asian Pacific Centre for Women and Development, 1980, 61 pp. (ISST).

Emphasises how research can be used as a tool for change and action and presents four case studies where this is being tried successfully.

2. **Banerjee** (Nirmala) : Why they get a worse deal—Report on unorganised women workers in Calcutta. *Manushi* No. 20, 1984, pp. 15–23.

Analyses the conditions under which women seek employment and observes that women have been conditioned to accept that they are primarily wives and mothers, not workers.

SECTION II

SECTION II

1

Employment Situation

1. **Acharya** (Sarathi): Employment of women and men in India—A historical review, 1901–1951. *Indian Journal of Labour Economics* V 22(3), 1979, pp. 138–60.

   Analyses the fall in the incidence of labour demand during this period when the development of the economy had frozen, and labour was unable to gain enhanced skill levels of social status.

2. **Adyanthnya** (N K): Women's employment in India. *International Labour Review* V 70(1), 1954, pp. 44–46.

3. **Agarwal** (R C): Women power—The neglected factor in development. *Manpower Journal* V 16(3), 1980, pp. 67–90.

   Discusses some aspects like education and employment and how working women were denied white-collar jobs.

4. **Ahmad** (Karuna): Studies of educated working women in India—Trends and issues. *Economic and Political Weekly* V 14(33), 1979, pp. 1435–40.

5. **Ahuja** (Kanta): Women and economic activities. Paper presented at the International Seminar on Women and Development, Jaipur, 1985 (ISST).

   The paper is in two parts. The first part discusses issues relating to women's economic activities. The second part consists of two alternative arguments regarding the policy and action implications as derived by two economists.

6. **Andhra Pradesh**, Directorate of Employment and Training: Employment and unemployment of women in Andhra Pradesh. Hyderabad, DET, 1977, 23 pp. (PC).

Gives an overview of the employment situation of women, both sector-wise and industry-wise.

7. **Andiappan** (P): Public policy and sex discrimination in employment in India. *Indian Journal of Industrial Relations* V 14(3), 1979, pp. 395–415.

Analyses the legal remedies for sex discrimination in employment in India with a view to suggesting changes in the public policy.

8. **Andiappan** (P): Remedies for sex discrimination in employment in India and the United States. *International Review of Administrative Sciences* V 45(3), 1979, pp. 268–74.

Argues on the basis of a comparison between the Indian situation and that of the USA that though the laws for equal pay are enacted women are still discriminated against in terms of wages and other benefits compared to men.

9. **Andiappan** (P): *Women and work—A comparative study of sex discrimination in employment in India and USA.* Bombay, Somaiya, 1980, 155 pp. (JNU).

10. **Anthuvan** (V L): Discrimination against women workers. *Southern Economist* V 20(2), 1981, pp. 16–18.

11. **Assam**, Directorate of Employment and Craftsman Training: Report on special study of women applicants in the live register of the employment exchanges in Assam as on 31 December 1975. Gauhati, DECT, 1976, 26 pp. (NL).

12. **Banerjee** (Nirmala): Women in the labour force—The Bengal experience. Paper presented at the Technical Seminar on Women's Work and Employment, New Delhi, 1982 (ISST).

Analyses how sex discrimination in the labour market has led to women working in lower, less skilled, monotonous jobs.

13. **Banerjee** (Nirmala): Women's work—Sex discrimination in

the labour market. Paper presented at the Workshop on Women and Poverty, Calcutta, 1983, 10 pp. (CSSS and ISST).

14. **Bardhan** (Kalpana) : Women's work, welfare and status—Forces of tradition and change in India. *Economic and Political Weekly* V 20(50), 1985, pp. 2207–17; V 20(51), 1985, pp. 2261–69.

Discusses how work is structured in relation to poverty and hierarchy, the differentials in the quantity and quality of work participation, the inequalities in work options, in renumeration, in access to the means and opportunities for better work and in the organised bargaining capacity to change the terms of existing employment.

15. **Batra** (V P) : Women and employment. *Yojana* V 26(8), 1982, pp. 36–37.

Reviews the employment situation in both public and private sectors and the number of persons registered with the employment exchange.

16. **Bharatiya** (L K) : The socio-cultural effects on the women working in village industries. *Journal of Anthropological Society of Bombay* V 14(2), 1972, pp. 16–28.

Summarises the trends in women's employment in various sectors of India's rural economy.

17. **Bihar**, Directorate of Employment and Training : Report on part-time employment potential of women residing in the new capital area of Patna. Patna, DET, 1967, 19 pp. (NL).

Report of a survey conducted to assess the availability of women workers for part-time jobs in Patna and the recommendations made by the Bihar Committee.

18. **Central Institute for Research and Training in Employment Service** : Creating your own job. Delhi, Controller of Publications, 1978, 10 pp. (PC).

19. **Central Institute for Research and Training in Employment Service**, Career Studies Centre : Careers for women. Second rev. ed. Delhi, Controller of Publications, 1976, 61 pp. (RUWS).

A list of various occupations with their scope.

20. **Centre for Women's Development Studies**: Women's work and employment—Selection from Indian documents. New Delhi, CWDS, 1983, 46 pp. (AIWC).

Contains extracts from (*a*) the summary of recommendation of the Committee on the Status of Women in India, (*b*) the blueprint of action points and the national plan of action for women, (*c*) the report of the Working Group on Employment of Women and (*d*) the report of the National Conference on Women's Development.

21. **Chakrabarti** (Ashok Kumar): Causes of women's unemployment in India. *Economic Affairs* V 22(5), 1977, pp. 177–84.

22. **Chakravarthy** (Kumaresh): Employment, income and equality. *Social Scientist* V 4(4–5), 1985, pp. 104–14.

23. **Chakravarthy** (Kumaresh) and **Tiwari** (G C): Regional variation in women's employment—A case study of five villages in three Indian states. New Delhi, ICSSR, 1975, 59 pp. (SSDC).

24. **Chakravarthy** (Renu): The working women. *Seminar* No. 52, 1983, pp. 34–38.

25. **Chatterjee** (Margaret): Trends of progress in the employment and welfare of women. *Social Welfare* V 2(5), 1955, pp. 6–7, 35–36.

26. **Chawdhary** (Pant): Employment of educated women. *Social Welfare* V 14(9), 1967, p. 9.

27. **Coe** (Jane Melevey): Employment and income generation for women in a resettlement colony of Delhi—The linkage between social action and research. *Social Action* V 30(3), 1980, pp. 285–300.

28. **Cooney** (Rosemary): Comparative study of work opportunities for women. *Industrial Relations* V 17(1), 1978, p. 64.

29. **Dasgupta** (Krishna): New careers for women. *Yojana* V 6(11), 1962, pp. 11–12.

30. **De** (Rama): Employment pattern of women workers in West Bengal—A sociological study. Calcutta, Calcutta

University, 1972. Thesis.

31. **Desai** (Armaity S): Women and part-time employment. *Social Welfare* V 19(7), 1963, pp. 40–41.
Discusses part-time employment for women who have dual responsibilities.

32. **Desai** (M M): Economic opportunities for women. *Social Welfare* V 22(6–7), 1975, pp. 25–28.
Analyses the economic opportunities available to women which are primarily determined by the system of production, differential valuation of the sexes, etc.

33. Eves to have reservation in Bombay mills. *Indian Worker* V 24(40), 1978, p. 8.

34. **Garg** (Saila): Industrial employment of women in UP. Lucknow, Lucknow University, 1952. Thesis.

35. **Gopalan** (Sarala): Employment of women—The Indian situation. New Delhi, Central Social Welfare Board, n.d., 20 pp. (CSSS).

36. **Goyal** (Santosh): Effective utilisation of women power resources in India. *AICC Economic Review* V 20(3), 1968, pp. 15–20.
Studies the available women power resources in India and the problems related to their utilisation, recent trends in employment and the need for reorientation of educational and training programmes accordingly.

37. **Guha** (P): Employment problems of uneducated women. *Social Welfare* V 10(7), 1963, p. 45.

38. **Gulati** (J S): Careers for women. Delhi, YMCA, 1956 (AIWC).

39. **Gulati** (Leela): Sex discrimination in work and wages. *Social Scientist* V 4(4–5), 1975, pp. 155–60.

40. **Gupta** (B N): Can women work at odd hours. *Social Welfare* V 11(8), 1964, pp. 23–24.
Argues that if married women have to work at odd hours they should be provided creche and other facilities.

41. **Gupta** (Manju): Study of job satisfaction among women workers. *Indian Journal of Industrial Relations* V 14(3), 1979, pp. 449–59.

42. **Hiraway** (Indira) : Employment problems of rural women in Gujarat. Ahmedabad, Sardar Patel Institute of Economic and Social Research, 1983, mimeo. Also in *Journal of Labour Economics* V 20(3), 1979, pp. 159–202.

43. **India,** Department of Social Welfare, Women's Welfare and Development Bureau : Report of the Working Group on Employment of Women. New Delhi, 1978, 88 pp. (RUWS).

44. **India,** Directorate of Employment, Training and Technical Education : Employment of women in Delhi, 1961–1964. New Delhi, DETT, 1965, 77 pp. (PC).

45. **India,** Ministry of Labour and Employment, Directorate General of Employment and Training : Report on the pattern of graduate employment. New Delhi, DGET, 1963, 95 pp. (PC).
Reveals the relationship between the academic curriculum and the nature of employment, statistical information regarding the choice of courses as well as employment and unemployment for both men and women alumni.

46. **India,** Ministry of Labour, Employment and Rehabilitation, Directorate General of Employment and Training : Careers for women. Delhi, Manager of Publications, 1971, 65 pp. (PC).

47. **India,** Ministry of Social and Women's Welfare : Women in India—Country paper. New Delhi, Ministry of Social and Women's Welfare, 1985, 80 pp. (ISST).
Paper produced for the UN End of Decade Conference for Women, Nairobi, July 1985. The chapter on employment reviews the changes that have taken place over the decade.

48. **India,** Ministry of Social Welfare : Report of the Working Group on Personnel Policies for bringing Greater Involvement of Social Welfare. 1981, 29 pp. (PC).

49. **India,** Ministry of Social Welfare, Working Group on Women and Development, Seventh Five-Year Plan : Report of the Sub-group on Women's Employment. 1983, 7 pp. (ISST).

50. **India,** Planning Commission : Report of the Study Group on Estimates of Requirements of Women Workers (1958–1966). New Delhi, Planning Commission, 1960, 68 pp. (PC).

51. **India,** Planning Commission : Some characteristics of women job-seekers on the live register of employment exchange. New Delhi, Government of India Press, 1966 (PC).

52. **Indian Council for Social Science Research,** Advisory Committee on Women's Studies : Critical issues on the status of women—Suggested priorities for action. New Delhi, ICSSR, 1977, 32 pp. (NL).

Describes the national neglect of women in the areas of health, employment, education and proposes priorities for the reversal of the present trend.

53. **Indian Council of Social Science Research and Central Statistical Organisation** : *Social information on India—Trend and structure.* Delhi, Hindustan Publishing Corporation, 1983, 302 pp. (ISI).

54. **International Labour Office** : Women's employment in India. *International Labour Review* V 79(4), 1959, pp. 440–44.

55. **International Labour Organisation** : Part-time employment for middle class women in India. *Industry and Labour* V 11(5), 1954, pp. 198–99.

56. **Jain** (Devaki) : Women's economic roles and women's employment —The linkages and policy implications. Paper presented at the International Seminar on Women and Development, Jaipur, 1985 (ISST).

Discusses issues in the debate on women's employment in India such as technological change, home-based work, primary and secondary workers and future strategies.

57. **Jain** (Devaki) : Women's employment, possibilities for relevant research. Copenhagen, Asian Pacific Centre for Women and Development, 1980, 61pp. (ISST).

Emphasises how research can be used as a tool for change and action and presents four case studies where this has been employed successfully.

58. **Jayalakshmi** (L) : The unutilised asset—Women labour. *Khadi Gramodyog* V 23(9), 1977, pp. 374–76.

59. **Joshi** (Heather) : Prospects and case for employment of women in Indian cities. *Economic and Political Weekly* V 11(31–33), 1976, pp. 1303–8.

60. **Kapoor** (Ranga) : Career opportunity for women. *Education Quarterly* V 27(2), 1975, pp. 10–12.

61. **Karlekar** (Malavika) : Some perspectives on the employment of scheduled caste women. *Social Action* V 32(3), 1982, pp. 292–302.

62. **Karnataka**, Planning Department, Manpower and Planning Unit : A paper on the size and pattern of female employment in Karnataka. Bangalore, Planning Department, 1979, 27 pp. (NCAER).

63. **Lakshmanan** (Leela) : Professions for women. *Social Welfare* V 12(1), 1965, pp. 11–12.

64. **Lakshmi Devi** (V) : Why controversy over jobs reservation ? *Mainstream* V 22(38), 1984, pp. 31–32.
Argues why jobs cannot be reserved for women.

65. **Lakshmi Raghu Ramaiah** (K) : Discrimination of sexes. *Social Welfare* V 15(2), 1968, pp. 13–14.
Discusses the discrimination against women in the fields of law and employment.

66. **Mandavat** (S L) : Myths about women's employment. *Yojana* V 22(1–2), 1978, p. 82.

67. **Mazumdar** (Vina) : Women workers in the changing economy. *Yojana* V 19(7), 1975, pp. 15–17.

68. **Menon** (L D) : Kerala's educated women in quest of jobs. *Social Welfare* V 10(7), 1963, pp. 42–43.
Discusses the problems faced by women in search of employment and suggests the necessity of partial employment.

69. **Mitra** (Asok) : Employment of women. *Manpower Journal* V 14(1), 1978, pp. 1–29.

70. **Mitra** (Asok) : *Status of women: Literacy and employment.* Bombay, Allied, 1979, 74 pp. (JNU, ISST).

71. **Murali Dhar** (B):Tough going in labour market. *Mainstream*
    V 22(46), 1984, pp. 14, 34.
    Discusses the decline in participation of women workers in
    traditional industries and the problems involved in finding
    employment.

72. **National Conference on Women's Studies**, Trivan-
    drum, 1984, Session on Work and Employment:
    Papers. New Delhi, Indian Association of Women's
    Studies, 1984 (ISST).
    The discussion is framed around issues of caste and class to
    consolidate the growing body of macro- and micro-level
    analysis and to explicitly address questions related to
    attitudes to women's work and the role of women's
    organisations in promoting collective struggles.

73. **National Federation of Indian Women**: Women's
    employment — A review at the end of the decade.
    Paper presented at NGO Consultation on Equality,
    Development and Peace — The Women's Decade in
    Review, New Delhi, 1985 (ISST).
    Reviews the employment situation of women with regard
    to their wages, work participation rates, disparities, dis-
    placement due to lack of technical training in India during
    the decade.

74. **Padmavalli Bharathi** (R): Special facilities for enhanc-
    ing the efficiency and quality of output by women
    labour force. Paper presented at the Seminar on the
    Optimum Utilisation of Women Power for. Develop-
    ment, New Delhi, 1975 (ISST).
    Focuses on the present position of the female labour force
    in the country and attempts to identify the special facilities
    needed for enhancing efficiency and the quality of their
    output in the economic sphere. Using secondary data, the
    author examines the employment pattern, employment
    opportunities, educational level, wage rates, nutritional
    level, and housing and medical facilities available for the
    female labour force.

75. **Pandey** (R N): Women's status and employment and
    wages disparity. *Indian Labour Journal* V 17(1), 1976,
    pp. 1–18.

Analyses the status of women and the historical development in terms of education, employment and wages.

76. **Papola** (T S) : Sex discrimination in the urban labour markets—Some propositions based on Indian evidence. Lucknow, Giri Institute of Development Studies, 1979, 13 pp. (GIDS).

77. **Papola** (T S) : Women workers in an urban labour market — A study of segregation and discrimination in employment in Lucknow (India). Lucknow, Giri Institute of Development Studies, 1982, 174 pp. (GIDS).

Shows that the work participation rate of women in the labour market in India is very low for socio-cultural and economic reasons.

78. **Parthasarathy** (G) : Pattern of employment on farms of Vidharbha. *Economic Weekly* V 11(33), 1959, pp. 1139–44.

79. **Perlee** (Diana Ashley) : Employment, ingenuity and family life—Rajasthani women in Delhi. London, University Microfilms International, 1982, 260 pp. (NIRD).

80. **Pillai** (Lakshmi Devi) : Sex discrimination in work and employment — The case of Kerala. Paper presented at the Second National Conference on Women's Studies, Session on Work and Employment, Trivandrum, 1984 (ISST).

81. **Pore** (Kumud) : A note on the integration of women in economic activity in India. Paper presented at the Seminar on the Optimum Utilisation of Women Power for Development, New Delhi, 1975 (ISST).

Suggests that in order to improve the situation of Indian women, the problem should be handled at two levels (*a*) measures for a fuller utilisation of the existing population of university educated women, and (*b*) measures to equip students to avail of the job opportunities.

82. **Ram Prakash** : Unprogressive pattern of women's employment in India. *Social Welfare* V 16(3), 1969, pp. 9–10, 19; V 16(5), pp. 4–5, 23.

Analyses the trends of distribution of women workers in the economic sectors.

83. **Rama Rao** (Rajalakshmi) : Shift in female work participation. *Social Welfare* V 31(12), 1985, pp. 4–5.

Notwithstanding the rampant illiteracy, there has been an appreciable improvement in the employment situation of women in the primary, secondary and tertiary sectors over the last ten years with the introduction of new laws and the amendment of old laws. The number of women engaged in occupations—professions once dominated by men—has also increased.

84. **Ranade** (S N) and **Ramachandran** (P) : Women and employment—Report of pilot studies conducted in Delhi and Bombay. Bombay, Tata Institute of Social Sciences, 1970, 60 pp. (BUL, JNU).

Stresses the need of part-time employment of women including training facilities on the basis of available statistics.

85. **Rao** (Usha N J) : *Women in a developing society.* New Delhi, Ashish, 1983, 180 pp. (IIPA).

Collation of research papers with special focus on women in Karnataka. The book includes the literacy level of women, the employment pattern of women workers, female work participation rates among scheduled castes, self-employment opportunities for scheduled caste women and utilisation of women in rural development.

86. **Saibaba** (G) : Public sector—A dynamic agent of women's employment. *Social Welfare* V 23(11), 1977, pp. 4–6.

87. **Saradamoni** (K) : Women in employment—Low in profile, high in discrimination. *Yojana* V 19(13&14), 1975, pp. 29–31.

88. **Sarojinibai** (K J) : Employment for women. *Kurukshetra* V 26(15), 1978, pp. 33–34.

89. **Savithri** (T S) : Structural changes in female employment in the non-agricultural sector in South India. *Economic Review* V 21(14), 1976, pp. 13–21.

90. **Sawant** (S D) and **Dewan** (Ritu) : Rural female labour and economic development. *Economic and Political Weekly* V 14(26), 1979, pp. 1091–99.

Examines the impact of economic development on rural

women particularly on their employment in Thane district of Maharashtra.

91. **Seminar on the Careers for Women**, Indore, 1956 : Papers and proceedings. New Delhi, All India Women's Conference, 1956, 103 pp. (AIWC).

92. **Seminar on the Optimum Utilisation of Women Power for Development**, New Delhi, 1975 : Papers and report (ISST). Also in *Social Change* V 5(3), 1975, pp. 34–37.

93. **Seminar on Sex Discrimination in Gainful Employment**, Pune, 1981 : Papers (CSSS).

94. **Seminar on Women — The Untapped Potential of Rajasthan**, Jaipur, 1975 : Proceedings. Jaipur, Rajasthan University, Department of Adult Education, 1975, 231 pp. (ISST).
Session on women and employment discussed the work participation rate, the categories of occupations women are involved in Rajasthan.

95. **Sengupta** (P) : Trends in women's employment. *Social Welfare* V 10(7), 1963, pp. 36–39.
Stresses the changing role of women and discusses the employment situation in India on the basis of data from the 1951 and 1961 Censuses.

96. **Sengupta** (P) : Protection for the women workers. *Social Welfare* V 5(2), 1958, pp. 6–7.
Voices concern about the fall in the rate of women's employment and argues that the protective laws for women employees as well as maternity and other benefits are partly responsible because the employers want to reduce the extra expenditure.

97. **Sengupta** (Padmini) : *Women in India.* New Delhi, Indian Book Company, 1974, 273 pp. (AIWC).

98. **Shah** (M S) : Wages and employment of women in India. *Indian Labour Journal* V 16(2), 1975, pp. 167–84.
Discusses the discrimination in employment and wages on the basis of: (a) Indian Labour Statistics—1971, (b) women in employment—Labour Bureau, (c) Report of

the Chief Inspector of Mines in India—1965, (*d*) Reports of the Central Wage Board for Coal Mining and Cement Industries, and (*e*) Handbook of the Central Wage Board's recommendation — 1968.

99. **Sharma** (G D) and **Apte** (M D) : Graduate unemployment in India. *Economic and Political Weekly* V 11(25), 1976, pp. 915–25.

100. **Sherwani** (Madeeha) : Creating more jobs for female workers. *Kurukshetra* V 32(4), 1984, pp. 28–32.
Discusses the motivation for work, different categories of female workers, their problems and gives suggestions for creation of employment.

101. **Sherwani** (Madeeha): Why more women entering work force ? *Yojana* V 28(10), 1984, pp. 23–25, 33.
Points out that there is an increasing trend of employment in professional jobs while it is decreasing in agriculture.

102. **Singh** (T R) and **Singh** (Kamal): Promoting self-employment among rural women. *Kurukshetra* V 29(10), 1981, pp. 24–25.
Emphasises the role of cooperatives in the promotion of self-employment.

103. **Sonarikar** (Sunanda) : Are economic opportunities dwindling for women? *Social Welfare* V 31(2), 1984, pp. 28–30.
Argues that the number of women workers covered by legislation is small. Also gives the occupational distribution of women workers.

104. **Sundar** (Pushpa) : Characteristics of female employment— Implication and research policy. *Economic and Political Weekly* V 16(19), 1981, pp. 863–71.
Highlights the way in which women's employment situation differs from the male employment situation and why it is necessary to consider female employment separately while formulating an employment policy.

105. **Sundar** (Pushpa) : Women's employment and organisation modes. *Economic and Political Weekly* V 18(48), 1983, pp. 171–76.

106. **Symposium on Women, Work and Society**, New Delhi,

1982 : Papers. New Delhi, Indian Statistical Institute, 1982 (ISST).

The symposium reviewed some of the Indian studies related to the field of women and work and discussed the data bases for Indian studies.

107. **Technical Seminar on Women's Work and Employment**, New Delhi, 1982: Report and papers. New Delhi, Institute of Social Studies Trust, 1982 (ISST).

Papers relating to women's employment, enumeration of women in the statistical sources, labour force participation rate and household work were presented at the seminar.

108. **Tilak** (Jandhyala B G): Education and labour market discrimination. *Indian Journal of Industrial Relations* V 16(1), 1980, pp. 95–114.

Based on data collected in a survey in West Godavary district, Andhra Pradesh, the study highlights two aspects of discrimination (*a*) in employment, and (*b*) in wages.

109. **Tilak** (Jandhyala B G): Inequality by sex in human capital formation, labour market discrimination and returns to education. *Margin* V 12(2), 1980, pp. 57–80.

Describes the discrimination in wages and suggests remedies to remove this discrimination.

110. **Usha** (S): Labour market discrimination against women. *Indian Journal of Industrial Relations* V 18, 1983, pp. 569–84.

Examines the magnitude of discrimination against women in an urban labour market with respect to wages.

111. **Usha Rani** (C): Women's employment. *Social Welfare* V 10(7), 1963, pp. 46–48.

Analyses the factors involved in taking up employment such as how many women are eager to do intellectual jobs, how many are able to face the trials and tribulations of taking up a career.

112. **Vanamala** (M): Employment status of women in Andhra Pradesh—State public enterprises in Hyderabad. Paper presented at the Conference on Women's Status and Development, Warangal, 1982 (ISST, SOWSTUD).

Analyses the condition of women in the public sector and points out that women are discriminated at all levels.

113. **Vasantha** (M) : Unemployed women graduates in the city of Madras, 1974–1977. Madras, Madras University, 1977, 83 pp. Thesis (MUL).

114. **Venkateswaran** (K) : Employment opportunities for women in rural areas. *Khadi Gramodyog* V 24(9), 1978. pp. 434–36.

115. **Vishwanath** (Vasantha) : Occupational structure of women in India—A geographical analysis. *Indian Geographical Journal* V 50(2), 1975, pp. 10–13.

116. **Wadia** (Avabai B) : *Some careers for women.* Bombay, Thacker & Company, 1947, 39 pp. (AIWC).

117. **West Bengal,** Directorate of National Employment Service : Unemployment among women in West Bengal, November 1958. Calcutta, West Bengal Government Press, 1959, 49 pp. (NL). Also in *Indian Labour Journal* V 1(1), 1960, pp. 146–49.

118. Women and unemployment. *Asian Labour* V 29(191–192), 1981, pp. 15–17.

119. Women — To work or not to work at night. *Social Welfare* V 23(2), 1976, pp. 15, 28.

120. **Workshop on Promotion of Self-Employment in Rural Areas,** Allahabad, 1982 : Report. New Delhi, ILO, 1982, 186 pp. (PC).
Some technologies with potential for self-employment of women were suggested (*a*) agro-based industries, (*b*) food processing, (*c*) manufacturing industries.

121. **Workshop on Women and Poverty,** Calcutta, 1983 : Papers. Calcutta, Centre for Studies in Social Sciences (ISST).
Papers relating to women's employment, health and nutrition in poverty households and discrimination in the labour market were presented and discussed at this workshop.

2

Employment Statistics

122. **Agarwal** (Bina): Work participation of women in rural India—Some data and conceptual biases. Sussex, Institute of Development Studies, 1984, 34 pp. (ISST).

Highlights the fact that there is a dearth of empirical research and reliable data on rural women and suggests that there are conceptual biases that affect the existing measurements of women's work participation.

123. **Ambannavar** (Jaipal P): Changes in economic activity of males and females in India, 1911–1961. *Demography India* V 4(2), 1975, pp. 345–64.

124. **Bardhan** (Pranab): Some employment characteristics of rural women—An analysis of NSS data for West Bengal, 1972–73. *Economic and Political Weekly* V 13(12), 1978, pp. A 21–A 26.

125. **Bhattacharya** (Sudhir): Women's activities in rural India—A study based on NSS 32nd round (1977–78 survey results on employment and unemployment). Calcutta, National Sample Survey Organisation, 1981 (ISST).

Report on labour force participation characteristics of rural women. It discusses the activities of rural women who are engaged in domestic work.

126. **Bose** (A): Census figures reveal discrimination against women. *Organiser* V 24(39), 1974, p. 5.

127. **Chandra** (R C): Female working force of rural Punjab. *Manpower Journal* V 2(4), 1976, pp. 47–62.
Discusses the female participation rate in Punjab which is low. The proportion of female workers to the female population is lower in urban areas than in rural areas.

128. **Dantwala** (M L): Rural employment—Facts and issues. *Economic and Political Weekly* V 14(25), 1979, pp. 1048–57.

129. **Deb Roy** (Rama): A note on statistics of the unorganised sector in India. Paper presented at the Fifth Data Base Seminar, Madras, 1978, 9 pp. (CSSS).

130. **D'Souza** (V S): Census data and theoretical framework—The case of female participation. Paper presented at the Indian Centenary Seminar, 1972 (CSSS).

131. **D'Souza** (Victor S): Family status and female work participation. An empirical analysis. *Social Action* V 25(3), 1975, pp. 267–76.

132. **Dholakia** (Bakul) and **Dholakia** (Ravindra R): Inter-state variation in female labour force participation rates in India. *Indian Journal of Labour Economics* V 20(4), 1978, pp. 290–307.
This study is based on data from the 1971 Census.

133. **Dholakia** (Ravindra H): Role of literacy and industrial structure in displacement of female workers. *Economic and Political Weekly* V 20(14), 1985, pp. 613–14.
Discusses the role and importance of literacy in the context of female work participation rate.

134. **Ghosh** (Bahnisikha) and **Mukhopadhyay** (Sudhin): Sources of variation in female participation—A decomposition analysis in India. Paper presented at the Technical Seminar on Women's Work and Employment, New Delhi, 1982, 72 pp. (ISST).
Analysis based on census data, suggests that during the last two decades in India females have lost ground in the work force. The most important factor is that displacement in the total work force is by their men.

135. **Ghosh** (Bahnisikha) and **Mukhopadhyay** (Sudhin) : Displacement of the female in the Indian labour force. *Economic and Political Weekly* V 29(47), 1984, pp. 1998–2002.

Analyses the available data on employment in India. It is found that there has been a drastic reduction in the number of women workers as well as in their work participation rates. There are three possible hypotheses—technology development, unemployment, and sex ratio.

136. **Gulati** (Leela): Female work participation—A reply. *Economic and Political Weekly* V 10(32), 1975, pp. 1215–18.

137. **Gulati** (Leela) : Female work participation—A study of inter-state difference. *Economic and Political Weekly* V 10(1–2), 1975, pp. 35–42.

138. **Gupta** (R N) : Correlates of female participation in economic activity. *Indian Labour Journal* V 25(3), 1984, pp. 345–55.

139. **Gupta** (Rajeswar Nath) : Influence of socio-economic characteristics of the household on female work participation rates. New Delhi, Jawaharlal Nehru University, 1980. Thesis.

140. **Hasalkar** (J B) : Spatial variations in urban female participation rates in India. Paper presented at the Seminar on Urban Population of India, Dharwar, 1968 (ISST).

141. **India**, Ministry of Labour, Labour Bureau : Statistical profile of women's labour. Simla, Labour Bureau, 1983, 223 pp. (ISST).

Analyses the sex-wise distribution of the working population by broad census industrial groups as per the 1971 Census.

142. **India**, Planning Commission : Statistics relating to employment and unemployment of women. Paper prepared for one day meeting of women workers and the role of the Ministry of Labour, New Delhi, March 1985, 2 pp. (ISST).

Discusses the work participation rates in the NSSO and census and changes in the employment status especially in the industrial sector and domestic work.

143. **Indira Devi** (M): Caste and women's participation in labour markets—A study of landless poor. Paper presented at the Second National Conference on Women's Studies, Trivandrum, 1984 (ISST).
States that the caste factor influences the work participation of girls and women. Caste also influences the wage market and labour market segmentation.

144. **Iyer** (V J) and **Jain** (H L): Some observations on field experience in NSSO surveys relating to the collection of data on women's participation in economic activities. Paper presented at the Technical Seminar on Women's Work and Employment, New Delhi, 1982 (ISST).

145. **Jacob** (Paul): The activity profile of Indian women, NSSO 32nd round. Paper presented at the Workshop on Women and Poverty, Calcutta, 1983, 15 pp. (CSSS).
Analyses the distribution of the population by educational attainment, labour force and participation in marginal work.

146. **Jacob** (Paul): The low female participation rates and related issues—Observations based on NSS results. Paper presented at the Technical Seminar on Women's Work and Employment, New Delhi, 1982, 10 pp. (ISST).
The NSS surveys show that there is a decline in women's participation rates, while the proportion of 'house worker' is very high. 'Household duties' contain elements of gainful work which need to be looked into.

147. **Jagannathan** (M): Profile of rural women in India. *Kurukshetra* V 33(3), 1984, pp. 37–40.

148. **Jain** (Devaki): Co-opting women's work into the statistical systems—Some Indian milestones. New Delhi, Institute of Social Studies Trust, 1983, 22 pp. (ISST). Also in *Samya Shakti* V 1(1), 1983, pp. 84–99.
Describes the attempts made in India to evaluate women's work and its enumeration in statistical sources.

149. **Jain** (Devaki): Household surveys as a source of statistics on women, children and youth. Paper prepared for the

Seminar on Household Surveys, Bangkok, 1980 (ISST).

150. **Jain** (Devaki) and **Chand** (Malini) : Domestic work—Its implication for enumeration of workers. Paper presented at the Golden Jubilee Symposium on Women, Work and Society, New Delhi, 1982, 16 pp. (ISST).
Examines the research and debate on the inadequacy of statistics on women's domestic work.

151. **Jain** (Devaki) and **Chand** (Malini) : Patterns of female work—Implications for statistical design, economic classification and social priorities. New Delhi, Institute of Social Studies Trust, 1981, 56 pp. (ISST).

152. **Kalpagam** (U) and **Usha** (P):|Female work force in Tamil Nadu. *Madras Development Seminar Series Bulletin* V 10(5–6), 1980, pp. 262–73 (MIDS).
Presents an overview of female work participation in Tamil Nadu on basis of data from the 1971 Census and highlights the inter-district variations and certain patterns of female participation occupation-wise.

153. **Kumar** (R S) : Women and economic activity. Paper presented at the International Conference on Women and Development, Jaipur, 1985 (ISST).
Discusses the statistical measurement of female participation, the dual roles played by women and prejudices regarding women's participation.

154. **Mathur** (R S) : Female labour force participation rates in India. *Indian Journal of Economics* V 21(1–2), 1978, pp. 113–19.

155. **Miller** (Barbara D) : Female labour participation and female seclusion in rural India—A regional review. *Economic Development and Cultural Change* V 30(4), 1982, pp. 777–94.

156. **Mitra** (Asok) and others : *The status of women: shifts in occupational participation—1961 to 1971*. New Delhi, Abhinav, 1980, 203 pp. (JNU).

157. **Mukherjee** (B N) : A study of some selected factors underlying married women's work participation. *NLI Bulletin* V 3(8), 1977, pp. 349–60.

158. **Mukhopadhyay** (Sudhir Kumar) : Economic development, female employment pattern, migration and human fertility in rural India. New Delhi, Indian Council of Social Science Research, 1982, 42 pp. (CWDS).
Deals with female labour force participation in rural India.

159. **Mukhopadhyay** (Swapna) : Women workers of India—A case of market segmentation. Paper presented at the Workshop on Women in the Indian Labour Force, Trivandrum, 1980 (ISST).
Reviews available evidence on segmentation of the female labour force in India.

160. **Mukhopadhyay** (Swapna): Work and women—Some pertinent issues. Paper presented at the National Conference on Women's Studies, Bombay, 1981 (ISST, IEG).

161. **Nath** (Kamala) : Female work participation and economic development—A regional analysis. *Economic and Political Weekly* V 5(21), 1970, pp. 846–49.

162. **Nath** (Kamala) : Urban women workers—A preliminary study. *Economic and Political Weekly* V 17(37), 1965, pp. 1405–12.
Describes the variation in work participation rates of urban women by levels of education and the distribution of workers among the principal occupational categories.

163. **Nath** (Kamala): Women in service occupations. *Economic and Political Weekly* V 2(1), 1967, pp. 25–30.
Describes the participation of women in various occupations and the changes that have taken place since 1951. Statistical data has been provided to show the percentage of distribution in different categories of service occupations.

164. **Nath** (Kamala) : Women in the working force in India. *Economic and Political Weekly* V 3(31), 1968, pp. 1205–13.
Discusses the decline in the work participation rates in areas like agriculture.

165. **National Sample Survey** : Employment and

unemployment situation in India during the seventies— A comparative study based on the results of the NSS 27th and 32nd round surveys. *Sarvekshana* V 3(3), 1980, pp. 1–75.

Gives statistical details regarding women workers—rural and urban—engaged in various sectors including the self-employed sector.

166. **National Sample Survey Organisation** : Women's activities in rural India—A study based on the NSS 32nd round (1977–78) survey results on employment and unemployment—Study report. New Delhi, NSSO, 1981, 123 pp. (ISST).

167. **Nayak** (Debendra Kumar) : Female participation in economic activity in rural areas—A geographical perspective with reference to selected regions in India. New Delhi, Jawaharlal Nehru University, 1982, 215 pp. (JNU).

168. **Neruaker** (Amaraju) : Segmentation of labour market in India with special reference to women. *Indian Journal of Labour Economics* V 23(1–2), 1980, pp. 52–65.

169. **Parthasarathy** (G) and **Rao** (G Dasaradharama) : Women in the labour force in India. Paper presented at the Workshop on Women in the Indian Labour Force, Trivandrum, 1980 (ISST).

Identifies some crucial relationships pertaining to the female labour force based on a review of available micro and macro studies.

170. **Patel** (B B) and **Dholakia** (R) : Female labour force participation rate—Direct verification of some hypotheses. *Indian Journal of Labour Economics* V 20(4), 1978, pp. 308–18.

171. **Paul** (Jacob) : Activity profile of Indian women. Paper presented at the Workshop on Women and Poverty, Calcutta, 1983 (CSSS).

172. **Punekar** (S D) and **Sharma** (J C) : Income and labour market participation of women in India. Bombay, Tata Institute of Social Sciences, 1976 (RUWS).

173. **Rajaraman** (Indira) : On the socio-economic condition of

women, the NSS and Labour Ministry surveys. Bangalore, Indian Institute of Management, n.d., 63 pp. (ISST).
Information collected on (*a*) labour force participation rates and (*b*) individuals identified by sex were used for this review. The issue of whether or not the NSS surveys themselves have been conceptually uniform has been examined in detail.

174. **Raju** (Saraswati): Regional patterns of female participation in the labour force of urban India. *Professional Geographer* V 34(1), 1982, pp. 42–49.
On the basis of the 1971 Census the paper examines variations in the level of female participation in the urban labour force in four States: Andhra Pradesh, Madhya Pradesh, Uttar Pradesh and Karnataka.

175. **Ramachandran** (Saroja): Methodology for valuating women's contribution to economic activities under conditions of irregular and uncertain participation. Paper presented at the Workshop on Women's Work and Employment, New Delhi, 1982, 15 pp. (ISST).
Suggests that women in the informal sector are not considered economically active though they are paid for the work and their contribution is not included in the gross national product. This is mainly due to the methodology adopted for measuring women's work which needs to be examined.

176. **Rao** (N T U): Female labour participation rates among scheduled castes of Karnataka *Indian Journal of Economics* V 21(1–2), 1978, pp. 76–100.

177. **Reddy** (Narasimha D): Female work participation in India—Facts and problems and policies. *Indian Journal of Industrial Relations* V 15(2), 1979, pp. 196–212.

178. **Reddy** (Narasimha D): Female work participation—A study of inter-state difference—A comment. *Economic and Political Weekly* V 10(23), 1975, pp. 902–5.

179. **Sahoo** (B) and **Mahanty** (B K): Female participation in work in Orissa—An inter-district comparison. *Journal of Labour Economics* V 20(4), 1978, pp. 329–35.

The study is based on census reports and other Government statistical sources.

180. **Seal** (K C) : Women in the labour force in India—A macro-level statistical profile. Paper presented at the Workshop on Women in the Indian Labour Force, Trivandrum, 1980 (ISST).

181. **Sen** (Gita) : Changing definitions of women's work—A study of the Indian census. Paper presented at the Golden Jubilee Symposium on Women, Work and Society, New Delhi, Indian Statistical Institute, 1982, 32 pp. (ISST).

Focuses on the reliability of the census over time and considers the data on female agricultural labour at the disaggregated State level.

182. **Sen** (Gita) : Women's work and women agricultural labourers—A study of the Indian census. Trivandrum, Centre for Development Studies, 1983, 43 pp. Also in *Economic and Political Weekly* V 20(17), 1985, pp. WS 49–WS 56.

Explains the relationship between women's dual roles, household work and women's place in the labour market. Labour force participation is based on women's responsibility for child care and other domestic work.

183. **Sen** (Gita) and **Sen** (Chiranjib) : Women's domestic work and economic activity—Results from National Sample Survey. Trivandrum, Centre for Development Studies, 1984, 28 pp. (CDS).

184. **Shareen** (Begum) : Labour force participation of women. Madras, Madras University, 1981, 96 pp. Thesis.

185. **Shastri** (P P) and **Ramachandran** (P) : Decadal rural Indian female participation rates and its variation, 1961–1971—A census analysis. *Journal of Family Welfare* V 36(4), 1980, pp. 3–17.

186. **Singh** (K P) : Economic development and female labour force participation—The case of the Punjab. *Social Action* V 30(2), 1980, pp. 128–37.

Compares the labour force participation rates in the various regions of Punjab focusing on the rural urban differences and the types of occupations in which women predominate. Analysis is based on the 1971 Census.

187. **Sinha** (J N): Female work participation—A comment. *Economic and Political Weekly* V 17(6), 1982, pp. 195–203.
Analyses the male and female work force as given in the census especially the female work participation rate.

188. **Srikantan** (K S) and others: Population and employment in area planning —Female and child work participation. *Demography India* V 7(1–2), 1978, pp. 194–210.
Gives data on the participation rates of women in different occupations.

189. **Srinivasan** (K N): Employment and unemployment —An assessment of two National Sample Surveys. *Economic and Political Weekly* V 17(38), 1982, pp. 1541–66.

190. **Thamarajakshi** (R): Statistics relating to employment and unemployment of women. Paper prepared for the Advisory Committee on Equal Renumeration Act, Ministry of Labour, 1984 (ISST).
Reviews the availability position of data on employment and unemployment of women and analyses the latest trends in work participation rates, the special characteristics of the marginal women workers, changes in the industrial composition of workers, etc.

191. **Tripathi** (B L): Female workers' participation in rural areas. *Indian Journal of Labour Economics* V 21(1–2), 1978, pp. 101–12.

192. **Visaria** (Pravin): Level and nature of work participation by age and marital status in India. *Economic and Political Weekly* V 28(19, 20, 21), 1983, pp. 901–18.
Gives the workers' population ratios and the distribution of workers in nine industrial categories by sex, age group and marital status in the rural and urban areas of a few Indian states.

193. **Visaria** (P M): Trends in labour force participation by age and sex in relation to education and skill. Bangkok, Asian Population Studies, 1972 (ISST).

194. **Wahan** (P) and **Venkat** (Dasappa) : Female work participation in Karnataka. *Indian Journal of Labour Economics* V 20(4), 1978, pp. 337–42.

195. **Wasi** (M) : Professional women in India—Dangerous corners. *Monthly Public Opinion Survey of IIPO* V 18(1), 1972, pp. 17–20.
      A survey of statistical data on women in different professions shows that there is an increase in the number of women in professions like teaching, secretarial jobs, social work, medicine, nursing, etc.

196. Women in India—A data compilation for the UN Decade for Women. New Delhi, United Nations Children's Fund, 1980 (ISST).

3

Women Workers: General Studies

197. **Anand** (P A): A comparative study of socio-economic conditions of women workers in Jabalpur. Saugar, Saugar University, 1949. Thesis.

198. **Baig** (Tara Ali): Ed. *Women of India.* New Delhi, Publications Division, 1958, 279 pp. (IIPA).
Collection of articles on women engaged in various professions, their participation in sports, politics, fine arts, etc.

199. **Bergstrom** (Greta) and **Paz** (Skoldolsson): Report on women's occupations in India, March–May 1975. Stockholm, ISDA, 1975 (ISST).
A list of occupations prepared in collaboration with the Ministry of Labour.

200. **Bhasin** (Kamla): Position of women in India. Bombay, Leslie Sawhny Programme of Training for Democracy, 1971, 131 pp. (ALHSCW).

201. **Billington** (Mary Frances): *Women in India—A study of medieval period.* New Delhi, Amarka, 1973, 269 pp. (AIWC).
Discusses the life of women workers engaged in agriculture and factory work.

202. **Central Institute of Research and Training in Public Co-operation**: Women in India—International Women's Year 1975. New Delhi, CIRTPC, 1975, 76 pp. (AIWC).

Discusses the economic contribution of women, the life and working conditions of women in construction work, industry and public life.

203. **Chadha** (S S) : Women in employment in Haryana. *Social Welfare* V 27(11), 1981, pp. 65–66.
Gives the occupational distribution of women in public and private sectors and in various industries.

204. **Correspondent** : Working class women and working class families in Bombay—Report of a survey. *Economic and Political Weekly* V 13(29), 1978, pp. 1169–73.

205. **Cour** (Ajit) : *Directory of Indian women today.* New Delhi, India International Pub., 1976 (ISST).
A directory of eminent women classified according to their professions.

206. **Despande** (S R) : Economic and social status of women workers in India. New Delhi, Ministry of Labour, 1953 (LML).

207. **Gandhi** (Madhu M) : Comparative occupational patterns among women in US and India. *Journal of Family Welfare* V 27(1), 1980, pp. 46–56.

208. **Gokhale** (Godavari) : A note on women workers in India. Bombay, Servants of India Society, n.d., 32 pp. (GUL).

209. **Golden Jubilee Symposium on Women, Work and Society**, New Delhi, 1982 : Papers. New Delhi, Indian Statistical Institute, 1982 (ISI, ISST).
The symposium had two important sessions (*a*) on the data bases for Indian studies on women and work and (*b*) a review of these studies.

210. **Gopalan** (Sarala) : Haryana women—A profile. *Social Welfare* V 27(11), 1981, pp. 52–55.
Gives the occupational distribution of women in the work force in Haryana.

211. **Gopalan** (Sarala) : Occupational distribution of women in Kerala. *Social Welfare* V 27(5–6), 1980, pp. 48–51, 53.
Suggests that the occupational distribution of women has to shift from low paid monotonous jobs to better paid

technologically superior work if the quality of working is to improve.

212. **Gopalan** (Sarala) : Women in white-collar professions. *Social Welfare* V 27(5–6), 1980, pp. 43–47, 63–64.

Deals with women who work as nurses, laboratory technicians and in the electronics industry.

213. **Gulati** (Leela) : Occupational distribution of working women and inter-state comparison. *Economic and Political Weekly* V 10(43), 1975, pp. 1692–704.

214. **India,** Ministry of Education and Social Welfare, Department of Social Welfare : Towards equality—Report of the Committee on the Status of Women in India. New Delhi, ICSSR, 1974, 480 pp. (ISST).

Contains a detailed chapter on employment presenting an overview of the employment situation till 1974.

215. **India,** Ministry of Labour : Women in employment. New Delhi, Government of India Press, 1964, 146 pp. (RUWS).

216. **India,** Ministry of Labour, Labour Bureau : Economic and social status of women workers in India. Simla, Labour Bureau, 1953, 97 pp. (RUWS).

217. **India,** Planning Commission and Labour Bureau : Women in employment, 1901–1956. New Delhi, Government of India Press, 1958, 41 pp. (LML).

218. **Institute of Applied Manpower Research** : Area manpower survey—Special problems of women and children. New Delhi, IAMR, 1965, 133 pp. (IAMR).

219. **International Labour Organisation** : Working women in changing India. New Delhi, ILO, 1963, 109 pp. (RUWS).

220. **Jain** (Devaki) : Women in employment—Some preliminary observations. New Delhi, Institute of Social Studies Trust, 1983, 26 pp. (ISST).

Report of the Workshop on Women and Poverty held in Calcutta, 17–18 March 1983.

221. **Jorapur** (P B) : A comparative picture of the demographic characteristics of working and non-working women.

Indian Journal of Social Work V 26(2), 1968, pp. 183–91.

222. **Jorapur** (P B) : Working women in Dharwar Taluka. *Journal of the Institute of Economic Research* V 1(2), 1966, pp. 20–25.

223. **Madras School of Social Work** : Working mothers in white-collar occupations. Madras, MSSW, 1966, 200 pp. (MSSW).

224. **Mankekar** (Kamala) : Women working against odds. *Yojana* V 24(16), 1980, pp. 13–14.
Emphasises that women's economic contribution goes unrecognised and highlights the problems faced by women in the organised and unorganised sectors.

225. **Manipur**, Directorate of Women and Children's Programme : Socio-economic status of women of Manipur. Imphal, DWCP, 1979 (NIRD).
Discusses the role of Manipuri women in agriculture, industry, commerce and trade.

226. **Mehta** (Sushila) : *Revolution and the status of women in India.* New Delhi, Metropolitan, 1982, 278 pp. (JNU).
Discusses the role of women workers in the organised sector.

227. **Nayak** (Sharada) : Ed. Profiles of Indian women. New Delhi, Educational Resources Centre, 1977, 56 pp. (ISST).
Profiles of working women and their innate ability to cope with diverse and difficult roles.

228. **Punjabi University**, Centre for Research in Economic Changes : Changing occupational structure of women in Punjab. Patiala, CREC, 1976, 73 pp. (LML).
Analyses the extent to which women participate in the economic activities and the different occupations they are engaged in. This is based on the analysis of data from the 1961 and 1971 Censuses, other statistical sources in addition to collecting primary data from Patiala district.

229. **Patel** (B B) : Blue-collar women workers in Ahmedabad—

Employment, occupational structure and earnings. Ahmedabad, Sardar Patel Institute of Economic and Social Change, 1979, 97 pp. (SPIESC).

230. **Patel** (Tara) : Report on a socio-economic survey of women in professions in the city of Ahmedabad. Ahmedabad, Gujarat University, 1958. Thesis.

231. **Pinchholiya** (K R) : Women workers in metropolitan city— A study of Ahmedabad. *Indian Journal of Labour Economics* V 20(4), 1978, pp. 319–28.

232. **Rai** (Ratna Prabha) : Women can do it—Adivasi women workers employed in Tata's. *Social Welfare* V 5(2), 1958, pp. 12–13.
Adivasi women are employed in all departments and are given suitable training.

233. **Rallia Ram** (Mayavanthi) : New facets of Muslim women. *Mainstream* V 11(19), pp. 29–34, 40.
Interviews with educated Muslim teachers, doctors, radio artists, librarians, journalists, etc.

234. **Ramanamma** (A) : *Graduate employed women in an urban seting.* Poona, Dastane Ramchandra, 1979, 159 pp. (JL).

235. **Ranadive** (Vimal) : *Women workers of India.* Calcutta, National Book Agency, 1976 (AIWC).

236. **Renuka :** Working women. *How* V 3(5), 1980, pp. 1–3.
The article deals with the dual roles performed by women—case studies of a teacher and a chikan worker.

237. **Sengupta** (P) : *Women workers of India.* Bombay, Asia Publishing House, 1960, 256 pp. (IIPA, AIWC).
The book is divided into two parts—(*a*) women in factories, mines, plantations and agriculture, (*b*) women in services, trades and professions.

238. **Sharma** (Kanta Devi) : Socio-economic study of women employees in Bhopal City. Ujjain, Vikram University, 1974. Thesis.

239. **Srivastava** (Ginny) : Problems of working women— Uncensored script on conditions of working women

—rural and urban—in Rajasthan prepared for AIR talk.
1983, 6 pp. (CWDS, AIWC).

240. **Strobel** (M) : Study of professional women in Delhi.
Delhi, University of Delhi, 1967. Thesis.

241. **Workshop on Women in the Indian Labour Force**,
Trivandrum, 1980 : Proceedings and papers. Bangkok,
Asian Regional Team for Employment Promotion,
1981, 137 pp. (ISST).

Discussions were organised around nine topics—the important ones being (*a*) concepts and definitions used in
national surveys, (*b*) labour unions and female workers, (*c*)
measures to improve statistical bases, (*d*) technological
change and its implication for women.

4

Women in Industries : General Studies

242. **Agnihotri** (V) : Women in industry. *Indian Labour Journal* V 4(9), 1963, pp. 895–917.
   Traces the participation of Indian women in economic activities historically and compares the situation with USA, France and UK.

243. **Bahl** (Sarojini) : Conditions of labour of working women in organised industries of Madhya Pradesh. Jabalpur, Jabalpur University, 1966. Thesis.

244. **Banerjee** (Nirmala) : The role of women workers in export oriented industries—Five case studies of West Bengal. Calcutta, Centre for Studies in Social Sciences, 1983, 109 pp. (SSDC).

245. **Champalakshmi** (R) : Working conditions of women, young workers, old workers and other special categories. *Productivity* V 23(1), 1982, pp. 41–48.

246. **Chatterjee** (Kamala) : Women in industry. *Modern Review* V 142(6), 1977, pp. 347–51; V 144(1&2), 1978, pp. 30–44, 85–89.

247. **Dayal** (P D) : The role of women power in industrial growth. *Social Welfare* V 9(9), 1962, pp. 21–22.

248. **Desai** (S F) : Role of small-scale industries in feeding large industries and women's part therein. Bombay, Author, 1959, 36pp. (NL).
   Gives statistics of women employed in small-scale

industries and compares it with the situation in Japan and America. Also emphasises the need for training women in business management and in the use of machines.

249. **Devadas** (R P) : Women workers in industry. Paper presented at the Conference on Human Relations in Industry, Coimbatore, 1962 (CSSS).

250. **Gulati** (Leela) : Women in the urban industrial labour force in India. Trivandrum, Centre for Development Studies, 1981, 24 pp. (CDS).

251. **Gulati** (Leela) : Women workers in industry—Kerala case studies. *State and Society* V 2 2(3), 1981, pp. 34–47.

252. **Halge** (Molly Juan) : Women power in industry. *Mainstream* V 13(34), 1975, p. 21.

253. **Hussain** (Sahiba) and **Rao** (V R) : Status of women in public sector industries—Impact of national policy, training facilities and special programme. New Delhi, ICSSR Programme of Women's Studies, mimeo, n.d., 84 pp. (CWDS).

Presents an analysis of the secondary data on employment in public sector industries such as coal, textiles, pharmaceuticals, electronics, heavy electrical and watch making regarding employment opportunities, training facilities, management policies and impact of technology on women.

254. **India**, Ministry of Labour, Labour Bureau : Study on employment of women in clothing, chemical and electronics industries. Chandigarh, Labour Bureau, 1978, 27 pp. (ISST).

255. **India**, Ministry of Labour, Labour Bureau : Women in industry. Delhi, Labour Bureau, 1975, 241 pp. (CWDS).

256. **Jai Prakash** : Women in industry. *Indian Labour Journal* V 16(8), 1975, pp. 1145–62.

Reviews the employment situation in various industries both in the organised and unorganised sectors.

257. **Jha** (Satyavathi) : Socio-economic conditions of women workers in organised industry of UP. Agra, Agra University, 1961. Thesis.

258. **Kalpagam** (U): Labour market segmentation in a multi-
     structural context and its implications on the female
     labour force. Paper presented at the Second National
     Conference on Women's Studies—Session on Work
     and Employment, Trivandrum, 1984, 23 pp. Also
     published as Working Paper No. 44, MIDS, 1984;
     and in *Labour, Capital and Society* V 17(2), 1984.
     The paper is in two parts. The first part deals with the
     nature of industrial structure and the characteristics of
     female industrial labour force in India. The second part
     deals with the implications for an analysis of the class
     dimensions of labour markets, job stratification, hierarchies
     and occupational segregation and how they affect the
     divisions of labour between men and women.

259. **Kalra** (Krishan Kumar): Study of women in employment—
     A study of one hundred working women. Delhi,
     University of Delhi, 1969. Thesis.
     A study of women working in industries manufacturing
     radio parts, optical goods and computers and as sales girls.

260. **Kanji** (Dwarkadas): Women and children in industry. *Indian
     Journal of Social Work* V 9(1), 1948, pp. 43–51.

261. **Kara** (M): Impact of industrialisation on women. *Janata*
     V 26(1–3), 1971, pp. 69–71, 76.
     With industrial development more women are trying to
     secure jobs in industries. It gives the percentage of women
     workers in different industries and the annual percentage
     of women seeking jobs in industries.

262. **Mehta** (V J): A survey of labour mobility of women indus-
     trial workers in Bombay City. Bombay, Tata
     Institute of Social Sciences, 1965, 92 pp. (TISS).
     Discusses the factors influencing mobility such as dis-
     semination of information about job opportunities and
     major obstacles to mobility of labour force.

263. **Oza** (Ghanshyambhai): Role of women in rural industries.
     Khadi Gramodyog V 22(1), 1975, pp. 9–14; V 22(8),
     1975, pp. 27–28.
     Discusses the reasons for the non-representation of women
     in rural industries.

264. **Patel** (B B) : Technology, employment and occupation of women workers—Manufacturing sector in Gujarat. Paper presented at the Workshop on Women, Technology and Forms of Production, Madras, 1984 (MIDS).

Presents an overview of women's economic activities in Gujarat. A majority of blue-collar women workers are employed in the textile industry. Also gives a break up for women in various industries.

265. **Rajula Devi** (A K) : Women in rural industries. *Kurukshetra* V 30(23), 1982, pp. 13–16.

Discusses the employment of women in the organised sector, industry-wise, outlines the drawbacks and suggests a three-fold strategy to increase the employment of women.

266. **Ranadive** (Vimal) : Working class women. *Social Scientist* V 4(4–5), 1975, pp. 146–59.

Deals with the problems of working women such as employment and unemployment, working conditions and other related problems in various industries.

267. **Rohatagi** (Rekha K) : Some observations of female participation rate in the industrial metropolis of Kanpur (UP). Paper presented at the National Conference on Women's Studies, Bombay, 1981, 5 pp. (ISST).

A comparison of female work participation with particular reference to industrial participation over the years 1951–1971.

268. **Sahay** (T) : Special problems of women in industries. *Social Welfare* V 7(5), 1960, pp. 7–8.

Deals with the special problems of women in industries particularly the ones relating to health and the extent to which the welfare measures adopted by the Government have helped them.

269. **Seminar on Women in Industry**, New Delhi, 1968 : Proceedings. New Delhi, Indian Council for Medical Research, 1969, 71 pp. (PC).

270. **Sengupta** (P) : Planning for women in industry. *Social Welfare* V 2(1), 1955, pp. 17–19.

Discusses why women in Indian industries are being

retrenched and suggests a solution for providing alternative employment.

271. **Sengupta** (P) : The problems of women in Indian industries. *Social Welfare* V 4(12), 1958, pp. 2–3.

   Expresses concern on the downward trend of employment of women in industries.

272. **Sengupta** (P) : Women in unregulated and miscellaneous industries. *Social Welfare* V 1(7), 1954, pp. 7–9, 45.

   Deals with the working conditions and wages of women working in unregulated industries such as cashewnut and chemical industries, rice mills and tobacco industry.

273. **Sharan** (Raka) : Working conditions and job satisfaction among industrial women workers—A case study. *Indian Journal of Industrial Relations* V 15(4), 1980, pp. 605–10.

   Shows that the working conditions are not satisfactory and women do not have job satisfaction whether in the public or private sector.

274. **Vijayalakshmi** (K) : Women and small industries in Goa. *Laghu Udyog Samachar* V 3(2), 1978, pp. 13–14.

5

Women in the Informal Sector : General Studies

275. **All India Women's Conference** : Artisans in the Indian society. Bombay, AIWC, 1979, 72 pp. (AIWC).
Discusses the struggle of women artisans for existence and their place in society.

276. **Banerjee** (Nirmala) : Unorganised women workers—Calcutta experience. Calcutta, Centre for Studies in Social Sciences, 1982, 188 pp. (CSSS).
Covers supari cutters, lifafa makers, papad makers, toy makers, etc.

277. **Banerjee** (Nirmala) : Why they get a worse deal—Report on unorganised women workers in Calcutta. *Manushi* No. 20, 1984, pp. 15–23.
Analyses the conditions under which women seek employment and observes that women have been conditioned to accept that they are primarily wives and mothers, not workers. This mental attitude only makes them more vulnerable to exploitation by employers.

278. **Banerjee** (Nirmala) : Women workers and development. *Social Scientist* V 6(8), 1978, pp. 3–15.
Deals with some aspects of the role of women workers in India's development. The growth of women's work in the unorganised sector does nothing to reduce poverty and contains within it the seeds of a state of increasing misery.

279. **Barve** (Jayashree) : Occupational life of self-employed Godadiya women. Baroda, Maharaja Sayajirao

University, 1979, 52 pp. Thesis.

280. **Bhatt** (Ela R) : Defending our rightful place in the city of Ahmedabad—SEWA's experience with urban poor women. Ahmedabad, Self Employed Women's Association, n.d. (ISST).

Describes the experience of SEWA in organising the unorganised labour and describes the different categories of workers in the informal sector.

281. **Bhatt** (Ela R) : Profiles of self-employed women. Ahmedabad, Self Employed Women's Association, 1976, 87 pp. (ISST).

Analyses the profiles of women workers in different fields and occupations—vegetable vendors, hand-cart pullers, garment makers, milkmaids, and junk-smiths.

282. **Bhatt** (Ela R) : The invisibility of home-based work—The case of piece-rate workers in India. Paper presented at the Asian Regional Conference on Women and the Household, New Delhi, 1985 (ISST).

Describes the working and living conditions of piece-rate workers.

283. **Buch** (A N) and **Bhatt** (Ela R) : SEWA marches ahead. Ahmedabad, SEWA, n.d., 12 pp. (ISST).

Discusses the different profiles of women such as firewood pickers, head loaders, garment workers, and milkmaids.

284. **Burman** (Kumar) : Social context of non-participation of women in labour among non-cultivating castes in Bholpur Block. Paper presented at the National Conference on Women's Studies, Bombay, 1981 (ISST).

Discusses the low work participation rates among women artisans.

285. **Dalaya** (C K) : Socio-economic study of unorganised women workers in the slum areas of Bombay City—A pilot project report. Bombay, SNDT, 1978, 71pp. (RDAS).

Presents the working and social conditions of women in the slum areas who are chiefly domestic workers and vegetable vendors.

286. **Dighe** (Anita) : Women's employment in the urban informal

sector—Some critical issues. *Social Change* V 15(2), 1985, pp. 3–6.

Opines that census data presents a distorted picture of women, particularly of their participation in the economy and labour force. At the micro-level a great deal of research remains to be done to understand how the informal sector relates to the wider urban economy.

287. **Eapen** (Mridul) : Women workers in the unorganised sector in Kerala. Paper presented at the Second National Conference on Women's Studies—Session on Work and Employment, Trivandrum, 1984, 17 pp. (ISST).

Focuses on the pattern of women's employment in the unorganised sector by detailed industrial categories in order to identify those activities in which women are predominant and discusses some issues concerning the organisation of women workers in the unorganised sector.

288. **Gambhir** (G D) : Labour in small-scale industries in MP with special reference to women and child labour in cotton ginning, bidi making, rice milling and shellac industries. Ujjain, Vikram University, 1970. Thesis.

289. **Gangrade** (K D) and **Gathia** (Joseph A) : Ed. *Women and child workers in unorganised sector—Non-governmental organisation perspectives.* New Delhi, Concept, 1983, 104 pp. (AIWC).

Analyses the problem of working women in the unorganised sector. The problems are discrimination and differentials in wages. This is due to lack of marketing links, lack of capital and non-availability of raw materials.

290. **Gulati** (Leela) : *Profiles in female poverty—A study of five poor working women in Kerala.* Delhi, Hindustan, 1981, 179 pp. (ISST).

A study of low income working women in Kerala engaged in five different occupations—agriculture, coir, brick, construction, and fish vending.

291. **Gulati** (Leela) : Women in the unorganised sector with special reference to Kerala. Trivandrum, Centre for Development Studies, 1982, 22 pp. (CDS).

292. **Heggade** (O D) : Development of women entrepreneurship

in India—Problems and prospects. *Economic Affairs*
V 26(1), 1981, pp. 39–50.

Suggests that the condition of female employment can be
efficiently tackled by improving entrepreneurship among
women.

293. **India**, Ministry of Labour, Directorate General of Employment and Training : Report of a survey to find out
the occupational structure of self-employed women in
resettlement colonies of Delhi. New Delhi, DGET,
1978, 38 pp. (JNU).

Gives the occupation-wise break up of the number of self-
employed women in Kalyanpuri and Mangolpuri and also
the monthly income for each occupation computed on basis
of daily wages.

294. **Indian Co-operative Union** : Women's employment in
handicraft industry—A monograph. New Delhi, ICU,
1979 (ISST).

Paper based on secondary data includes the following
industries : textile, hand-printing, tie and dye, zari industry, crochet lace industry, cane, bamboo and willow work,
pottery, lacquerware, metalware, and agarbathi industry.

295. **Jain** (Devaki), **Singh** (Nalini) and **Chand** (Malini) : *Women's
quest for power—Five Indian case studies.* New Delhi,
Vikas, 1980, 272 pp. (ISST).

Discusses five instances where Indian women in large
numbers have organised themselves in pursuit of better
food, shelter and wages. The case studies are (*a*) street vendors of Ahmedabad, (*b*) milk producers of Kaira, (*c*) papad
rollers of Lijjat, (*d*) painters of Madhubani and (*e*) night
patrollers of Manipur.

296. **Kar** (Indrani) : Women in Indian society. *Capital* V 188
(4698), 1982, pp. 11–19.

Describes women's contribution in agricultural and non-
agricultural operations and in the unorganised sector.

297. **Kumar** (G) : Entrepreneurial development among women—A
comparative view. Paper presented at the Conference on Women's Status and Development,
Warangal, 1982, 14 pp. (ISST).

298. **Lebra** (Joyce) and others : Eds. *Women and work in India—Continuity and change.* New Delhi, Promilla, 1984, 310 pp. (TISS).

299. **Mazumdar** (Vina) : Women in the unorganised sector. Paper presented at the Seminar on Optimum Utilisation of Women Power for Development, New Delhi, 1975 (ISST).
Stresses that the unorganised sector which includes 94 per cent of women workers requires much more understanding because the entire decline in women's participation is seen there.

300. **Murali Manohar** (K) : *Socio-economic status of Indian women.* Delhi, Seema, 1983, 317 pp. (AIWC).

301. **Nadkarni** (Sulochana A) : Women entrepreneurship and economic development. Paper presented at the National Conference on Women's Studies, Bombay, 1981, 8 pp. (ISST).
Identifies the special difficulties and problems faced by women entrepreneurs in different industries and provides guidelines to solve their problems.

302. **Nair** (G R) : International conference on women entrepreneurs. *Social Welfare* V 27(9), 1980, pp. 7–9, 22, 28.

303. National Conference of Women Entrepreneurs. *Fisme Review* V 2(1), 1982, pp. 1–53 (AIWC).

304. **Ninan** (Sevanti) : Sisterhood is self-help. *Voluntary Action* V 24(8), 1982, pp. 332–34.
Focuses on self-employed women, whose percentage in the unorganised work force is higher than men.

305. **Radha Devi** (D) and **Ravindran** : Women's work in India. *International Social Science Journal* V 35(4), 1983, pp. 683–99.
Discusses the overall participation rate of women in occupations like agriculture, plantation, construction work, industry, etc.

306. **Rai** (Prabha) : Unorganised labour force. *Social Welfare* V 22(6–7), 1975, pp. 16–18, 93.
Discusses the participation of women in non-agricultural

occupations like chikan, beedi and cigarette industries.

307. **Rajula Devi** (A K) : Women entrepreneurs. *Yojana* V 22(17), 1978, pp. 19–22.

308. **Sebstad** (Jennefer) : Struggle and development among self-employed women—A report on the SEWA Ahmedabad, India. Ahmedabad, SEWA, 1982, 340 pp. (ISST).
Emphasises the role of self-employed women in the labour market in Ahmedabad. They are grouped into three categories (*a*) vendors, traders of vegetables, fish, (*b*) home-based producers of beedi, papad, (*c*) those selling services, e.g., scrap pickers, construction labourers.

309. **Second International Conference of Women Entrepreneurs**, New Delhi, 1981 : Report. 21 pp. (ISST).

310. **Shobha** (V) : Women in unorganised sector—A study. Warangal, Kakatiya University, 1984. Thesis (KU).

311. **Srinivasan** (Viji) : Rural marketing—A micro-level study of Pullampatti Village in Omalur Block, Salem District, Tamil Nadu and of periodic markets of Omalur Village (Tuesdays) and Muthunaickampatti Village (Fridays). New Delhi, Ford Foundation, 1983 (ISST).

312. **Sundar** (Pushpa) : Education and socialization of professional women—The case of women entrepreneurs. Paper presented at the Seminar on Socialisation, Education and Women, New Delhi, 1985 (ISST).

313. **Third International Conference of Women Entrepreneurs**, New Delhi, 1984 : Proceedings. New Delhi, National Alliance of Young Entrepreneurs, 1984 (ISST).

314. **Varadappan** (Sarojini) : Emergence of women entrepreneurs. *Social Welfare* V 23(8), 1976, pp. 1–3, 10.

6

Women Workers : Studies by Occupation/ Industry

6.1 Agarbatti Making

315. **India**, Ministry of Labour and Rehabilitation, Labour Bureau : The working and living conditions of workers in the agarbathi industry in Karnataka—A report. Chandigarh, Labour Bureau, 1981, 66 pp. (ISST).

A survey conducted in fifty-six units to examine the working and living conditions, welfare amenities, housing problems, industrial relations, etc., of workers in the agarbathi industry.

316. The lines on their palms are worn away. *Manushi* No.15, 1983, p. 21.

Report of the survey conducted in the Vikas Agarbatti factory in Raipur, Maharashtra. It describes the working conditions of women agarbatti rollers and the impact on their health.

6.2 Agriculture

317. **Achanta** (Lakshmi Devi) : Role of rural women in agricultural development. *Kurukshetra* V 31(2), 1982, pp. 15–20.

318. **Agarwal** (Bina) : Women, rural poverty and agricultural

growth in India. Paper presented at the National
Seminar on Structural Constraints to Growth with
Equality. Delhi, Institute of Economic Growth, 1985,
101 pp. (IEG).

319. **Agarwal** (Bina) : Women, agricultural development strategies
and ecological imbalances—The Indian context.
Paper presented at the Asian Regional Seminar on
Women and the Household, New Delhi, 1985 (ISST).
Examines the implications of strategies vis-a-vis agriculture
and forestry for women from poor rural households.

320. **Agarwal** (Bina) : Water resource development and rural
women. Delhi, Institute of Economic Growth, 1981,
94 pp. (IEG).

321. **Andhra University**, Department of Co-operative and
Applied Economics : Factorisation of agriculture,
employment and productivity—An inquiry in West
Godavary District. Waltair, Andhra University, 1974
(AUL).

322. **Arunachalam** (Jaya) : Women in rice farming systems—
Experiment Working Women's Forum, alternative
employment options for Indian rural women. Madras,
Working Women's Forum, 1983 (WWF).

323. **Atchi Reddy** (M) : Female agricultural labourers of Nellore,
1881–1981. *Indian Economic and Social History Review*
V 20(1), 1983, pp. 67–80.

324. **Bhatnagar** (Suman R) : In Rajasthan—Tribal women play a
significant role. *Indian Farming* V 25(8), 1975, p. 81.

325. **Bhatt** (Kokila P) : Leading role in agriculture and animal husbandry. *Indian Farming* V 25(8), 1975, p. 39
Highlights the importance of women's work in these basic
and extremely significant sectors.

326. **Bose** (Sukla) : Caste, tribe and female labour participation.
Social Change V 15(2), 1985, pp. 15–20.
Examines the relationship between tribe, caste and female
labour participation among the poorer households in four
villages of Bengal. Focuses on the caste hierarchy and sex-

based division of labour. The households selected for analysis are those of agricultural labourers and poor peasants in Bengal.

327. **Chakravarthy** (Shanti) : Farm women labour-waste and exploitation. *Social Change* V 5(1–2), 1975, pp. 9–16.

328. **Chakravarthy** (S) : Women power in agriculture. *Kurukshetra* V 24(4), 1975, pp. 8–9, 12.

329. **Chatterjee** (Attreyi) : Landless agricultural women workers —A statistical profile. *Indian Farming* (V 25(8), 1975, pp. 30–32.

330. **Chatterjee** (R) : Marginalisation and the induction of women into wage labour, case study of Indian agriculture. Geneva, International Labour Organisation, 1984, World Employment Programme Research Working Paper No. 32 (ILO).

331. **Chattopadhyaya** (Manabendu) : Role of female labour in Indian agriculture. *Social Scientist* V 10(17), 1982, pp. 43–54.

332. **Chawdhari** (T P S) and **Sharma** (B M) : Female labour of the farm family in agriculture. *Agricultural Situation in India* V 16(6), 1961, pp. 643–50.

333. **Chopra** (Kusum) : Female work participation in three group regions of India—An inter-temporal study of rural India between 1951, 1961, 1971. New Delhi, Indian Council of Social Science Research, 1977, 33 pp. (SSDC).

Analyses the trends in female work participation rates in major wheat, rice and millet growing areas in sixty-two districts of the country. Its main focus is on women workers in the agricultural sector.

334. **Das** (Arvind Narayan) : Agricultural labour in bonded freedom. *Economic and Political Weekly* V 11(20), 1976, pp. 724–26.

335. **Dasgupta** (Arunava) and **Deshpande** (Ragini Shankar) : Sericulture, more employment through waste utilisation—The scope of utilisation of silk wastes for providing women with gainful employment.

Bangalore, Social Action Foundation India, 1983, 139 pp. (ISST).

A study conducted in Bangalore, Mysore, Mandya and Kolar and Malda in West Bengal discusses in detail the utilisation of silk wastage and the need for better technological climate.

336. **Datt Sharma** (Krishna) : Female participation in rural agricultural labour in North India—A spatial interpretation. *Manpower Journal* V 3(4), 1971, pp. 52–57.

337. **Deshpande** (Anjali) : Agrarian women, unanswered questions. *Mainstream* V 20(35), 1982, pp. 23–24.

Discusses the statistics, wages and other benefits like creches and maternity leave available to agricultural labourers and plantation workers.

338. **Devadas** (Rajammal P) : Role of women in modern agriculture. *Indian Farming* V 25(8), 1975, pp. 15–17.

339. **Devadas** (Rajammal P) : Women in agricultural productivity and home improvement. *Voluntary Action* V 20(6), 1978, pp. 3–7.

Describes the role of women in the agricultural sector and recommends training programmes for women in new technology, skill development, management and obtaining credit facilities.

340. **Devadas** (P R Muthu) and **Thangamani** (K) : Role of selected farm women in agricultural operation. *Indian Journal of Home Science* V 6(1), 1972, p. 50..

341. **Dholakia** (Anila R) : Let the other half participate—Women and agrarian reforms in Gujarat. Paper presented at the National Seminar on Agrarian Reforms in India, Bangalore, 1983. Ahmedabad, SEWA, 9pp. (SEWA).

342. **Dholakia** (Anila R) : Rural women and a challenge to food production. Paper presented at the Expert Consultation on Women and Food Production at FAO, UN, Rome, 1983 (ISST).

A survey of 200 women farmer trainees of Gujarat Vidya Peeth Agriculture Training Institute, Ahmedabad reveals that majority of them suffered heavily because of lack of irrigation facilities, bullock carts, bullock improved fertilisers and seeds.

343. **Girija Rani** : Female work participation in Indian agriculture. Warangal, Kakatiya University, 1984, 162 pp. Thesis.

344. **Gulati** (Leela) : Profile of a female agricultural labourer. *Economic and Political Weekly* V 13(12), 1978, pp. A27–A35.

   Attempts to answer questions regarding female labour and its value. A case study of an agricultural labourer from Kerala is also included in the article.

345. **Gulati** (Leela) : Sex discrimination in farm wages. Trivandrum, Centre for Development Studies, 1976, 10 pp. (CDS).

346. **Gulati** (Leela) : Unemployment among female agricultural labourers. *Economic and Political Weekly* V 11(13), 1976, pp. A31–A39.

347. **Haragopal** (G) and others : Female agricultural labour in Andhra Pradesh—A micro analysis. Paper presented at the Conference on Women's Status and Development, Warangal, 1982 (SOWSTUD).

   Studies and analyses the problems of female labour in Medak and Godavary districts of AP. Gives data regarding income and caste.

348. **Horowitz** (B) and **Kishwar** (Madhu) : Family life, the unequal deal—Women's conditions and family life among agricultural labourers and small farmers in Punjab village. *Manushi* No. 11, 1982, pp. 2–18.

   A detailed study of the work, income indebtedness, working hours, nutrition, and health of women agricultural labourers and small farmers.

349. **India**, Ministry of Agriculture : Country review and analysis of the role and participation of women in agriculture and rural development—Report of the national level committee appointed by the Ministry of Agriculture. New Delhi, 1979, 53 pp. (NIRD).

350. **International Labour Organisation** : Agricultural labour

in India—Summary of the second inquiry into the conditions of agricultural labour of the Ministry of Labour. *International Labour Review* V 85(1), 1962, pp. 248–61.

351. **Janaki Ammal** (E K) : While the men went hunting. *Indian Farming* V 25(8), 1975, p. 34.
Analyses the primitive women's participation in economic activities such as cattle breeding when their husbands were out hunting.

352. **Kala** (C V) : Female participation in farm work in Central Kerala. *Sociological Bulletin* V 24(2), 1976, pp. 185–206.

353. **Kumar** (Dinesh) and **Singh** (A K) : Role of women in rural economy. *Kurukshetra* V 31(7), 1983, pp. 13–14.

354. **Lahiri** (R K) : Inter-state and seasonal variation in agricultural labourers' work participation. Paper presented at the Seminar on Optimum Utilisation of Women Power for Development, New Delhi, 1975.
Examines the work pattern of women workers in the agricultural sector. The paper is based on data from the 25th round of NSS. It clearly describes the seasonal variation in the employment of women agricultural labourers.

355. **Malhans** (Nirlep) : Role of women in agricultural and rural development. New Delhi, Jawaharlal Nehru University, 1982, 84 pp. (JNU).

356. **Mazumdar** (Vina) : Women in agriculture. *Indian Farming* V 25(8), 1985, pp. 5–9.
Describes the participation of women in agriculture and emphasises that development has sometimes led to a shrinking of women's role in agriculture.

357. **Mazumdar** (Vina) and others : Country review and analysis of the role and participation of women in agriculture and rural development in India. New Delhi, ICSSR, 1979, 51 pp. (CSSS).

358. **Mencher** (John P) : *Agriculture and social structure in Tamil Nadu.* Bombay, Allied, 1978. 314 pp. (ISST).
Examines the relationship between the structure of society

and agriculture in Chingleput district of Tamil Nadu and women's role therein.

359. **Mencher** (John P) and **Saradamoni** (K): Muddy feet, dirty hands--Rice production and female agricultural labour. *Economic and Political Weekly* V 17(52), 1982, pp. A 149–A 67.

360. **Misra** (Sridhar): Women and child labour in agriculture in UP. *Rural India* V 11(17), 1951, pp. 264–68.

361. **Mukherji** (A B): Female participation in agricultural labour in UP—Special variations. *National Geographer* No. 6, 1971, pp. 13–18.

362. **Mukherji** (A B): Female participation in rural agricultural labour in Andhra Pradesh — A study in population geography. *Deccan Geographer* V 12(1), 1974, pp. 1–25.

363. **Mukherii** (A B) and **Mehta** (Swaranjit): Female participation in agricultural labour in India and patterns of association. *Punjab University Research Bulletin AMIS* V 4(2), 1973, pp. 165–79.

364. **Mukherjee** (Mukul) and **Jain** (Devaki): Statistics on women, children and aged in agriculture in India. New Delhi, Institute of Social Studies Trust, 1983, 133 pp. (ISST).

365. **Mulay** (Sumati) and **Singh** (Jagdish): Farm work in Delhi villages—Role of women. *Kurukshetra* V 12(2), 1964, pp. 10–17.

366. **Nair** (G Ravindran): The unenviable lot of rural working women. *Kurukshetra* V 30(3), 1981, pp. 4–6.

367. **Omvedt** (Gail): The downtrodden among the downtrodden —An interview with a Dalit agricultural labourer. *Signs* V 4(4), 1979, pp. 763–74.

368. **Palriwala** (Rajani): Agrarian change and women. Paper presented at the National Conference on Women's Studies, Bombay, 1981.
    Raises a methodological issue in social research in order to identify and tackle two major problems, viz., exploitation and oppression that women face in the rural sector.

369. **Parthasarathy** (G) and **Adishesh** (K) : Growth fluctuations and real wages in AP agriculture—An inter-district analysis. Waltair, Andhra University, Agro-Economic Research Centre, 1982 (AERC).

Gives data on wages of female agricultural labour for the periods 1968–69 and 1978–79 for the State of Andhra Pradesh and different districts of Andhra Pradesh.

370. **Reddy** (Narasimha D) : Women in economic development. The scheduled caste female agricultural labourers in India—A target group approach. Paper presented at the Conference on Women's Status and Development, Warangal, 1982, 13 pp. (SOWSTUD and ISST).

Deals with the role, work status, inter-state variations based on the 1971 Census among scheduled caste women.

371. **Round Table on Women in Agriculture**, New Delhi, 1984 : Papers. New Delhi, Ministry of Rural Development, 1984 (ISST).

Papers relating to women's contribution in agriculture, the various development programmes initiated for their welfare, a case study of Achhaya village and the situation of women in the Seventh Plan were presented.

372. **Roy** (Burman) : Agricultural revolution—Loss and gain for women. *Indian Farming* V 25(8), 1975, p. 29.

373. **Saikia** (Anuva) : Seasonal variation of female participation in farm work. *Kurukshetra* V 31(9), 1983, pp. 15–17.

374. **Saikia** (Anuva) : State of female agricultural labour in Assam. *Kurukshetra* V 32(6), 1984, pp. 11–13.

375. **Saikia** (P D) and **Gogoi** (Kala) : Women labour in North East India. *Yojana* V 25(12), 1981, pp. 11–12.

Describes the types of jobs performed by women. Most of them are engaged in agriculture and do odd jobs like uprooting, planting, seedling, transplanting, harvesting and threshing.

376. **Saradamoni** (K) : Women's status in agrarian relations—A Kerala experience. *Economic and Political Weekly* V 17(5), 1982, pp. 155–62.

377. **Saradamoni** (K): Women's work—Need for indepth look. Paper presented at the Golden Jubilee Symposium on Women, Work and Society. New Delhi, Indian Statistical Institute, 1982, 21 pp. (ISST).

The first part of this paper is devoted to the definitional problem of what constitutes women's work. The second part is based on a study of involvement of women in the production processing of paddy in Kerala, giving details about the employment earnings and the contribution of women to household work.

378. **Sen** (Gita): Inter-regional aspects of the incidence of women agricultural labourers' (district level) employment earnings. Paper presented at the Workshop on Women and Poverty, Calcutta, 1983 (ISST).

Looks closely at the relationship between incidence and agricultural growth, productivity, land inequality, and the cultivation of coarse grains at the district level. It also examines some of the regional features of unemployment and differential earnings among women agricultural labourers.

379. **Sen** (Gita): Paddy production, processing and women workers in India—The south versus the north case. Trivandrum, Centre for Development Studies, 1983, 26 pp. (CDS).

380. **Sen** (Gita): Women agricultural labourers—Regional variations in incidence and employment. Trivandrum, Centre for Development Studies, 1983, 39 pp. (CDS).

381. **Seth** (Padma): The exploited labour force. *Social Welfare* V 22(6–7), 1975, pp. 19–20.

Deals with the problems of women in the agricultural sector, bonded labour and women in the unorganised sector in general.

382. **Sethi** (Raj Mohini): Female labour in agriculture. Chandigarh, Punjab University, 1982, 157 pp. (ISI).

Studies intensively the condition of female labourers and analyses the reasons for low participation rates in various types of economic activities.

383. **Sharma** (Krishan Datt): Female participation in rural agricultural labour in Northern India. *Manpower Journal* V 8(4), 1973, pp. 52–67.

384. **Sharma** (Ursula M): Women's participation in agriculture in India. *Current Anthropology* V 23(2), 1982, pp. 194–95.

385. **Shobha** (V): Women agricultural labourers in India—A study. Warangal, Kakatiya University, 1984. Thesis.

386. **Singh** (R P): Employment of family labour and its productivity in agriculture. Varanasi, Banaras University, 1969. Thesis.

387. **Singh** (T R): Role of farm women in decision-making— Their participation in subsidiary occupations. Paper presented at the National Conference on Women's Studies, Bombay, 1981 (ISST).
Discusses women's role in agricultural operations. A large proportion of women participate in seed storage, winnowing, care of animals and harvesting. Focuses on the decision-making power of women.

388. **Sridharan** (Sumi): In Chhatera, Maya, Bhim Kaur and Chalthi. *Indian Farming* V 25(8), 1975, pp. 43–46.
A collection of case studies of women in agriculture.

389. **Thamarajakshi** (R): Women in Indian agriculture. New Delhi, Planning Commission, n.d., 17 pp. (ISST).

390. **Vanamala** (M): Hired and family labour among women—A case study. *Mainstream* V 20(28), 1983, pp. 28–30.

391. Women in India—Decline in sex ratio—High incidence of illiteracy, fall in work opportunities, increase in agricultural labour. *How* V 2(4), 1979, pp. 28–30.
Gives details regarding women workers in India with special emphasis on the rural sector.

6.3 *Armed And Civil Services*

392. **Arora** (Gulshan): Study of women working in All India Radio. Delhi, University of Delhi, 1969. Thesis (DSSW).

393. **Bhardwaj** (Aruna) : Police modernization in India—A study of women police in Delhi. *Indian Journal of Social Work* V 37(1), 1976, pp. 39–48.

394. **Chaturvedi** (Gita) : *Women administrators of India—A study of the socio-economic background and attitudes of women administrators of Rajasthan.* Jaipur, RBSA Publishers, 1985, 328 pp. (ISST).

Analyses the socio-economic background and attitudes of women administrators of India with special focus on senior bureaucrats holding important administrative positions and the heads of educational institutions.

395. **Dharampal** : Work and living conditions of P & T Workers at Parliament Street Head Post Office. Delhi, University of Delhi, 1968. Thesis (DSSW).

396. **Ghosh** (S K) : *Women in policing.* New Delhi, Light & Life, 1981, 155 pp. (GUL, NIEPA).

397. **Mahajan** (A) : Women in the armed forces in India. *Indian Journal of Social Work* V 42(4), 1982, pp. 393–402.

398. **Mahajan** (Amrit) : *Indian police—A sociological study of a new role.* New Delhi, Deep and Deep, 1982, 198 pp. (AIWC).

399. **Mahajan** (Amarjit) : Police women in the States of Punjab, Himachal Pradesh and Union Territories of Chandigarh—A sociological study of a new role in Punjab, 1976–78. Chandigarh, Punjab University, n.d. Thesis.

400. **Maharashtra**, Committee to Examine the Problems facing Women Employees in Government Services : Report. Bombay, Government Central Press, 1972, 172 pp. (GUL).

401. **Mehrotra** (Deepti) and **Virdi** (Jyotika) : Women on the lowest rung—A report on the working conditions of telephone operators in Delhi. *Manushi* No. 6, 1980, pp. 10–13.

402. **Mitra** (Aruna) : From a gram sevika diary. *Kurukshetra* V 6(2), 1957, pp. 238–40.

403. Post woman knocks twice. *Yojana* V 11(2), 1967, p. 13.

404. **Ramanamma** (A) and **Bambawale** (U): Telephone operators— Women without faces. *Social Science Research Journal* V 3(3), 1979, pp. 93–111.

405. **Richards** (M D): Socio-economic survey of girls serving in Central Government offices residing in Vinay Nagar, colony of New Delhi. Delhi, University of Delhi, 1954. Thesis (DSSW).

406. **Sharma** (Kama): Women in employment. Delhi, University of Delhi, 1969. Thesis (CRL, DU).
Study of women working in the Eastern Court Telephone Exchange, New Delhi.

407. **Swarnalatha**: Women in the All India Services. *Prashasnika* V 11(4), 1982, pp. 39–48.
A historical review of women in the civil services, also gives details regarding women IAS officers recruited during the years 1951–78.

408. **Titus** (Aruna): Study of women police in Delhi. Delhi, University of Delhi, 1970. Thesis (DSSW).

409. **Vithayathil** (Teresa): Women in the IAS *Journal of National Academy of Administration* V 16(4), 1971, pp. 91–98.

410. Women employees in Indian Railways. *Indian Railways* V 20(5), 1975, pp. 57–64.

6.4 Banks

411. **Kelkar** (G): Women in the world of banks. Paper presented at the Seminar on Women and Development, Anand, 1977 (ISST). Also in *National Labour Institute Bulletin* V 5(9 & 10), 1979, pp. 303–10.
A survey conducted in seven nationalised banks in Maharashtra found that in none of the banks women were in charge of the personnel department.

412. **Nair** (G Ravindran): Syndicate Bank—The story of all women's branches. *Social Welfare* V 22(8), 1975, pp. 20–22.

413. **Sekaran** (Uma): A study of sex role difference in the Indian

banking industry. *Human Futures* V 19(2 & 3), 1981, pp. 184–87.

6.5   Beedi Rolling

414. **Abraham** (Amrita) : Beedi workers of Bombay. *Economic and Political Weekly* V 15(44), 1980, pp. 1881–82.
Report of the struggle of beedi workers regarding the supply of tendu leaves and minimum wages.

415. **Avachat** (Anil) : Beedi workers of Nipani. *Economic and Political Weekly* V 13(29), 1978, pp. 1176–78; V 13(30), 1978, pp. 1203–5.

416. **Baxi** (Upendra) : State, seths and sikhsa—The saga of Sattemma. Paper presented at the Asian Regional Conference on Women and the Household, New Delhi, 1985.
Describes the struggles/problems of women beedi workers when they participated in the activities of the Andhra Pradesh Beedi Workers Union.

417. Beedi workers of Sinnar. *Economic and Political Weekly* V 9(24), 1974, pp. 945–46.
Describes the working conditions of workers in Sinnar taluka of Nasik district in Maharashtra.

418. **Bhatty** (Zarina) : Economic role and status of women—A case study of women in the beedi industry in Allahabad. Geneva, ILO, 1980, 77 pp. (ISST). Also in *Manushi* No. 27, 1985, pp. 29–32.
Paper is based on an intensive study of women beedi workers in three tehsils of Allahabad district of Uttar Pradesh regarding the organisation of the industry, women's contribution to household income as a result of beedi-making and housework.

419. **Jayasingh** (J Visuthas) : Women beedi workers of Vellore. *Social Welfare* V 31(11), 1985, pp. 26–27.
Report of a socio-economic survey conducted by the Department of Social Work to investigate the difficulties and problems of beedi workers.

420. **Maheshwari** (Prakash Chandra) : Condition of labour in the beedi industry—In Central India. Agra, Agra University, 1962. Thesis.

421. **Mehta** (Prayag) : We are made to mortgage our children—Interviews with women beedi workers of Vellore. *Manushi* No. 22, 1985, pp. 14–17.
Report of the survey conducted for the National Labour Institute—interviews with fifty women beedi-makers.

422. **Mohandas** (M) : Beedi workers in Kerala—Conditions of life and work. *Economic and Political Weekly* V 15(36), 1980, pp. 1517–23.

423. **Murali Manohar** (K) and others : Beedi workers. Paper presented at the Conference on Women's Status and Development, Warangal, 1982 (SOWSTUD).
Study undertaken in the Nizamabad and Warangal districts of Andhra Pradesh. It intends to highlight the socio-economic background, work situation and life pattern of beedi rollers.

424. **Omvedt** (Gail) : Women roll beedis—Factory owners roll in wealth. *Manushi* No. 7, 1981, pp. 63–65.
Describes the struggle and suffering women have to go through in Nipani while the factory owners make money by exploiting these women.

425. **Pillai** (Lakshmi Devi K R) : Women beedi workers in a Kerala village. Paper presented at the Asian Regional Conference on Women and the Household, New Delhi, 1985 (ISST).
Compares the situation of women beedi workers working in a factory system with those working at home in relation to employment, work output of production, wages, working and health conditions, benefits, etc.

426. **Pujari** (Gobardhan) : A study of beedi-makers in Orissa. Delhi, University of Delhi, 1970. Thesis.

427. **Self Employed Women's Association** : Socio-economic survey of women workers employed in hand rolled beedi trade. Ahmedabad, SEWA, 1979, 6 pp. (ISST).
Survey was conducted around the city of Ahmedabad by SEWA with a view to organise the beedi-makers.

6.6 Block Printing

428. **Bhatt** (Ela R) : Socio-economic survey of Chipa women. Ahmedabad, SEWA, n.d., 36 pp. (ISST, SEWA).
A survey of Chipa women, i.e., those engaged in hand printing in Ahmedabad. The study analyses the socio-economic problems and suggests measures to make them economically stronger.

429. **Krishnaswami** (Lalita) : Workers become entrepreneurs— Story of block printers. Ahmedabad, Self Employed Women's Association, 1981, 13 pp. (ISST).
Highlights the efforts made by SEWA to train women hand block printers in new designs and selling techniques.

6.7 Brick Kilns

430. **Gulati** (Leela) : Female labour in the unorganised sector— Profile of a brick worker. Trivandrum, Centre for Development Studies, 1977, 27 pp. Also in *Economic and Political Weekly* V 14(16), 1979, pp. 744–52.

6.8 Cashew Industry

431. **Nair** (Aravindakshan K) : Women workers in cashew industry. New Delhi, Indian Council for Social Science Research, 1979, 185 pp. (SSDC).
Reviews the various jobs performed by women in the cashew industry and their socio-economic condition.

432. **Ranadive** (Vimal) : Women in the cashew industry among the lowest paid workers in Kerala. *Manushi* No. 12, 1982, pp. 33–35.
Describes the various jobs performed by women and the health hazards faced by women workers in the cashew industry in Mangalore.

6.9 Chikan Embroidery

433. **Ahmed** (Huma) : Socio-economic conditions of women in

chikan embroidery industry of Lucknow. 1982, 56 pp. (ISST).

Discusses the use of contract labour and explores the reasons why women are continuing with chikan work.

434. **Singh** (K P) : Embroidery workers in Patiala. Chandigarh, Punjab University, 1984. Unpublished thesis.

6.10 Coir Industry

435. **Mathew** (Molly) : Constant underemployment—Women in Kerala's coir industry. *Manushi* No. 9, 1981, pp. 27–29.

Examines the conditions of women, their contribution, wages, structure and the state of the coir industry in Kerala.

436. **Mathew** (Molly): Women workers in the unorganised sector of coir industry in Kerala. New Delhi, ICSSR, 1979, 133 pp.

437. **Velayudhan** (Meera): Struggles of women coir workers in the spinning sector, 1950–1970. *The Voice of the Working Woman* V 5(6), 1984, pp. 3–5.

Describes the struggles of women workers for minimum wages and their retrenchment.

6.11 Construction Work

438. **Atchi Reddy** (M) : Socio-economic conditions of women construction workers in Hyderabad. Paper presented at the Workshop on Women and Work, Hyderabad, 1985 (ISST).

A survey of twenty families in the city of Hyderabad to look into the working and living conditions and compares it with their counterparts in the villages.

439. **Mathur** (R N) and **Mathur** (Anju): Improving the working and living conditions of migrant women construction workers. Paper presented at the National Conference

on Women's Studies, Bombay, 1981 (ISST).

Discusses the problems faced by women migrant workers in Delhi.

440. **Mehta** (Pratibha) : Women construction workers with particular reference to legal security and social justice— A case study of Delhi. Delhi, National Institute of Urban Affairs, 1982, 103 pp. (CED).

441. **Murali Manohar** (K) and others: Women construction workers of Warangal. *Economic and Political Weekly* V 16(4), 1981, pp. 97–99.

Examines the life style, socio-economic background and work situation in Warangal city.

442. **Patna University**, Department of Labour and Social Welfare : Women construction workers—An inquiry into the conditions of women workers employed in major construction projects in and around Patna. Patna, Patna University, 1974, 123 pp. (ISST).

The study examines the socio-economic, working and living conditions of women workers.

443. **Ranade** (S N) and **Sinha** (G P): *Women construction workers—Reports of two surveys.* New Delhi, Allied, 1975, 79 pp. (ISST).

Surveys conducted in Delhi and Bihar to secure information about the social, economic and work life of construction workers. The Bihar study also provides a comparative glimpse into the life and habits of tribal women workers of Chotanagpur area of Bihar and non-tribals drawn from areas around Patna.

444. **Sengupta** (Padmini): Women in municipality and public works. *Social Welfare* V 1(8), 1954, pp. 13–15.

Describes the working conditions of sweepers, cleaners and construction labourers in various cities and towns.

6.12 Dairying

445. **Atreya** (Gita) : Sathmadurai women's dairy co-operative—A case study. New Delhi, Ford Foundation, 1985, 27 pp. (ISST).

446. **Atreya** (Gita) and **Chen** (Marty): Case study of women's dairy programme—Bhagavatula Charitable Trust. New Delhi, Ford Foundation, 1985, 30 pp. (ISST).

447. **Chen** (Marty) and **Dholakia** (Anila R): Case study of women's dairy co-operatives. Ahmedabad, Self Employed Women's Association, n.d. (ISST).
Documents the collaboration between NDDB and SEWA in promoting dairy co-operatives in sixty villages in Gujarat.

448. **Dholakia** (Anila R): Rural women in white revolution. Paper presented at the Seminar on Women and Dairy Co-operatives, New Delhi, UNICEF, 1984, 35 pp. (ISST).
Describes the efforts of some members of the rural wing of Self Employed Women's Association to form a diary co-operative.

449. **Mitra** (Manoshi): Integration of rural poor women into co-operative dairying—A case study from Andhra Pradesh. New Delhi, Ford Foundation, 1985, 49 pp. (ISST).
Attempts to look at the problems and prospects of providing women from poor households with an asset base and income source through acquisition of milch bovines and provision of adequate inputs and services in three districts of AP.

450. **Mitra** (Manoshi): A study of women in dairying in Andhra Pradesh—Report of the baseline survey on dairy producers' cooperatives in select villages in Andhra Pradesh. 1983, 268 pp. (ISST).
Survey conducted in five villages each in Nalgonda, Chitoor and Krishna districts.

451. **Mitra** (Manoshi): The women and the sacred cow—Women in dairy production. Paper presented at the Conference on Women, the State and the Household Economy, New Delhi, 1985. To be published by the Institute of Social Studies, The Hague (ISST).

452. **Mitra** (Manoshi): Women and work in the livestock company—An introduction. New Delhi, Ford Foundation, 1985, 23 pp. (ISST).

453. **National Seminar on Women in Dairying**, Tirupati, 1985 : Papers. Hyderabad, Dairy Development Co-operative Federation Ltd (ISST).

454. **Sunder** (Pushpa) : Khadgodhra—A case study of women's milk co-operative. *Social Action* V 31(1), 1981, pp. 79–98.
Examines the impact of co-operatives on the lives of women in the villages. Also evaluates how successful women have been as managers, and whether there has been a real shift in the traditional balance of power in rural society between men and women.

6.13   Development Work

455. **Annapurna** (P) : Role of mukhya sevika in community development programme—Study conducted in West Godavary District, Andhra Pradesh. Delhi, University of Delhi, 1962. Thesis.

456. **Baker** (D) : Women and social work. *Social Action* V 13(3), 1963, pp. 121–28.

457. **Hariharan** (V) : Development work among rural women. *Khadi Gramodyog* V 4(3), 1957, pp. 31–34.
Based on the Report of the National Seminar on Development Work among Rural Women organised by the IAEA and Bhartiya Grammena Sangh.

458. **Howarth** (Mary) : Swastia sevika—Health workers. *Kurukshetra* V 8(2), 1959, pp. 21–22.

459. **Nandkeolyar** (Subhalakshmi) and **Singh** (R P) : Job satisfaction of gram sevikas. *Kurukshetra* V 22(11), 1974, p. 12.

460. **Nimbakar** (Krishna Bai) : Development work among rural women—A guide boom. Delhi, Indian Adult Education Association, 1958, 45 pp. (GUL).

461. **Nimbakar** (Krishna Bai) : Rural women and development work. *Kurukshetra* V 3(1), 1954, pp. 39–41, 45.
Suggests that there should be training programmes for women and underlines the importance of bringing women within the purview of development.

462. **Odeyar** (D Meggade) : How women development functionaries are changing the rural scene. *Kurukshetra* V 31(6), 1982, pp. 4–6.

463. **Papanek** (Hanna) : The women field workers in a purdah society. *Human Organisation* V 23(2), 1974, pp. 160–63.

464. **Seetharam** (Mukkavalli) : Problems of women development functionaries in rural area. *Yojana* V 26(12), 1982, pp. 15–16.
    Describes the problems faced by development functionaries such as low scales of pay, lack of specialised education and training, confusion and ambiguity at work.

465. **Shaheen** : Anganwadi workers struggle for minimum wages. *Manushi* No. 21, 1984. p. 8.
    Report of the march organised by the All India Anganwadi Helpers and Workers Union to press the need for minimum wages for anganwadi workers.

466. **Singh** (R P) and **Nandkeolyar** (Subhalakshmi) : Personal characteristics and job satisfaction—Grama sevika (Haryana). *Khadi Gramodyog* V 20(8), 1974, pp. 408–11.
    A survey conducted on gram sevikas regarding their job satisfaction, it concludes that widows experienced more satisfaction than others.

6.14 Domestic Work

467. **Baboo** (Balgovind) and **Panwar** (Laxmi) : Maid servants—A case study in Haryana. *Mainstream* V 23(1), 1984, pp. 22–23.
    A survey of fifty maid servants in Rohtak city regarding their working conditions.

468. **Bhaiya** (Abha) : A report on the life and work of women domestic workers. *How* V 5(1), 1982, pp. 15–19.
    Report on the life and working conditions of women domestic workers of Poona.

469. **Elenjimitiam** (A) : Emancipation of domestic servants. *Social Action* V 10(2), 1960, pp. 65–68.
    Compares the working conditions and wages of domestic

servants with the general working class and concludes that
their condition is static.

470. **Gharpure** (Prabha Mahadev) : Life and labour of full-time
domestic servants. Poona, Poona University, 1959.
Thesis.

471. **Kasturi** (Leela) : Domestic servants in urban Delhi—Some
conclusions. New Delhi, Indian Council for Social
Science Research, 1977, 19 pp. (CWDS).
Survey conducted in Delhi covering a hundred Tamil
female domestic workers.

472. **Khanderia** (J G) : Domestic servants of Bombay. *Indian
Journal of Social Work* V 8(2), 1947, pp. 162–72.

473. **Mehta** (A B) : *The domestic servant class.* Bombay, Popular
Book Depot, 1960, 324 pp. (JNU).

474. **Murali Manohar** (K) and **Shobha** (V) : Servant maids in
semi-urban area. *Mainstream* V 19(34), 1980, pp. 24–
26.
Presents the life style, working and socio-economic conditions of servant maids and the factors that influence them
to take up and continue in these jobs.

475. **Pawar** (Amarja) : Organisation of the unorganised domestic
servants in Pune—Struggle for better working conditions. *Manushi* No. 21, 1984, pp. 19–23.
An indepth study of Pune Malkarni Sanghatana, its
struggle for better working conditions.

476. **Ramachandran** (P) : A fair wage for domestic servants.
Indian Journal of Social Work V 19(1), 1958, pp. 27–29.

477. **Rocoo** (C.) : A survey of domestic servants. *Social Action*
V 8(3), 1958, pp. 105–14.

478. **Schenk-Sandbergen** (Loes) : Women work without status
Outdoor household servants in Allepey—Kerala.
Amsterdam, Centre for Anthropological and
Sociological Studies, 1982, 32 pp. (CESS).

479. **School of Social Work**, Research Department : A national
socio-economic survey of domestic workers. Madras,
Catholic Bishops' Conference of India, 1980, 243 pp.
(ISST).

Gives a profile of a domestic worker. Discusses the family background, reasons for taking up domestic work, wages and other benefits, working conditions and job satisfaction.

480. **Sengupta** (P) : Women as domestic servants and in small trades. *Social Welfare* V 1(19), 1954, pp. 7–8, 46.
Discusses how women domestic servants are deprived of almost all benefits which other workers in large-scale industries enjoy and suggests five-year plans for small industries in municipal and rural areas which can be developed by the Planning Commission.

481. **Singh** (A) : A study of socio-economic conditions of domestic servants employed in R.P. Bagh and Shakti Nagar areas of Delhi. Delhi, University of Delhi, 1971. Thesis (DSSW).

6.15 Electronics Industry

482. **Pillai** (Indira Ramakrishna) : Needy women make radios for Keltron. *Social Welfare* V 39(3), 1983, p. 11.
Case study of an organisation in Trivandrum, which has a radio assembling unit as an ancillary to Keltron.

483. **Ramanamma** (A) and **Bambawale** (U) : Women in electronic industry. 1983, 317 pp. (JL).

484. **Sharma** (R N) and **Sengupta** (Chandan) : Women's employment at Seepz, Bombay—Report prepared for ICRIER. Bombay, Tata Institute of Social Sciences, 1984, 211 pp. (ISST).
Analyses the various aspects associated with the phenomenon of female preponderance in the work force at SEEPZ, and the problems arising thereof.

485. **Workshop for Identifying Occupational Skill Requirements of Electronics Industry**, Bombay, 1982 : Summary discussions (ISST).
The Workshop organised by the Ministry of Labour discussed mainly the future of technological development in electronics and designing of a training system.

6.16 Firewood Collection

486. **Bhaduri** (T) and **Surin** (V): Community forestry and women head-loaders. Paper presented at the Seminar on Community Forestry and Women, Dehra Dun, 1980 (ISST). Also in *Manushi* No. 17, 1983, pp. 14–16.

Condensed from the survey report conducted by the Xavier Institute of Social Sciences, Ranchi covering 170 households regarding the socio-economic condition of women engaged in head-loading operations.

487. **Buch** (A N) and **Bhatt** (Ela R): The economic status of women firewood pickers from Mount Girnar. Paper presented at the Seminar on Role of Women in Community Forestry, Dehradun, 1980 (ISST).

Describes the process of firewood collection, its sale and the socio-economic condition of the firewood pickers.

6.17 Fishing

488. **Anbarasan** (Karuna): Factors influence the role and status of fisherwomen—A study of three villages in Chingleput District, Tamil Nadu. Paper presented at the Workshop on Women, Technology and Forms of Production, Madras, 1984, 31 pp. (ISST).

Points out that socio-cultural barriers prevented fisherwomen from equal participation in decision-making and in economic development.

489. **Drewes** (Edelstrand): Three fishing villages in Tamil Nadu—A socio-economic study with special reference to the role and status of women. Madras, Development of Small-Scale Fisheries in Bay of Bengal, 1982, 65 pp. (ISST).

490. **Ram** (Kalpana): The coastal fisherwomen of Kanyakumari —The contradiction of capitalism and gender. Paper presented at the Second National Conference on Women's Studies—Session on Work and Employment, Trivandrum, 1984, 19 pp. (ISST).

Discusses women's work in the fishing communities and particularly the contradictory impact of change.

6.18   Food Processing Industry

491. **Deshpande** (Anjali) : Worse than slavery. *Mainstream* V 21(10), 1982, p. 23.
     Describes the working conditions of women workers in beef exporting factories in Delhi, where sexual harassment is rampant.

492. **Institute of Social Studies Trust** : Employment of women from Kerala in the fish processing units of Gujarat—A report. New Delhi, ISST, 1984, 55 pp. (ISST).
     A study of the working conditions of migrant women from Kerala employed as contract labour in the fish processing units of Veraval.

493. **Jetley** (Surinder) : Women workers in the food processing industry, Uttar Pradesh and Delhi. New Delhi, Centre for Women's Development Studies, 1983, 98 pp. (CWDS).

494. **Loening** (Ariane) : Prawn fish head cutters of Haroa. *Manushi* No. 24, 1984, pp. 36–37.
     A study of the prawn export business in West Bengal where women are involved in the cutting of scalps.

495. **Ranadive** (Vimal) : Kerala fisherwomen in Veraval. *The Voice of the Working Woman* V 5(6), 1984, pp. 11–13.
     Summary of the findings of the study conducted by the Institute of Social Studies on the Employment of Women from Kerala in the Fish Processing Units of Kerala.

6.19   Forestry

496. **Agarwal** (Anil) : Try asking the women first. New Delhi, Centre for Science and Environment, 1983 (CSE).

497. **Chambers** (Robert) : Women and agro-forestry—Four myths

and three case studies. New Delhi, Ford Foundation, 1984, 30 pp. (ISST).

The involvement of women in agro-forestry projects and activities are examined in the case studies from the Dominican Republic, India and Kenya. Considerations for including women in agro-forestry projects are also discussed.

498. **Chand** (Malini) and **Bezboruah** (Rekha) : Employment opportunities for women in forestry. Paper prepared for the Seminar on the Role of Women in Community Forestry, Dehra Dun, 1980 (ISST).

Report of a survey conducted in Betul district of Madhya Pradesh describes the tasks in forestry prevalent in the area and the issues and recommendations at the macro-level.

499. **Chowdhary** (R L) : Employment of women in forestry—A case study of Chandrapur district of Maharashtra State. Paper presented at the Seminar on the Role of Women in Community Forestry, Dehra Dun, 1980 (ISST).

Gives estimates of self-employment, direct and indirect employment provided by forestry. It is found that one-third of the jobs in this sector, particularly in the unskilled categories of direct employment, are held by women.

500. **Gopalan** (Sarala) : Involvement of women in the production and utilisation of forest resources as part of the overall national forest conservation and production programme. Paper presented at the Expert Group Meeting on Women and Forest Industries, Bangkok, 1980 (ISST).

Reviews the role of women in forest management, agro-forestry and forest industries.

501. **Hegde** (Pandurang) : A handful of grain for the cause. *Manushi* No. 22, 1984, pp. 38–39.

Report on women's participation in the Appiko movement, Karnataka, which is aimed at preserving the forest wealth from the depravations of profiteers.

502. **Pant** (M M) : Employment of women in forestry—Scope and discrimination in employment, case studies. Paper pre-

sented at the Seminar on the Role of Women in Community Forestry, Dehra Dun, 1980 (ISST).

Emphasises that forestry provides direct employment mainly in the form of casual labour and self-employment in the form of grazing, looping, grass cutting, collection of firewood, etc.

503. **Roy** (Burman B K) and others: Scope of employment of women in forestry—A case study of Awomgkhul, Manipur. Paper presented at the Seminar on the Role of Women in Community Forestry, Dehra Dun, 1980 (ISST).

Survey of land and forest resources to assess the scope of employment for women.

504. **Seminar on Role of Women in Community Forestry**, Dehra Dun, 1980: Papers and report. Dehra Dun, Forest Research Institute (ISST).

505. **Singh** (Ashbindhu) and **Chowdhary** (R L): Role of women in collection and disposal of minor forest products—A case study of Manipur State. Paper presented at the Seminar on the Role of Women in Community Forestry, Dehra Dun, 1980 (ISST).

Describes the role of women in the collection and disposal of forest product and offers suggestions so that the women engaged in this work derive economic benefits commensurate with the efforts involved in this work.

506. **Srivastava** (K C): Women labour in grass industry of Uttar Pradesh. Agra, Agra University, n.d. Thesis.

6.20   Garment Making

507. **Gurucharan Prasad** : Study of hundred women workers working in a spinning factory, industrial area, Rajpura, District Patiala, Punjab. Delhi, Universtiy of Delhi, 1969. Thesis (CRL, DU).

508. **Hussain** (Sahiba) and **Rao** (V Rukmani): Women employees in a Garment Export Co. Pvt. Ltd. New

Delhi, National Labour Institute, 1978, mimeo. 40 pp. (ISST).

Case study of a garment export company investigating into the general work process, different types of work performed by women, their family background, etc.

509. **Jyothi Rani** (T) : Socio-economic status of self-employed women in a semi-urban city—Case study of women tailors. Paper presented at the Conference on Women's Status and Development, Warangal, 1982, 7 pp. (ISST).

Examines the living standards of self-employed women and whether economic independence is a sufficient condition for female liberation on the basis of data collected in Warangal, Andhra Pradesh.

510. **Kalpagam** (U) : Female labour in small industry—The case of export garments. Madras, Madras Institute of Development Studies, 1981, 47 pp. (MIDS). Also in *Economic and Political Weekly* V 16(48), 1981, pp. 1957–68.

Focuses on the structure of the garment export industry and highlights the characteristics of the so-called informal sector and also examines the nature of the labour force in the export industry and raises crucial questions of unionisation in small industries.

511. **Krishnaraj** (Maithreyi) : New opportunities on old terms—The case of the garment industry in India. Paper presented at the Workshop on Women, Technology and Food Production, Madras, 1984 (MIDS).

Describes the situation of women working in the garment industries of Delhi and Bombay.

512. **Krishnaraj** (Maithreyi) : Socio-economic condition of women workers in the garment industry in Bombay. New Delhi, ICSSR, 1983 (RUWS).

513. **Rao** (V Rukmani) and **Hussain** (Sahiba) : One step forward, two steps back—Women's work and struggles in the garment export industry—A case study of Delhi. Paper presented at the Second National Conference

on Women's Studies—Session on Work and Employment, Trivandrum, 1984, 21 pp. (ISST).
Paper based on interviews with women working in thirty
companies of Delhi regarding their working conditions,
wages, etc. Highlights the attitudes of women towards
unions.

6.21 Handlooms and Handicrafts

514. **Awasty** (Indira) : *Rural women of India*. Delhi, B.R. Pub.
Corporation, 1982, 482 pp. (AIWC).
Describes the role of unmarried women working in the
Phulkari Co-operative Society.

515. **Bahuguna** (Anjali) : Role of Bhotiya women of Garhwal in
home-based production of wool. Paper presented at
the Asian Regional Conference on Women and
the Household, New Delhi, 1985 (ISI).

516. **Bhatt** (Ramesh M) : Full employment for women in handloom sector—A special report on potential for full
employment of women in the weavers' households in
Mahesana District, Ahmedabad. Ashish, n.d., 15 pp.
(CWDS).

517. **Brouwer** (J) : A matter of liminalities—A study of women
and crafts in South India. Paper presented at the
Asian Regional Seminar on Women and the Household,
New Delhi, 1985 (ISI).
Describes the traditional divisional labour between the
sexes in fourteen different crafts in South India.

518. **Dhamija** (Jasleen) : Handicrafts—A source of employment
for women in developing rural economics. *International Labour Review* V 112(6), 1975, pp. 459–65.

519 **Goswami** (T D) : The handloom and women. *Khadi
Gramodyog* V 7(2), 1960, pp. 76–78.
Emphasises the importance of handloom in solving the problem of unemployment of women as it gives them pleasure
and employment in their leisure time.

520. **Jain** (L C) : The phenomenon, scale and process of displace-

ment of women in traditional industries—Some instances and issues. Paper presented at the Workshop on Women, Technology and Food Production, Madras, 1984, 17 pp. (MIDS).

A study of three traditional industries—woollen, handloom and hand block printing, where there is a high rate of displacement.

521. **Khan** (M E) and others : Women in handloom industry—A case study of handloom centres in Uttar Pradesh. Paper presented at the Workshop on Women, Technology and Forms of Production, Madras, 1984 (ISST).

522. **Nigar** (Fatima Abidi) : Home-based production—A case study of women weavers in a village of Eastern Uttar Pradesh. Paper presented at the Asian Regional Conference on Women and the Household, New Delhi, 1985 (ISI).

Discusses the problems relating to production, weaving processes, marketing faced by women in the home-based textile industry.

523. **Patel** (Manibhai T) and **Sharma** (Mohan) : Co-operatives of women for Khadi and Village Industries. *Cooperator* V 20(24), 1983, pp. 641–42, 652.

524. Women in the handloom industry. *Manushi* No. 15, 1983, p. 23.

Survey conducted in the weaving households of Mahesana district of Gujarat. Most women know more than one skill related to weaving. Although they support the men they are not paid separately.

6.22 *Hotel Industry*

525. **Singh** (Preeti) : Women in professions—A study of women in hotel industry. Paper presented at the Seminar on Socialization, Education and Women, New Delhi, 1985 (ISST).

Study conducted in twenty hotels of Delhi (*a*) to collect employment data before and after Asiad 1982, (*b*) to analyse the project demand for women employees in future with a view to looking into the possibility of opening training centres in colleges as part of non-formal employment oriented educational programmes.

6.23 Jute Industry

526. **Rao.** (M N) and **Ganguli** (H C) : Women in the jute industry of Bengal—A medico-social study. *Indian Journal of Social Work* V 11(2), 1950, pp. 181–91.
Shows the impact of the working conditions on their health.

527. **Sengupta** (P): Women in jute industry. *Social Welfare* V 1(3), 1954, pp. 17–19, 43.
Discusses women's working conditions and suggests measures for their benefit.

6.24 Lace Making

528. **Azad** (Nandini) : Profiles in exploitation—Women lace artisans of Narsapur. Madras, Working Women's Forum, 1982, 11 pp. (CWDS).

529. **Lalitha** (K) : Women in politics of development—A case study of Narsapur women lace artisans. Hyderabad, Osmania University, 1980. M. Phil. Dissertation.

530. **Mies** (Maria) : Dynamics of sexual division of labour and capital accumulation—Women lace makers of Narsapur. *Economic and Political Weekly* V 16(10,11,12), 1981, pp. 487–501.

531. **Mies** (Maria) : *The lace makers of Narsapur—Indian housewives produce for world market.* London, Zed Press, 1982, 196 pp. (AIWC, ISST).

532. **Ninan** (Sevanti) : Lace makers of Narsapur. *Voluntary Action* V 24(8), 1982, pp. 333–38.

6.25   Law

533. **Chaudhary** (P) : Women lawyers in a man's world. *Social Welfare* V 19(12), 1973, pp. 2–3, 26–27.
Interviews with a few women lawyers of Delhi to ascertain their views on vital questions such as the reason for their getting into this profession, the difficulties experienced by them and women's contribution to the legal profession.

534. **Mukherji** (Tapati) : Women's role in dispensing justice. *Social Welfare* V 7(5), 1960, pp. 13–14.
Suggests that women make better judges.

535. **Sarkar** (Lotika) : In Law. *Seminar* No. 165, 1973, pp. 13–15.
Deals with the provisions of law for women as enshrined in the Constitution and how far these provisions have been implemented in India.

6.26   Leather Industry

536. **Usha** (P) : Mechanisation and labour utilization—Leather industry in Tamil Nadu. *Economic and Political Weekly* V 20(4), 1985, pp. 167–72.
Describes briefly the jobs performed by women and the work participation of women in the leather industry.

6.27   Librarianship

537. **Chatterjee** (Mridula) : Musings on Indian women's role in library profession. *Indian Librarian* V 30(3), 1975, pp. 114–15.

538. **Kumar** (P S G) : Women and librarianship. *Herald of Library Science* V 14(4), 1975, pp. 221–24.

539. **Morris** (Berjye) : Women in senior library management. *Herald of Library Science* V 12(1–2), 1983, pp. 72–76.

6.28   Literature

540. **Desai** (Anita): Aspects of Indo-Anglian novel—Women writers. *Quest* No. 65, 1970, pp. 39–43.
Suggests that women have had till recently, less chances to education than men thus, in a country with a strong tradition in story-telling, women have been the chief upholders of this tradition.

541. **Hussain** (Saliha Abid): Women writers in Urdu literature. *Indian Horizons* V 23(2–3), 1974, pp. 5–14.
A brief survey of the contribution of women writers to Urdu language and literature.

542. **Lakshmi** (CS): Tradition and modernity of Tamil women writers. *Social Scientist* V 4(9), 1976, pp. 37–45.
Deals with certain trends in order to understand what is written today. It is essential to go back and examine the status and role of Tamil women and the social change they have undergone.

6.29   Management

543. **Amba Rao** (Sita C): The managerial mainstream and Indian women. *Indian Management* V 18(11), 1979, pp. 2–9.

544. **Bombay University**, Department of Economics, Business Management Section: Women executives in Bombay City. Bombay, Bombay University, 1962 (BUL).

545. Can women be successful executives. *Industrial Times* V 19(21), 1968, pp. 16–20.

546. *Crossfield directory of women executives in India.* New Delhi, Crossfield, 1977, 321 pp. (MUL).

547. **Rai** (Usha): Success or failure in executive position. *Social Change* V 2(1), 1972, pp. 43–49.

548. **Sankaran** (Laxman): Women executives—Today's phenomenon and tomorrow's reality. *Integrated Management* V 14(4), 1979, pp. 5–11.

Discusses the capability of women as executives. According to the author, they are generally above average in intelligence, hard working and committed to their job responsibilities.

549. **Singh** (D R) . Women executives in India. *Management International Review* V 20(2), 1980, pp. 53–60.

550. **Tewari** (Harish C) :|*Understanding personality and motives of women managers.* Michigan, UMI Research Press, 1980, 148 pp. (AIWC).

Study of the participation of women in the labour force and motivation among women to work.

551. **Unwalla** (Jerro Maneck) : Beyond the household walls—A study of women executives at work and at home. Bombay, Tata Institute of Social Sciences, 1977. Thesis.

552. Women executives—Can they execute? *Integrated Management* V 13(7), 1978, pp. 9–11.

6.30   Match Box Making

553. **Shinde** (P R) : Poona Match Factory—A social welfare experiment. *Social Welfare* V 6(7), 1959, p. 35.

Case study of a particular factory where women are employed to make match boxes and sticks.

6.31   Medicine

554. **Adranwala** (T K) : Women in the nursing profession. *Social Welfare* V 7(5), 1960, pp. 11–12.

555 **Ahmad** (Karuna) : Hospital, doctors and nurses. *Economic and Political Weekly* V 16(38), 1981, pp. 15–31.

556. **Ambekar Institute of Labour Studies** : An enquiry into the situation of nursing personnel in India. Bombay, AILS, 1981, 88 pp. (AILS).

557. **International Labour Office** : Survey of the nursing pro-

fession in India. *Industry and Labour* V 14(11), 1955, pp. 468–74.

558. **Juneja** (Harpal) : A study of socio-economic background of ayas in the Delhi hospitals. Delhi, University of Delhi, 1970. Thesis.

559. **Keskai** (S A) : Enquiry into working conditions of nurses in Government hospitals in Poona. Poona, Pune University, 1979. Thesis.

560. **Khan** (Praveen) : Personality structure of women in the nursing profession. Kanpur, Kanpur University, 1974. Thesis.

561. **Namjoshi** (Virodini) : Social background of nurses in two districts of Gujarat State (Ahmedabad and Bhavnagar Districts). Bombay, SNDT Women's University, 1975. Thesis.

562. **National Conference of Women Doctors in India**, New Delhi, 1975 : Proceedings. 96 pp. (NML).

563. **Oommen** (T K) : *Doctors and nurses—A study in occupation role structure.* Delhi, Macmillan, 1978.

564. **Padmavati** (S) : Higher medical education for women. *Journal of Higher Education* V 1(13), 1975, pp. 256–58.

565. **Prakash** (Padma) : Nurses striking the core issues. *Economic and Political Weekly* V 16(14), 1981, p. 618.

566. **Ramanamma** (A) and **Bambawale** (U) : Comparative analysis of the nursing profession in USA and India. 1984 (JL).

567. **Ramanamma** (A) and **Bambawale** (U) : Nurses—A sociological analysis. 1979, 250 pp. (JL).

568. Rewards of service in rural area. *Mainstream* V 19(52), 1980, p. 12.

569. **Shanta Mohan** (N) : Status of nurses in India. New Delhi, 1985, 105 pp. (ISST).

Examines the social and educational background of girls who take up this career, records their reasons for becoming nurses and studies the treatment they receive and the conditions under which they work in government and private hospitals.

570. **Singh** (Shyama) : Employment, income and conditions of work and life of nurses—A study of urban working group in Lucknow. Lucknow, Giri Institute of Development Studies, 1981, 93 pp. (GIDS).

571. **Suryamani** (E) : The organisation and the semi-professionals—A sociological study of nurses. Waltair, Andhra University, 1982. Thesis.

572. **Vasudevan** (Jayshree) : Women in medicine and teaching—A trend analysis. New Delhi, Jawaharlal Nehru University, 1979, 141 pp. (JNU).

6.32 Mining

573. **Dasgupta** (S) : Employment of women in mines. *Indian Worker* V 11(9), 1962, p. 4.

574. **Ghosh** (Anjan) : Escalating redundance dispensability of women labour in the coal mines of Eastern India. Paper presented at the Workshop on Women, Technology and Forms of Production, Madras, 1984, 12 pp. (MIDS).
Analyses the process of dispensability of women labour in the coal mines of Raniganj.

575. **Mattan** (A) : Tribal women as contract labourers in Meghatuburu Iron Ore Project. *Manushi* No. 23, 1984, pp. 16–18.
Describes the miserable conditions under which the tribal women from Ranchi and Keonjhar have to work, as they are handicapped by illiteracy and lack of skills.

576. **Sengupta** (P) : Women in mining industry. *Social Welfare* V 1(6), 1954, pp. 9–11, 46–48.
Reviews the condition of women workers in the mining industry and gives comparative data on women in iron, mica and coal mines.

577. **Talpallikar** (M B) : Life and labour of women workers in

the Bellampalli mines. *Indian Journal of Social Work* V 9(3), 1948, pp. 208–17.

578. They give us light but live in darkness—Survey report. *Manushi* No. 4, 1980, pp. 57–61.

Summary of the survey conducted by the Labour Bureau in 1975 on the condition of women workers in mines, who are covered under the Mines Act, 1952.

6.33   Paper Bag Making

579. **Mehrotra** (Deepti) : Invisible labour force—Women paper bag makers in Delhi. *Manushi* No. 14, 1983, pp. 38–43.

Case studies of women engaged in making paper bags in the Himmatgarh area of New Delhi.

6.34 Pappad Rolling

580. **Alaka** and **Chetna** : Pappad rollers of Lijjat—A mockery in the name of a cooperative. *Manushi* No. 19, 1983, pp 37–38.

Article describes the problems faced by women in the Lijjat pappad cooperative in Valod.

581. Pappad rollers of Lijjat. *How* V 3(4), 1980, pp. 23–27.

6.35 Pharmaceutical Industry

582. **Gothaskar** (Sujata) and **Banaji** (Rohini) : Making the work place a better place for women. *Manushi* No. 24, 1984, pp. 118–22.

Discussions with women workers engaged in packing, hand labelling, counting and filling tablets in twenty pharmaceutical and two biscuit companies regarding their work and work place.

583. **Gothaskar** (Sujata) and **Banaji** (Rohini) : A challenge of unions—Women's employment in pharmaceuticals

and food industries. *Manushi* No. 23, 1984, pp. 36–39. A study conducted in Bombay in these industries to investigate their working conditions such as hours of work, creches, and maternity benefits.

6.36 Plantations

584. **Bhowmik** (Shanti Kumar) : Sociological study of tea plantation labour in Eastern India—A case study in the Dooais area of West Bengal. Delhi, University of Delhi, 1979. Thesis (CRL, DU).

585. **Bhowmik** (Sharit) : Wages of tea garden workers in West Bengal. *Economic and Political Weekly* V 17(40), 1982, pp. 1600–1.

586. **Gupta** (Vimala) : A socio-economic survey of the working and living conditions of women workers at tea gardens in UP. Agra, Agra University, 1968. Thesis.

587. **India,** Ministry of Labour, Labour Bureau : Socio-economic conditions of women workers in plantation. Chandigarh, Labour Bureau, 1980, 102 pp. Also in *Indian Labour Journal* V 22(3), 1980, pp. 327–33 (M L).

588. **Jayasingh** (J Visuthas) : Women workers in tea plantations. *Social Welfare* V 25(12), 1979, pp. 7–9. Analyses the findings of a research study conducted by the Madurai Institute of Social Work on the living conditions of female plantation workers in Munnar, Kerala.

589. **Saikia** (P D) and **Phukan** (U) : Ex-tea garden labour women in Assam. Jorhat, Agro-Economic Research Centre for North East India, 1979, 47 pp. (PC). Also in *Social Welfare* V 29(11–12), 1983, pp. 8–10.

590. **Sengupta** (P) : Women in plantations. *Social Welfare* V 1(5), 1954, pp. 9–12, 42. Gives data on women working in tea, coffee, rubber and cardamom plantations, their working conditions and the legislative measures available to them.

591. **Sharma** (Kumud) : Women plantation workers. *Indian*

Farming V 25(8), 1975, pp. 66–68.

Gives an account of the working and living conditions of women in tea and rubber plantations—their wages, the benefits provided to them, etc.

6.37   Rag Picking

592. **Shah** (Nandita) : Study of women rag pickers–Profile and work pattern. Bombay, Nirmala Niketan, 1983, 153 pp. Thesis (NN).

6.38   Sales Promotion

593. **Parameswaran** (T S) : Women in employment—Study of sales girls conducted in the Central Cottage Industries Emporium, Janpath. Delhi, University of Delhi, 1969. Thesis.

594. **Sadasivam** (Bharati) and **Singh** (Sunila) : Submissive and cheap labour force—Sales girls in Madras. *Manushi* No. 13, 1982, pp. 36–37.

Report on the living and working conditions of sales girls based on interviews with thirty women.

6.39   Sanitation Work

595. **Dang** (Satyapal) : Plight of women sweepers. *Mainstream* V 12(5), 1974, pp. 20–22.

Considers briefly the working conditions and wage structure of sweepers in various cities of Punjab.

596. Garbage is women's work. *Voluntary Action* V 25(9–10), 1983, p. 293.

597. **Jayakar** (Samuel) : *Rural sweepers in the city.* Mysore, Wesley Press, 1952, 310 pp. (RUWS).

598. **Karlekar** (Malavika) : *Poverty and women's work—A study of*

sweeper women in Delhi. New Delhi, Vikas, 1982, 158 pp. (AIWC).

599 **Murali Manohar** (K) and **Sambaiah** (P) : The plight of women sanitary workers in a semi-urban city—An empirical observation. *Nagarlok* V 12(4), 1980, pp. 85–96.

Survey conducted in the Nagaram City (AP) to examine the socio-economic background, roles in the family, and problems involved in discharging their responsibilities both as a member of the family and as employees of the Municipality.

600. **Searle-Chatterjee** (Mary) : *Reversible sex roles—The special case of Benaras sweepers.* Oxford, Pergamon Press, 1981, 112 pp. (CWDS).

6.40   Science and Technology

601. **Chakravarthy** (Radha) : The status of women scientists in India. New Delhi, National Institute of Science, Technology and Development Studies, 1984, 28 pp. (ISST).

602. **Gandhi** (Indira) : Women engineers and scientists. Faridabad, Government of India Press, 1981, unpaginated (NMML).

603. **India**, Department of Science and Technology : Employment pattern of women in the research and development organisations—A statistical analysis. New Delhi DST, 1980, 27 pp. (CWDS).

604. **Jaiswal** (R P) : Status of working men and women engineers—An analysis based on fifty engineers of Kerala. A paper based on M.Phil. dissertation, Jawaharlal Nehru University, New Delhi, n.d. (AIWC).

Interviews with women engineers regarding their working conditions and problems.

605. **Jaiswal** (R P) : Women in science, engineering and

technology—A trend analysis. New Delhi, Jawaharlal Nehru University, 1979. Thesis.

606. **Krishnaraj** (Maithreyi) : The status of women in science. Paper presented at the Seminar on Women and Development, Anand, 1982, 16 pp. (ISST).

Reviews the place of women in scientific hierarchy which can be adjudged by numerical preponderance, salary levels, positions of prestige, decision-making power, etc.

607. **Sengupta** (B) : Our women engineers. *Yojana* V 19(14), 1967, p. 18.

6.41   Sports

608. **Mathur** (Madhu) : Women and sports. *Education Quarterly* V 27(2), 1975, pp. 26–28.

Describes the participation of women in sports, its implication on the various aspects of their life such as menstruation, exercise, fertility, pregnancy, body-building, injuries, emotions and differences with men.

609. **Sundaresan** (P N) : Women in Indian cricket. *Swarajya* No. 27, 1976, pp. 22–23.

6.42   Stone Quarrying

610. **Choudhury** (Arun) : Contract labour—To crush the stone crushers. *Economic and Political Weekly* V 9(50), 1974, pp. 2051–53.

A study of the problems faced by women stone crushers such as denial of minimum wages, security against cave-ins and accidents, and harassment by the employers.

611. **Prabhakar** (Raj) : Study of hundred Rajasthani scheduled caste women working at a quarry in Delhi. Delhi, University of Delhi, 1955. Thesis (DSSW).

6.43   Street Vending

612. **Alaka** and **Chetna** : Struggling at every step—Pheriwalis of
     Bombay. *Manushi* No. 27, 1985, pp. 37–38.
     Discusses the life and struggle of pheriwalis who have to
     provide financial support to their families and have to face
     harassment by the traders and police.

613. **Azad** (Nandini) : The social context and micro-economics of
     women—Idli sellers of Madras City. Madras, Work-
     ing Women's Forum, 26 pp. (ISST).
     Report of a survey conducted in Madras.

614. **Azad** (Nandini) : Women vegetable vendors of Madras
     City—A case study of the economic and social milieu
     of 400 vegetable vendors. Madras, Working Women's
     Forum, 1983, 27 pp. (WWF).
     A detailed survey of the socio-economic background, living
     conditions and the process of trading in the city of Madras.

615. **Lessinger** (Joanna) : Caught between work and modesty.
     The dilemma of women traders in South India. Paper
     presented at the Asian Regional Conference on
     Women and the Household, New Delhi, 1985 (ISI).
     Discusses female marginalisation in petty trades in
     Madras.

6.44   Teaching

616. **Lila** (Kanchana) : Enslaved   Saraswatis—Women   primary
     school teachers. *Manushi* No. 8, 1981, pp. 29–38.
     Discusses the working conditions of teachers working in
     private, unrecognised and unaided schools.

617. **Malti** (M) : Comparative study of teachers in Government
     and private schools. Delhi, University of Delhi, 1970.
     Thesis (DSSW).

618. **Paranjape** (Lata S) : Problems of women primary teachers
     in the Poona revenue region. Poona, Poona Univer-
     sity, 1970. Thesis.

619. **Pethe** (Vasanth P) : *Living and working condition of primary school teachers—Sholapur survey.* Bombay, Popular Book Depot, 1962, 70 pp.

620. **Rajalakshmi** (N) : Women and work—A case study of teachers and nurses. Madras, Madras University, 1981. Thesis.

621. **Saradamoni** (K) : The off-beat school teachers. *Mainstream* V 14(42), 1975, p. 13.

622. **Shukla** (Sheela) : Problems of women teachers working in predominantly male educational institutions. Paper presented at the National Conference on Women's Studies, Bombay, 1981 (ISST).

6.45   Textiles

623. **Baud** (Isa) : Women's labour in the South India textile industry. Tilburg, Tilburg University, 1983, 54 pp. (ISST).
A study conducted in and around the city of Coimbatore, reviews the influence of production and mobilisation in the gender division of labour.

624. **Chatterjee** (Renuka) : A study of problems and prospects of women workers in a textile ·mill with particular reference to textile mills of Vidharbha. Nagpur, Nagpur University, 1976. Thesis.

625. Cotton mills in Ahmedabad—Condition of women workers. *Commerce* V 14(2913), 1967, p. 416.

626. **Desai** (Rajani) : Problems of married women labourers working in a cotton textile mill. Bombay, Nirmala Niketan, 1969. Thesis (N N).

627. **James** (R C) : Discrimination against women in Bombay textiles. *Industrial and Labour Relations Review* V 15(2), 1962, pp. 202–20.

628. **Jhabvala** (Renana) : From the mill to the streets—A study of retrenchment of women from Ahmedabad textile mills. *Manushi* No. 26, 1985, pp. 21–23, 29–41.

Discusses the displacement of women in the industrial sector in general and in the textile industry in particular.

629. **Kumar** (Radha) : Family and factory—Women workers in the Bombay cotton textile industry. *Indian Economic and Social History Review* V 20(1), 1983, pp. 81–110.

630. **Nadkarni** (Nalini) : Problems of married women labourers in a cotton textile mill. Bombay, Nirmala Niketan, 1969. Thesis (NN).

631. **Nair** (Devaki K) : Conditions of women workers in the textile industry of Madhya Pradesh. Saugar, Saugar University, 1960. Thesis.

632. **Parliwala** (Palwin) : Problems of the married women labourers working in a cotton textile mill. Bombay, Nirmala Niketan, 1969. Thesis (NN).

633. **Savara** (Mira) : Changing trends in women's employment— A case study of the textile industry in Bombay. Bombay, Bombay University, 1981, 313 pp. (BU).

634. **Savara** (Mira) : Factory and home, the contrary pulls—Lives of women workers in the textile industry. *Manushi* No. 12, 1984, pp. 14–19.
Examines how women working in the textile industry view their lives at work and at home.

635. **Savara** (Mira) : Working class women view their own lives. Bombay, Feminist Resource Centre, n.d., 43 pp. (RUWS).

636. **Sengupta** (P) : Women in the cotton industry. *Social Welfare* V 1(4), 1954, pp. 19–22.
Gives a statistical profile of women in cotton industries in India.

637. **Singh** (Vijay Pal) : Women in the cotton textile industry, Ahmedabad—A survey conducted by TLA. *How* V 3(12), 1980, pp. 5–7

638. **Ved** (R G) : Cultural and social change among women in industry. *Social Welfare* V 11(5), 1964, pp. 19–20.
Survey report on rural women who have migrated and are employed in industries—especially the textile industry in the cities.

639. **Women's Research Centre** : Report of an investigation into the history and present conditions of women workers of the cotton textile industry in West Bengal. Calcutta, WRC, 1984. Also in *Manushi* No. 23, 1984, pp. 30–34.

6.46   Transportation

640. **Brahme** (Sulabhe) : Economic plight of Hamal women in Pune. New Delhi, Indian Council of Social Science Research, 1979, 97 pp. Also in *Manushi* No. 6, 1980, pp. 47–52.
Summarised version of a survey report on Hamal women in Pune working in five centres of the city. Their work includes carrying various kinds of goods on the head or in hand-carts, from trucks or Railway wagons to godowns.

6.47   Zari

641. **Deepti** and **Mehta** (Pushpa) : Behind the glitter—Zardozi workers in Delhi. *Manushi* No. 24, 1984, pp. 8–12.
Interviews with Zardozi workers regarding their work and their lives.

7

Women and Political Participation

642. **Agnew** (Vijay) : *Elite women in Indian politics.* New Delhi, Vikas, 1979, 163 pp. (ISST, JNU).
    Discusses the role of women in the freedom movement, in extremist politics, in the Congress Party and the suffragette movement.

643. **Annapurna Devi** and **Pati** (N M) : Women in state politics. *Political Science Review* V 21(4), 1981, pp. 117–44.

644. **Annapurna Devi** : Women's participation in the politics of Orissa—A sociological analysis. New Delhi, Jawaharlal Nehru University, 1981. Thesis (JNU).

645. **Chattopadhaya** (Kamala Devi) : *Indian women's battle for freedom.* Delhi, Abhinav, 1982 (ISST).

646. **D'Lima** (Hazel) : *Women in local government—A study of Maharashtra.* New Delhi, Concept, 1983, 211 pp. (GUL).
    Looks at the different social and political groups from which women representatives are drawn, their outlook and the extent of their awareness of their special role as women representatives, and examines the scope and the actual degree of participation of these members in the local government bodies.

647. **Hamsa** (N) : Impact of socialisation on political participation of women in an Indian urban community. New Delhi, Jawaharlal Nehru University, 1980. Thesis.

Discusses the active participation of women in politics, local government and the electoral role of women.

648. **Mazumdar** (Vina) : Ed. *Symbols of power—Studies on the political studies of women in India.* Bombay, Allied, 1979, 373 pp. (ISST).

The studies provide quantitative data on women's political participation and also examine their impact on the process; identifies the gap that exists between popular notions and opinions and empirical realities, between what the law provides and the polity demands on the one hand and what society actually permits on the other.

649. **Mehta** (Usha) : Indian women and their participation in politics. *Social Change* V 8(3), 1978, pp. 31–34.

650. **Minault** (Gail) : Ed. *Extended family—Women and political participation in India and Pakistan.* Delhi, Chanakya, 1981, 312 pp. (ISST).

Explores the beginnings of women's involvement in public activities beyond the realm of their families; the relationship of movements for women's rights to the freedom movement and women's political participation after independence.

651. **Pallegar** (D N) : Woman chairman gives panchayat a new look. *Yojana* V 8(14), 1964, pp. 14–15.

652. **Pathankar** (Indumati) : Confronting male power—An all women panel contests panchayat election. *Manushi* No. 25, 1984, pp. 2–4.

Describes the problems and conflicts faced by women candidates who contested in elections in Indoli village in Maharashtra.

653. **Pearson** (Gail Olina) : Women in public life in Bombay city, with special reference to civil disobedience movement. New Delhi, Jawaharlal Nehru University, 1979. Thesis.

654. **Sen** (S) : The role of women legislatures. *Janata* V 29(43), 1974, pp. 11–12.

Describes the historical background of women's role in politics.

655. **Sen** (Shipra) : Political women in India—An assessment of
her status and role. New Delhi, Jawaharlal Nehru
University, 1977. Thesis (JNU).
Describes the participation of women in politics, before and
after independence and their impact on the political
process.

8

Welfare Schemes for the Economic Participation of Women

656. **Ahmed** (Zubeida): The plight of women—Alternatives for action. *International Labour Review* V 119(4), 1980, pp. 425–37.

Describes the impact of technology on the life of rural women and suggests socio-economic programmes that could be designed to help women.

657. **Amrit Kaur** (Rajkumari): Women and community projects. *Kurukshetra* V 1(3), 1952, pp. 9–10.

658. **Baliga** (B V S) and others: Developing income generating activities among rural women. *Financing Agriculture* V 15(3), 1983, pp. 5–11.

659. **Chari** (T V R): Employment and self-employment for needy women and the handicapped. *Social Welfare* V 30(3), 1983, pp. 8–10, 13.

Describes the socio-economic programmes of the CSWB, and other schemes for which financial support is given.

660. **Chari** (T V R): Vistas of employment for needy women and disabled—CSWB's economic programmes. *Social Welfare* V 28(11), 1982, pp. 10–13, 32.

Analyses the various economic programmes of the Central Social Welfare Board.

661. **Chen** (Marty): Development projects for women. OXFAM America's programme in India and Bangladesh.

Paper presented at the Conference on the International Women's Decade and Beyond, New York, 1984 (ISST).

662. **Chen** (Marty) : Strategies to increase the economic productivity of rural women. Experience from India and Bangladesh. 1983, 16 pp. (ISST).

663. **Chopra** (S L) : Socio-economic programme—Wide opportunities for needy women. *Social Welfare* V 25(1), 1978, pp. 7–9.

664. **Costa-Pinto** (Selena) : Towards self reliance, income generation for women. *Social Welfare* V 26(7), 1979, pp. 1–3.

665. **Course on Identification and Planning of Income Generating Activities for Rural Women**, Hyderabad, 1984 : Papers (NIRD).

666. **Dalaya** (C K) : Economic activities of voluntary women's organisations (Mahila Mandals) in the city of Bombay. Bombay, Shreemati Nathibai Damodar Thackersay Women's University, 1982, 85 pp. (ISST).

667. **Dandekar** (Kumudini) : Employment Guarantee Scheme— An employment opportunity for women. Pune, Gokhale Institute of Politics, 1983, 76 pp. (ISST).
Assesses the impact of the Employment Guarantee Scheme on the rural employment situation in Maharashtra and the benefits derived by women. It is based on a survey of sixty Employment Guarantee Scheme work sites.

668. **Dandekar** (Kumudini) and **Sethi** (Manju) : Employment Guarantee Scheme and food for work. *Economic and Political Weekly* V 15(15), 1980, pp. 1707–13.

669. **District Level Conference on Dakshina Kannada**, Mangalore, 1983 : Background paper. Bangalore, Institute of Social Studies Trust, 1983, 11 pp. (ISST).
Describes the socio-economic condition of women, their work participation rate in Dakshina Kannada and the extent of utilisation of development schemes by these women.

670. **Dixon** (R B) : Four programmes of employment for rural

women in India and Bangladesh. *Development Digest* V 17(1), 1979, pp. 75–88.
Describes the different employment programmes for rural women with particular reference to the Amul Project and Lijjat Pappad.

671. **Foundation to Aid Industrial Recovery** : Alternative economic schemes—Some options for Annapurna Mahila Mandal. New Delhi, FAIR, 1985, 35 pp. (ISST).

672. **Gopalan** (Sarala) : An experiment in co-operation of Government and voluntary organisations for welfare and development of women—The Central Social Welfare Board. New Delhi, CSWB, n.d. (ISST).
Discusses the role of the Central Social Welfare Board and voluntary organisations in introducing income generating projects to provide employment opportunities to needy and poor women.

673. **Hiraway** (Indira) : Employment planning according to labour force characteristics—The case of rural women. *Indian Journal of Labour Economics* V 22(4), 1979, pp. 71–82.
Analyses the labour force characteristics in rural areas and the process of planning schemes.

674. **India**, Ministry of Industries, Small-Scale Industries, Development Commissioner : Industrial enterprises for women. New Delhi, Ministry of Industries, 1976, 164 pp. (AIWC).
An overview of different kinds of industrial enterprises which women can take up.

675. **Indian Co-operative Union** : Income generating activities for women—Some case studies. New Delhi, UNICEF, 1980, 144 pp. (AIWC).
Describes the endeavours which have been effective in supporting women in their quest for income—includes case studies of selected projects like Lijjat pappad, handloom work in Tamil Nadu, Kashmir and sikki grass handicraft work of Bihar.

676. **Institute of Applied Manpower Research** : National Plan

for women's employment. New Delhi, IAMR, n.d., 15 pp. (ISST).

677. **Institute of Social Studies Trust**: An assessment of women's roles—The Karnataka Sericulture Development Project. Bangalore, ISST, 1982, 59 pp. (ISST).

Study examines the principal aims of the project, its employment potential and the nature of such employment, the type and number of functionaries that the project intends to employ, their roles, pay scales, educational level, etc.

678. **Institute of Social Studies Trust**: Impact on women workers, Maharashtra Employment Guarantee Scheme—A study. New Delhi, ISST, 1979, 300 pp. (ISST).

A detailed study of eight work sites to assess (*a*) the impact of the scheme on women's work, household life, (*b*) to assess the designing and implementation of the scheme.

679. **Institute of Social Studies Trust** : Inter-State Tasar Project. A report on a field survey (Chandrapur District, Maharashtra). New Delhi, ISST, 1982, 125 pp. (ISST).

The basic aim of the survey is to identify ways and methods by which the Inter-State Tasar Project could improve the living conditions of the tribal population particularly women through the Tasar Development Programme.

680. **Institute of Social Studies Trust** : Women's employment— Some preliminary observations. Paper presented at the Seminar on Women and Poverty, Calcutta, 1983. Bangalore, ISST, 1983.

Attempts to explore the possibilities of integrating woman's interest into the planning process perceiving her both as a primary bread winner and as a mother.

681. **Jain** (Devaki) : Women in the tea plantation—A study of plantation workers in the Nilgiri Wynad area of South India. New Delhi, Institute of Social Studies Trust, 1977, 52 pp. (ISST).

682. **Jain** (Devaki) and **Srinivasan** (Viji) : Women's roles in

large employment systems. New Delhi, Ford Foundation, 1983, 90 pp. (ISST).

The two case studies raise issues regarding the development of sericulture in Karnataka and Tamil Nadu and particularly the question of the unequal access of women to the benefits of development due to the unequal presence of women in the personnel network.

683. **Karnataka**, District Rural Development Society: Development of Women and Children in Rural Areas (DWCRA), Chikmagalur District—Annual Plan 1984–85. 53 pp. (ISST).

District level plan for the Development of Women and Children in Rural Areas Scheme which aims to improve the economic condition of women by pursuing useful and suitable income generating activities in the Chikmagalur District of Karnataka.

684. **Krishnan** (Prabha): Appropriate technology—Income and convenience for rural women. *Voluntary Action* V 24(9), 1982, pp. 363–65.

Report of the workshop-cum-exhibition on science and technology for rural women. Suggests ways for employment generation—mushroom cultivation, bee keeping, match box and agarbathi making, rope-making.

685. **Kumaraswamy** (Jacintha): A socio-economic survey for creating employment among the women in Tilak Nagar—Report. Bangalore, SEARCH, 1981, 44 pp. (CWDS).

686. **Law** (Preeta): Rural development—Its impact on women. *Social Action* V 35(1), 1985, pp. 81–90.

Evaluates the impact of rural development programmes on women and the particular problems faced by rural women in India.

687. **Mehra** (Rekha) and **Saradamoni** (K): *Women and rural transformation—Two studies.* New Delhi, Concept, 1983, 176 pp. (CWDS).

Provides a critical view of rural transformation and planned policies for the transformation of women.

688. **Mitra** (Manoshi): Designs implementation of development

project—A look into organised dairying in India. New Delhi, Ford Foundation, 1985 (ISST).

689. **National Seminar on a Fair Deal to the Self-Employed and the Seventh Plan**, Ahmedabad, 1983 : Policy recommendations for the Seventh Plan. 15 pp. (ISST).

Policy recommendation covers the following areas—planning philosophy, organisational structure, minimum real income policy, right to shelter, health services, introduction of new technology, etc.

690. **National Workshop for the Promotion and Training of Rural Women in Income Raising Activities**, Bangalore, 1978 : Report. 1979, 65 pp. (ISST).

Five case studies on income raising projects were presented which provide the framework for the discussions.

691. **Pinto** (Selena Costa) : A feasibility study for an income generating programme for women. Bombay, Tata Institute for Studies in Social Science, 1980. Thesis.

692. **Prasad** (Aruna) and others : A review of the economic schemes for the development of women in the past decade with special reference to Karnataka State. Paper presented at the Second National Conference on Women's Studies—Session on Work and Employment, Trivandrum, 1984 (ISST).

693. **Radha Devi** (D) : Future prospects of employment of women in India. *Indian Journal of Social Work* V 45(3), 1984, pp. 287–95.

Describes the type of projects worked out by both public and private agencies for providing employment for women.

694. **Sarin** (Madhu) : Women's co-operative— Learning from the rope-makers of Sukhomajri. Paper presented at the Workshop on Women and Employment—Needs and Trends, New Delhi, 1982 (ISST).

Describes how women of Sukhomajri in Haryana were taught rope-making with the help of machines as part of the irrigation programme of ICAR and were helped to form a co-operative.

695. **Shamala Devi** (L N) : Report on the project of women

sericulture extension workers at TSC Kanakpura.
New Delhi, Ford Foundation, 1984, 13 pp. (ISST).
Assesses the role and effectiveness of women extension
workers in developing the technical skills of women rearers.

696. **Sharma** (Kumud) : Place of women in rural development.
Mainstream V 19(16), 1980, pp. 7–8.
Discusses the development schemes for promoting rural
women's participation in all aspects of rural life.

697. **Sharma** (Kumud) : Policies for employment generation—
Impact on women. New Delhi, Indian Council for
Social Science Research, 1980, 37 pp. (ISST).

698. **Sinha** (Frances) and **Sinha** (Sanjay) : Woollen textile pro-
duction in the Kumaon Hills—A review of the ITIS/
ATDA Wool Spinning Project. Lucknow, Economic
Development Associates, 1983, 46 pp. (ISST).
A critical review of the methodology of project develop-
ment and administration applied in wool technology.

699. **Small Industries Service Institute** : Small industries for
women entrepreneurs. New Delhi, SISI, 1979, 149 pp.
(ISST).
Gives guidelines for choosing a small-scale industry and a
scheme of assistance for small-scale industries. Project profiles are included for chemicals, food, hosiery, leather, electronics and ceramics industries.

700. **Tellis-Nayak** (Jessie B) : Education and income generation
for women—Non-formal approaches. New Delhi,
Indian Social Institute, 1982, 79 pp. (GUL).

701. **Tellis-Nayak** (Jessie B) and **Pinto** (Selena Costa) : Eds.
Towards self-reliance—Income generation for women.
Indore, Divine World Publications, 1979, 101 pp.
(DSSW).
Gives guidelines to enhance the income of women, and
planning of small-scale activities.

702. **United Nations Children's Fund** : Schemes for rural
development—Scope for women. New Delhi,
UNICEF, 1982, 125 pp. (ISST).
Lists the schemes under the Ministries of Rural Development, Social Welfare, Health and Family Welfare,

Industry, Commerce, Education and Culture, and Works and Housing.

703. **Working Women's Forum** : Rural women and development needs of today—Experiences of the Working Women's Forum, India. Madras, WWF, 1984, 29 pp. (ISST).

704. **Workshop for Organisers of Income Generating Projects for Women**, New Delhi, 1977 : Report. New Delhi, Gandhi Peace Foundation, 1977, 136 pp. (ISST).

Report of the discussion between the organisers and potential organisers of income generating projects for women, on the basis of case studies of the Bharatiya Grameen Mahila Sangh and the Stree Seva Mandir and others.

705. **Workshop on the Integration of Women in Agriculture and Rural Development**, Hyderabad, 1980 : Report and papers. Hyderabad, National Institute of Rural Development, 1980 (NIRD).

9

Women and Labour Welfare

706. **Acharji** (Nilima): Social policy and women labour in an emergent country. *Social Welfare* V 10(2), 1963, pp. 1–2, 8.

Suggests that there should be protective legislation to safeguard their rights.

707. **Acharji** (Nilima): Social responsibility of employers and employment of women. *Social Welfare* V 20(9), 1973, pp. 4–6.

708. **Agarwal** (Bina): Exploitation in employment. Paper presented at the Seminar on Optimum Utilisation of Women Power for Development, New Delhi, 1975, 23 pp. (ISST).

Investigates the problem of exploitation of women in the labour force by their employers, the social structure and often by the attitudes of women themselves to work.

709. **Balasubramanyan** (Vimal): Women, work and occupational health. *Mainstream* V 23(16), 1984, pp. 20–22.

Discusses why there should be a focus on women's occupational health and the present state of research on this topic.

710. **Banerjee** (G R): Hostels for working mothers. *Indian Journal of Social Work* V 16(3), 1955, pp. 133–40.

711. **Bhoite** (Anuradha): A study of the problems of employed women in rural areas. Poona, Poona University, 1975. Thesis.

712. **D'Souza** (C): A case study of working mothers. *Social Action*

V 13(11), 1963, pp. 640–46.
Suggests services that could be offered to working mothers.

713. **Dighe** (Anita) : Housing for working women—Need for realistic assessment. New Delhi, Council for Social Development, 1975, 12 pp. (CSSS).

714. **Dixit** (D K) : A bank by women for women. *Voluntary Action* V 26(3 & 4), 1983, pp. 62–63.
Describes the working of a bank managed by women for the welfare of women in Nagpur.

715. **Everett** (Jana M) and **Savara** (Mira) : Bank credit to women in the informal sector—A case study of DRI in Bombay city. Bombay, SNDT Women's University, 1983, 192 pp. (ISST). Also in *Signs* V 10(2), 1984, pp. 272–90.
Examines the amount of bank credit available to lower class women in the city of Bombay and describes the extent to which self-employed women are getting bank credit, how and with what effect.

716. **Iyengar** (Ashok K) : Credit facilities for rural women. *Social Welfare* V 29(9), 1982, pp. 13–16, 26.
In order to raise the socio-economic status of women adequate credit facilities coupled with training in skills have to be provided. The article emphasises the need for providing credit facilities and the role of Mahila Mandals in extending these facilities.

717. **Joshi** (Dina Nath) : The problems of the welfare of women workers. *Indian Journal of Social Work* V 22(3), 1961, pp. 179–85.
Emphasises that employers should be educated regarding the welfare of women workers and also emphasises the need to solve the problems of women workers.

718. **National Institute of Public Co-operation and Child Development** : Social problems of working women. New Delhi, NIPCCD, 1975, 120 pp. (NIPCCD).
Discusses the socio-economic problems like accommodation, discriminatory practices and attitude of the employees.

719. **Pais** (H) : Employment of women in India. *Indian Labour*

Journal V 21(4), 1980, pp. 533–44.
Explains how special measures and facilities can be provided for women workers. This has been studied with reference to select industries as well as employment in general.

720. **Purohit** (Manju) and others: Occupational and environmental health hazards. New Delhi, Department of Science and Technology, 1984, 40 pp. (ISST).
Discusses the health problems faced by women working in agriculture, non-agricultural occupations and plantations and suggests remedies.

721. **Ranadive** (Vimal): National Convention of Working Women—Report. Madras, Centre of Indian Trade Unions, 1979, 34 pp. (CWDS).
The convention discussed the problems of Indian working women such as (a) security of jobs, (b) maternity benefits, and (c) creches.

722. **Ranadive** (Vimal): Women and the labour movement. *Manushi* No. 1, 1979, pp. 9–10.
Describes the demands of women workers in plantations and in industries for creches and maternity benefits.

723. **Sengupta** (P): Welfare of women in industries. *Social Welfare* V 10(7), 1963, pp. 36–37, 39.

724. **Sengupta** (Padmini): Women and labour welfare. *Social Welfare* V 1(2), 1954, pp. 3–4.
Describes the legal and social welfare measures and medical benefits programmes adopted by the State and Central Government.

725. **Shastree** (Tara): Working women's hostels. *Social Welfare* V 21(3 & 4), 1974, p. 102.

726. **Subramaniam** (K) and **Yadav** (M S): Working women's hostel in India—A study. New Delhi, National Institute of Public Co-operation and Child Development, 1981, 244 pp. (NIPCCD).
Study of nineteen hostels in four cities of India. Outlines the structure and functioning of the working women's hostels, assesses the extent to which hostel facilities satisfy the needs of the residents.

727. **Sundar** (Pushpa): Credit for self-employment of women—
    Discussion paper series. Delhi, Ford Foundation,
    1983, 95 pp. (ISST).
    Collection of three papers on self-employed women's need
    for bank credit, difficulties faced by them in availing credit,
    and policy measures needed to improve their access to and
    utilisation of bank credit.

10
Women and
Labour Legislation

728. **Agarwal** (S L) : Position of women in labour law. *Awards Digest* V 9(2), 1983, pp. 109–37.

729. **Andhra Pradesh**, Office of the Chief Inspector of Factories and Boilers : Running report on the administration of Maternity Benefit Act and rules in the State of Andhra Pradesh. Hyderabad, 1978 (NL).

730. **Balachandran** (Geeta) : Equal remuneration for equal work. *Social Welfare* V 31(2), 1984, pp. 17–19, 35, 36.
Discusses how this Act has become an obstacle to women's employment.

731. **Balachandran** (Geeta) : Women and labour laws— Maternity benefits, ensuring the basic rights of women labour. *Social Welfare* V 30(4), 1983, pp. 29–30, 35.
Analyses the benefits under (*a*) the Employee's State Insurance Act, 1948, (*b*) Maternity Benefit Act, 1961 and (*c*) The Factories Act.

732. **Bihar**, Labour Department, Factory Inspection Department : Annual report on the working of the Bihar Maternity Benefit Act, 1947 in the State of Bihar for the year 1957. Ranchi, Bihar Secretariat Press, 1959 (NL).

733. **Committee for the Advancement of Legal Literacy** : Women and labour law. Bombay, n.d. (ISST).

734. **India**, Lok Sabha, Joint Committee on the Maternity Benefit

Bill, 1960 : Report. New Delhi, Lok Sabha Secretariat, 1961, 27 pp. (NL).

735. **India**, Ministry of Law and Justice : The Maternity Benefit Act, 1961 (Act No. 53 of 1961). Delhi, Manager of Publications, 1972, 9 pp. (NL).

736. **International Labour Organisation** : The new Maternity Benefit Act in India. *International Labour Review* V 86(4), 1962, pp. 395–467.

737. **Jha** (Sadananda) : Maternity benefits at present and their future in India. *Journal of Indian Law Institute* V 18(2), 1976, pp. 332–43.

738. **Mahajan** (O P) : Women and labour laws. *Social Welfare* V 28(5), 1981, pp. 1–3, 42–43.
Analyses the provisions contained in the labour laws and argues the need for strict implementation of these laws.

739. **Mir** (Ghulam Qadir) : Women workers in India. *Commercial Law Gazette* V 2(9), 1979, p. 3.
Discusses the place of women in the labour force and the legal provisions for protection against exploitation of employees.

740. **Sengupta** (P) : Women in the labour code. *Social Welfare* V 1(12), 1955, pp. 20–147.
Deals with the Acts which have been passed in connection with women on the basis of the ILO convention.

741. **Sharan** (Raka) : Women workers' employment and its policies—A study of industries of Kanpur. Paper presented at the Workshop on Women, Technology and Food Production, Madras, 1984 (MIDS).
Focuses on the problems of social legislation in relation to women employees in industries.

742. **Shri Balram** : Women workers and the labour legislation in India. *Indian Labour Journal* V 25(10), 1984, pp. 1527–42.
Survey of the implementation of the Labour Acts.

743. **Sinha** (N N) : Labour legislation and women's employment in India. *Indian Labour Journal* V 22(8), 1981, pp. 1117–23.

11

Women Workers and Automation

744. **Acharya** (Sarathi): Transfer of technology and women's employment in India. New Delhi, Indian Council of Social Science Research, 1979, 17 pp.
Review of the current debate on the requirements, criteria and choice of technology for developing countries with reference to the impact of technology transfers on the employment of women and some data based evidence of the effects of technology.

745. **Acharya** (Sarathi) and **Patkar** (Pravin): Technological infusion and employment conditions of women in rice areas. Paper presented at the Conference on Women in Rice Farming System, Manila, 1983 (TISS).

746. **Agarwal** (Bina): Agricultural mechanisation and labour use—A disaggregated approach. *International Labour Review* V 120(1), 1981, pp. 115–27.

747. **Agarwal** (Bina): Agricultural mechanisation and Third World women—Points from the literature and an empirical analysis. World Employment Programme Research, Working Paper No. 10/WD 21. Also presented at the Seminar on Women and Work and Development—Methodological Issues, New Delhi, 1982, 21 pp. (ISST).

748. **Agarwal** (Bina): Rural women and the high yielding variety rice technology in India. Delhi, Institute of Economic Growth, 1984, 66 pp. (ISST, IEG). Also in *Economic*

and Political Weekly 31 March; *Agricultural Review*
V 19(13), 1984, pp. A39–A52.

749. **Agarwal** (Bina) : Women and technological change in
agriculture, Asian and African experience. Delhi,
Institute of Economic Growth, 1984, 55 pp. (ISST,
IEG).

Examines agricultural modernisation and how it has affected the position of women in the labour market.

750. **Billings** (Martin H) and **Singh** (Arjun): Mechanisation and
the wheat revolution—Effects on the female labour in
Punjab. *Economic and Political Weekly* V 5(52), 1970,
pp. 169–74.

Discusses the fact that mechanisation in agriculture has led
to a decrease in women's participation in Punjab and
Haryana.

751. **Brandtzeez** (Brita) : Women, food and technology—A
village study from India. Landsseminaret, Oslo
University, 1982, 45 pp. Also in *Economic and Political
Weekly* V 15(47), 1979 pp. 1921–24.

Discusses the technological displacement of women in the
process of modernisation and the technological change in
Third World countries with examples from public as well
as domestic sectors.

752. **Centre of Science for Villages** : Science and technology
for women. New Delhi, Department of Science and
Technology, 1982 (ISST).

Deals with employment generating technologies to improve
the condition of women.

753. **Desai** (Neera) and **Gopalan** (Prema) : Changes in the food
processing industry from traditional to modern forms
and its impact on women's role and status. Bombay,
SNDT Women's University, Research Unit on
Women's Studies, 1983, 67 pp. (CSSS).

Modernisation and industrialisation processes have
resulted in a tremendous decline of the household sector
units over the last ten years, a rise in employment has been
in the non-household sector.

754. **Deshpande** (Anjali) : Women and mines mechanisation.

Mainstream V 22(14), 1983, pp. 30–31.

Expresses concern about the increasing mechanisation of mines. A report of the seminar organised by PUDR on mines, mechanisation and people.

755. **Grover** (I) and **Sharma** (S) : Technology to the aid of rural women. *Kurukshetra* V 29(17), 1981, pp. 26–27.

756. **Gulati** (Leela): Fishing technology and women—Two parts—Case studies. Trivandrum, Centre for Women's Development Studies, 1983, pp. 1–142, 253 (CDS).

757. **Gulati** (Leela) : Fisherwomen in Kerala—The impact of new technology on their lives. *Manushi* No. 21, 1984, pp. 33–34.

758. **Gulati** (Leela): Role of women from fishing households—A study of three fishing villages. Trivandrum, Centre for Development Studies, 1982, 11 pp. (CDS).

759. **Gulati** (Leela): Technological change and women's participation and demographic behaviour—A case study of three fishing villages. *Economic and Political Weekly* V 19(49), 1984, pp. 2089–94.

760. **Haq** (Luqmanual L): The plight of women in industrial sector. *Social Welfare* V 31(2), 1984, pp. 12–14, 34.

Analyses the factors affecting women's employment, such as the introduction of modern and automatic machinery, division of labour market into male and female, and lack of mobility.

761. **Hiraway** (Indira) : Women and technology—A study of Khadi and Village Industries in Gujarat. Paper presented at the Workshop on Women, Technology and Food Production, Madras, 1984, 19 pp. (MIDS and ISST).

Shows that the contribution of Khadi and Village Industries Board is nominal in nature and the real issues of women are hardly touched. The sexual division of labour is not favourable to women. Technology is helpful to women only in a limited way.

762. **Institute of Social Studies Trust** : A case study in the

modernization of the traditional handloom weaving industry in the Kashmir Valley. Kuala Lumpur, Asian and Pacific Centre for Women and Development, 1979, 14 pp. (ISST).

763. **Jain** (Devaki): Displacement of women workers in three traditional industries—Cotton handlooms, woollen cottage industry and hand block printing. Paper presented at the Second National Conference on Women's Studies—Session on Work and Employment, Trivandrum, 1984 (ISST).

Reviews the employment situation and the impact of new technology in these three industries. It also gives implications for policy design.

764. **Jain** (Devaki): Technology planning for promoting women's employment. Paper presented at the Workshop on Science and Technology for Rural Women, New Delhi, 1982, 19 pp. (ISST).

Discusses the various kinds of technology which are useful/harmful to women and the various innovations that have taken place. It also suggests guidelines to design suitable projects for women.

765. **Kelkar** (Govind): Impact of green revolution on women's work, participation and sex roles. Paper presented at the Asian Regional Seminar on Rural Development and Women, Mahabaleshwar, 1982, 110 pp. (ISST).

Explains how the Green Revolution technology is only in favour of large landowners. It has increased the disparity between men and women and widened the gulf between the large farmer and small cultivator. Women are denied the opportunity to learn modern technology though they play a significant role in agriculture.

766. **Malhans** (Nirlep) and **Sanghera** (Jyoti): Women in development. Appropriate technology and women, the case of Gobar Gas. Paper presented at the National Conference on Women's Studies, Bombay, 1981 (ISST).

Based on a case study of a community Gobar Gas plant, it endeavours to explore the degree to which the stated objective of mass participation of the appropriate technology programmes has been achieved. These projects have failed to involve and integrate women in the development process because of their lack of understanding of women's economic roles.

767. **Mukherjee** (Mukul) : Impact of modernization on women's occupation—A case study of the rice husking industry of Bengal. *Indian Economic and Social History Review* V 20(1), 1983, pp. 27, 45.

Opines that female employment can survive if there is scope for alternative employment of workers who are displaced, but in the case of rice mill technology this did not happen because (a) the employment potential of such mills was limited, (b) women were in a minority, (c) there were socio-cultural constraints.

768. **Patel** (Vibhuti) : Impact of modern technology on the employment and conditions of work of women in India. Paper presented at the Workshop on Women, Technology and Food Production, Madras, 1984 (MIDS).

Analyses how agricultural mechanisation affected women's employment, making masses of women jobless. Technological advancement has displaced female labour, a section of women have been completely ignored in industries and there are no labour laws protecting the interests of women workers.

769. **Raghuvanshi** (Kalpana) : Appropriate technology to help rural women. *Kurukshetra* V 30(19), 1982, pp. 18–21.

770. **Raghuvanshi** (Kalpana) : Technology for rural women. *Voluntary Action* V 25(4–5), 1982, pp. 161–65.

Emphasises the advancement of technology which would effectively help to improve the condition of rural women. Science and technology should provide appropriate alternatives to rural women to improve their economic condition rapidly.

771. **Rai** (Prabha) : Women labour—Uniform discrimination. *Yojana* V 19(7), 1975, pp. 18–20.

772. **Regional Workshop on Women and Technology** Surat, 1983 : Papers. Surat, South Gujarat University.

Department of Rural Studies (ISST).
The workshop aimed to see how technology has affected the working conditions of women and offered some suggestions how research could improve the condition of women.

773. **Sandhu** (H K): Technological development versus economic contribution of women in rural Punjab. *Social Change* V 6(3–4), 1976, pp. 18–22.
Survey conducted to assess : (*a*) the contribution of women to household activities to form incomes, (*b*) the role of women in farm decisions, (*c*) contribution to outdoor farm activities.

774. **Seminar on Appropriate Technologies for Rural Women**, Hyderabad, 1985 : Report. Hyderabad, NIRD, 1985 (NIRD).

775. **Sen** (Amartya) : Women technology and sexual division. Oxford, All Souls College, 1984, 55 pp. (ISST).
Concerned with the problems of sexual division in general and sex bias in particular and why we should take a broader view of technology.

776. **Sinha** (S P) : Impact of technological development in agriculture on women in rural areas—A two village profile. New Delhi, Indian Council for Social Science Research, 1981, 97 pp. (ISST).
Study conducted in the rural areas of Bihar to analyse how technological change in agriculture has affected the living and working conditions, the time disposition and employment pattern of rural women and highlights aspects of exploitation.

777. **Srivastava** (J C) : Technology for development of rural women. *Khadi Gramodyog* V 28(4), 1982, pp. 198–209; V 28(5), 1982, p. 239.

778. **Workshop on Women, Technology and Forms of Production**, Madras, 1984 : Report. Madras, Madras Institute of Development Studies, 1984, 23 pp. (MIDS). Also in *Economic and Political Weekly* December 1984; *Yojana* V 29(8), 1985, pp. 8–10.

12

Women : Organisation and Unionisation

779. **Acharji** (Nilima): Safeguarding the interests of women workers. *Social Welfare* V 28(10), 1982, pp. 4–6, 22.
Analyses the effectiveness of women's participation in unions and factors which have been either hostile or acted as hindrances to their career.

780. **Acharji** (Nilima): Women workers in trade unions. *Social Welfare* V 28(11), 1982 pp. 14–16, 31.

781. **Ahmedabad Women's Action Group**: Fire was kindled within the coal labourers and AWAG acts as a catalyst. Ahmedabad, AWAG, 1984, 19 pp. (ISST).
Describes the efforts made by AWAG to organise women labourers working in the coal-mines of Ahmedabad.

782. **Ali** (Mohd. Iqbal): Socio-economic conditions of members of Mahila Mandals—A study in Hanumakonda Block, Andhra Pradesh. Paper presented at the Conference on Women's Status and Development, Warangal, 1982, 9 pp. (ISST).
The purpose of the present study was to examine (*a*) the socio-economic characteristics of Mahila Mandal members, (*b*) whether caste division playing an important role determined the socio-economic status of Mahila Mandals, (*c*) whether or not the involvement of low caste members in Mandals was limited.

783. **Arunachalam** (Jaya): Role of women's organisation in organising women's labour in rural areas who pursue vocations either jointly or separately with men and which have their own problems and peculiarities—A

case study. Paper presented at the National Seminar
on Organising the Unorganised Labour, New Delhi,
1984 (ISST, WWF).
Gives reasons why women need to be organised and suggests ways in which it can be done.

784. **Arunachalam** (Jaya): Role of women and children in infor-
mal sector—A case study of the Working Women's
Forum, Madras.   Paper presented at the National
Seminar on Productivity in the Informal Sector, New
Delhi, 1985 (ISST).
A note on the informal sector and the activities of the
Working Women's Forum.

785. **Azad** (Nandini) : Women micro entrepreneurs of Madras city,
experiment in credit-system—A case of Working
Women's Co-operative Society Limited. Madras,
Working Women's Forum, 1982, 14 pp. (WWF).

786. **Bahuguna** (Sunderlal): Protecting the sources of community life, women's non-violent power in the
Chipko movement. *Manushi* No. 6, 1981, pp. 34–36.

787. **Balasubramanyan** (Vimal): Do trade unions care for
women workers. *Mainstream* V 22(52), 1984, pp. 27–28.
Trade unions are being formally accepted as an important
forum for serious action, vital for improvement, in employment. Historically, it has been found that male dominated
trade union movements must take the blame for the low
participation of women at leadership levels.

788. **Bhan** (Jai Kishore): Find women aiffesiens to vitalise co-
operatives. *Kurukshetra* V 11(6), 1963, pp. 17–18.

789. **Bhatt** (Ela R):   Self Employed Women's Association—A
symbol of unity of the blue blouse. *Social Welfare*
V 22(6–7), 1975, pp. 33–36, 64.
A case study of SEWA—their experience in organising
unorganised women workers like garment dealers, vegetable vendors, hand-cart pullers, junk-dealers.

790. **Biswas** (Kali) : A thousand women and one purpose to live by
—Their own work. *Yojana* V 5(20), 1961, pp. 10–11, 29.

791. **Centre for Women's Development Studies** : A directory

of women's co-operatives in India. 4 vols. New Delhi, CWDS 1982 (ISST, CWDS).

792. **Chakravarthy** (Gargi) : Trade union vista. _Mainstream_ V 22(32), 1984, p. 31.

Proceedings of the Working Women's Convention held under the auspices of the All India Trade Union Conference.

793. **Chari** (T V R) : Co-operative societies for women—Role of Central Social Welfare Board. _Social Welfare_ V 12(2), 1965, pp. 5–6.

794. **Chaudhary** (Paul P) : Change through Mahila Mandals. _Kurukshetra_ V 226(10), 1978, pp. 14–18.

795. **Chaudhary** (Pawan) : Women in trade unions. _Social Welfare_ V 24(6), 1977, pp. 22–23.

796. **Dass** (Usha) : Housewives against profiteers—Lucknow women organised co-operative stores. _Yojana_ V 9(17), 1965, pp. 22–23.

797. **Deshpande** (Anjali) : Right issue, wrong direction. _Mainstream_ V 21(25), 1983 p. 24.

Report of the march organised by various women's organisations to campaign for women's employment and for welfare benefits.

798. **Despande** (R) : Women workers get organised. _World Trade Union Movement_ V 5, 1964, pp. 27–29.

799. **Dholakia** (Anila R) : Rural women in white revolution. Ahmedabad, Self Employed Women's Association, 1984, 21 pp. (SEWA).

Describes SEWA's initiative in organising a diary co-operative and in matters relating to cattle loan.

800. **Dwivedi** (Sudha) : Role of co-operative movement in the International Women's Year. _Kurukshetra_ V 23(14), 1975, pp. 12–13.

801. **Garg** (Sadhana) : Role of women in co-operatives. _Social Welfare_ V 27(8), 1980, pp. 40–41.

Evaluates the participation of women in co-operatives in Punjab, Gujarat, Maharashtra and Jammu and Kashmir.

802. **Gawankar** (Rohini) : Annapurna—Case study of grass-root self-employed women's organisation, Bombay. Paper presented at the Asian Regional Conference on Women and the Household, New Delhi, 1985 (ISST).
Describes the activities and obstacles faced by the organisation in organising textile workers.

803. **Gothaskar-Kanhare** (Sujata) : Organising working class women. *How* V 5(1), 1982, pp. 11–14.
Report of the experience of the author in organising the working class women in Shahada and Taloda Talukas in Maharashtra.

804. **Guha** (P) : Women's industrial co-operatives in national development. *Cooperator* V 5(20), 1963, pp. 5–6.

805. **Guha** (Sunil) : Co-operatives for rural women. *Social Welfare* V 7(4), 1960, pp. 8–9.

806. **Hanumappa** (H G) and **Sujata** (T M) : The changing status of rural women. *Yojana* V 28(16), 1984, pp. 15–16.
Study of thirty-six Mahila Mandals in Bangalore District to assess the functional impact of the Mandals in the process of socio-economic upliftment of women.

807. **India**, Ministry of Agriculture and Irrigation : Development of village level organisation—Report of the Working Group on Development of Village Level Organisations of Rural Women. New Delhi, Department of Rural Development, 1978 (ISST).

808. **Jain** (Devaki) : From dissociation to rehabilitation—Report on an experiment to promote self-employment in an urban area. Bombay, Allied, 1975, 32 pp. (ISST).
Describes the initial founding and activities of SEWA.

809. **Jain** (S P) and **Reddy** (V Krishnamurthy) : Role of women in rural development—A study of Mahila Mandals. Hyderabad, National Institute of Rural Development, 1979, 93 pp. (NIRD, ISST).
Assesses the working of fifteen Mahila Mandals in Gujarat, Jammu and Kashmir, Orissa, Punjab and Tamil Nadu.

810. **Jain** (Shobita) : Women's and people's ecological movement —A case study of women's role in the Chipko

movement in Uttar Pradesh. *Economic and Political Weekly* V 19(41), 1984, pp. 1788–94.

The study is based on an investigation in Chamoli district. The mobilisation of women for the Chipko movement has led to a situation of conflict wherein women want to be a part of the decision-making process and men oppose this.

811. **Jayalakshmi** (L) : Co-operatives for rural women. *Khadi Gramodyog* V 25(10), 1979, pp. 410–14.

812. **Jeffers** (Hilde) : Organising women petty traders and processors—A case study of Working Women's Forum, Madras. Madras, Working Women's Forum, 1981, 82 pp. (ISST).
Study conducted to (*a*) examine the Forum's organisational structure and leadership, (*b*) evaluate the impact of the organisation's key programme, and (*c*) assess the potential of this type of organisation as a model for urban development and women's progress.

813. **Jhabvala** (Renana) : Neither a complete success nor a total failure—Report of SEWA's campaign to organise beedi workers. *Manushi* No. 22, 1984, pp. 18–22.
Gives an idea of the actual process which most organising efforts have to go through and the persistence required to make small gains.

814. **Jhabvala** (Renana) : Organising home-based workers. Paper presented at the Technical Seminar on Women's Work and Employment, New Delhi, 1982 (ISST).
Describes the different kinds of home-based workers, their socio-economic condition and the need to organise them around issues.

815. **Jhurani** (Kamlesh) : Rural women's work and organisation, role of intervening agencies—Some lessons from Tejpur Mahila Mandal, Punjab. Paper presented at the Second National Conference on Women's Studies, Trivandrum, 1984 (CWDS).

816. **Joshi** (Gopa) : Protecting the sources of community life. *Manushi* No. 7, 1981, pp. 22–23.
Describes the problems faced by Chipko activists because

men do not appreciate their participation in the movement.

817. **Kanhare** (Sujata) and **Savara** (Mira) : A case study on the organising of landless tribal women in Maharashtra. Bangalore, Asian and Pacific Centre for Women's Development, 1980, 13 pp. (CSSS).

818. **Kanthi Mathi** (A B) : Women's co-operatives. *Kurukshetra* V 19(17), 1977, p. 7.

819. **Kapur** (Mohinder) : Women and the co-operative movement. *Kurukshetra* V 12(1), 1963, pp. 37–38.

820. **Manohar** (Mukta) : Difficulties of women workers and limitations of trade union organisations. Paper presented at the National Conference on Women's Studies, Bombay, 1981 (ISST).
    Difficulties faced by most women workers are cultural. The author opines that the form of trade union organisation is not sufficient to involve women in it.

821. **Mitra** (Manoshi) : Tribal women and tribal movements. *Samya Shakti* V 1(2), 1984, pp. 80–91.
    Focuses on tribal women's participation in the tribal movement in Bihar where women active in peasant and workers' movements are facing a hostile reaction from male workers who are attempting to prevent the emergence of a women workers' movement.

822. **Naponen** (Helzi) : Organising women petty traders and home-based producers. A case study of Working Women's Forum, India. Paper presented at the Asian Regional Conference on Women and the Household, New Delhi, 1985 (ISI).
    Evaluates the grass-root efforts of the Working Women's Forum which has an innovative credit programme to unionise women workers in the informal sector.

823. **National Workshop on Organising Self-Employed Women in India**, Ahmedabad, 1981 : Report. Ahmedabad, Self Employed Women's Association, 1981, 35 pp. (ISST).
    Describes some of the successful strategies for organising self-employed women in India.

824. **Omvedt** (Gail): Women and rural revolt in India. *Social Scientist* V 6(1), 1977, pp. 3–18.
    Describes the revolt by women agriculture labourers in Maharashtra.

825. **Orissa,** Planning and Co-ordination Department: Evaluation of Mahila Samities in Orissa. Cuttack, Government Press, 1969, 60 pp. (NL).

826. **Rao** (G R S): Co-operative movement—Potential field for women. *Social Welfare* V 12(2), 1965, pp. 7–8.

827. **Rathod** (C S): Women's co-operatives—Progress and scope. *Kurukshetra* V 16(7), 1968, pp. 14–15.

828. **Ruikar** (Malathi): Women in trade unions. *Indian Journal of Social Work* V 13(4), 1953, pp. 250–56.
    Analyses the reasons for women's unwillingness to share the responsibility of leadership and points out the necessity of more leisure as well as better education and training in trade union organisation and leadership.

829. **Savara** (Mira): Organising the Annapurna. *Institute of Development Studies Bulletin* V 12(3), 1981, pp. 48–53.

830. **Self Employed Women's Association**: We, the self-employed—Organising self-employed women. Ahmedabad, SEWA, 1982 (ISST).

831. **Selvam** (V Solomon): Role of women in Indian peasant movement. New Delhi, JNU, 1982, 158 pp. (JNU).
    Describes women's participation in the peasant movement in 1947.

832. **Shah** (Radhika): Feasibility study of setting up a credit co-operative for women in Gujarat. Ahmedabad, Indian Institute of Management, 1979, 43 pp. (ISST).

833. **Sharan** (Raka) and **Dhanagare** (D N): Trade unions and women workers. *Indian Journal of Industrial Relations* V 15(3), 1980, pp. 447–57.

834. **Sharma** (Kumud): Women in struggle—A case study of the Chipko movement. *Samya Shakti* V 1(2), 1984, pp. 55–62.
    Describes the role of women in the Chipko movement

which has given women a strong forum to articulate their concerns but so far it has not helped them in their own struggle against oppression.

835. **Srinivasan** (Viji) : Working Women's Forum—A case study. New Delhi, Ford Foundation, 52 pp. (ISST).

Describes the structure, functioning, future plans of the Working Women's Forum.

836. **Subramaniam** (K) and **Ramanathan** : Study of Mahila Mandals in India. New Delhi, National Institute of Public Co-operation and Child Development, 1978, 200 pp. (NIPCCD).

837. **Tellis-Nayak** (Jessie B) : *Indian womanhood, then and now— Situation efforts and profile.* Indore, Satprakasan Sanchar Kendra, 1983, 303 pp. (NN).

Includes various efforts made by women to form organisations like SEWA and Working Women's Forum.

838. Women's industrial co-operatives in States. *Cooperator* V 5(19), 1968, pp. 14–18, 23.

Discusses the different problems of co-operatives and gives the statistics of women in these co-operatives.

839. **Workshop on the Unorganised Sector**, Ahmedabad, 1983 : Report. Ahmedabad, SEWA, 1984, 73 pp. (ISST).

Collation of experiences of activists working with workers in the unorganised sector.

13

Education and Training of Women

840. **Ahuja-Patel** (Krishna): Women, technology and the development process. *Economic and Political Weekly* V 14(36), 1979, pp. 1549–54.

Attempts to delineate the significant elements of inequalities of access to technical education and technological know-how between men and women and stresses the need for policy measures to improve the technological level of women.

841. **Aiyer** (K B): Industrial institute for blind women, Bombay. *Social Welfare* V 16(7), 1969, pp. 16–17.

842. **Bhandari** (K G) and **Vidyarthi** (G S): Training village level workers and gram sevikas. *Kurukshetra* V 9(9), 1961, pp. 23–26.

843. **Centre for Women's Development Studies**: Extension of vocational centre facilities for rural women—Report on Punjab, District Jullunder. New Delhi, CWDS, 1981, 67 pp. (CWDS).

844. **Centre for Women's Development Studies**: Extension of vocational training facilities for rural women—Report on West Bengal, District Bankura. New Delhi, CWDS, 1980, 73 pp. (ISST).

845. **Centre for Rural Development and Human and Natural Resources Research Society**: Women's training needs—Rural Ambala (Haryana). Delhi CRD and HNRRS, 1981, 564 pp. (ISST)

846. **Centre for Rural Development and Human and**

Natural Resources Research Society: Women's training needs—Rural Bharuch (Gujarat). New Delhi, CRD and HNRRS, 1981, 478 pp. (ISST).

847. **Chakravarthy** (S): Training farm women for effective decision-making. *Indian Farming* V 25(8), 1975, pp. 53–54.

848. **Chakravorti** (S): Role of rural women in development— Their training and extension needs. Paper presented at the Seminar on Women and Development, Anand, 1977, 6 pp. (ISST).

849. **Dasgupta** (A): Women in management profession for economic welfare. *Office Management* V 6(4), 1966, pp. 6–7.
Discusses some professional courses and considers many activities in the professional side of management which are suitable for women and emphasises that women have the right to participate in all spheres of economic activity.

850. **Dasgupta** (Krishna): Women's organisations—What they can do to serve the community. *Yojana* V 6(9), 1962, pp. 3–5.
Describes the training courses in sewing and embroidery conducted by women's organisations.

851. **Deshmukh** (Durgabai): Women as full partners. *Social Welfare* V 21(6), 1974, pp. 11–12.
Stresses the need for training women and increasing employment opportunities.

852. **Deulkar** (Durga): Welfare of rural women—Role of education. *Kurukshetra* V 13(5), 1965, pp. 23–25.

853. **Devadas** (Rajammal P): Improving the status of Indian women. *Kurukshetra* V 24(4), 1975, pp. 10–12.
Emphasises the importance of education and employment and suggests that efforts must be made to explore all possibilities for part-time jobs for women and for educating them in the profitable use of leisure time.

854. **Eleventh Congress of the National Federation of Indian Women**, Calcutta, 1984: Education, training and employment. New Delhi, NFIW, 31 pp. (WL).

855. **India**, Ministry of Labour, Directorate General of Employment and Training: A priority profile—Training rural women. New Delhi, DGET, 1980, 62 pp. (ISST).

Summary of a large-scale survey conducted by DGET to assess the vocational training needs of rural women in various states.

856. **India**, Ministry of Labour, Directorate General of Employment and Training: Report of a survey on the employment of ex-trainees of National Vocational Training Institute, New Delhi. New Delhi, DGET, 1980, 21 pp. (ISST).

Evaluation conducted to make a quick assessment of the employment situation among the trainees who have been trained in various courses by Vocational Training Institutes in India.

857. **India**, Ministry of Labour, Directorate General of Employment and Training: Workshop for identifying occupational skill requirement of electronic industry, Bombay, 1982. New Delhi, DGET, 1982, 44 pp. (ISST).

Workshop was organised to assess the training needs of urban women workers in new occupations on the basis of a survey of the electronics industry conducted in Bombay.

858. **Indian Institute of Public Administration**, Centre for Rural Development Administration: Vocational training programmes for rural women—Kerala. New Delhi, IIPA, 1981, 170 pp. (ISST).

Reviews (*a*) the existing training facilities in selected industries, (*b*) identifies training needs and areas in which the training needs are to be expanded, (*c*) suggests the nature of training courses and organisational pattern at various levels.

859. **Indian Institute of Rural Workers**: Assessment of vocational training needs of women in rural areas—Report of the study. Aurangabad, IIRW, 1980 (ISST).

860. **Institute of Applied Manpower Research**: Vocational training programme for women in rural areas—

Jammu and Kashmir. New Delhi, IAMR, 1981, 153pp. (ISST).

861. **Institute of Applied Manpower Research** : Vocational training programme for women in rural areas—Uttar Pradesh. New Delhi, IAMR, 1981, 179pp. (ISST).

862. **Institute of Applied Manpower Research** : Women in the labour force and their educational composition. New Delhi, IAMR, 1973 (RUWS).

863. **Institute of Cultural Affairs** : Survey for assessing the vocational training needs of women in the rural areas of the Kolaba district. Bombay, Institute of Cultural Affairs, 1981, 66 pp. (ISST).

864. **Institute of Social Studies Trust** : A study of utilisation and wastage of the training programme—National and Regional Vocational Training Institutes for Women. New Delhi, ISST, 1984 (ISST).
Follow up study of ex-trainees trained by the NVTI and RVTIs in India.

865. **Kamala** (V) and **Sinha** (M N) : Training in modern dairying for rural women. *Khadi Gramodyog* V 26(3), 1979, pp. 159–62.

866. **Kamalanathan** (Godavari) and **Seethalakshmi** (S) : Extension training. *Indian Farming* V 25(8), 1975, p. 60.

867. **Kamat** (A R) : Women's education and social change in India. *Social Scientist* V 5(1), 1976, pp. 3–27.
Highlights the importance of education for occupational diversification. Describes the recent job trends in women's occupational pattern.

868. **Karnataka Conference on New Perspectives on Women's Vocational Training**, Bangalore, 1983 : Report. New Delhi, Ministry of Labour and Rehabilitation, 1983 (CSSS).

869. **Khan** (Q U) : Women in the labour force and their educational composition. Paper presented at the Seminar on Optimum Utilisation of Women Power, New Delhi, 1975 (CSSS).

870. **Kumar** (K) and **Mago** (Snehlata) : Training needs of farm

women in Haryana. *Indian Journal of Adult Education* V 30(10), 1974, pp. 72–76.

871. **Mehta** (Prayag): Vocational training needs of rural women. New Delhi, National Labour Institute, 1980, 115 pp. (NLI).

872. **National Institute of Rural Development**: Assessment of vocational training needs of rural women—A plan for Anantapur District of Andhra Pradesh. Hyderabad, NIRD, 1981, 205 pp. (ISST).

873. **National Institute of Rural Development**: Assessment of vocational training needs of rural women—A plan for Kanyakumari District of Tamil Nadu. Hyderabad, NIRD, 1981, 213 pp. (ISST).

874. **National Labour Institute**: Vocational training needs of rural women—Santhal Paraganas (Bihar) and Sundargarh (Orissa). New Delhi, NLI, 1980, 111 pp. (ISST).

875. **National Workshop of the ESCAP/FAO Inter-Country Project for Promotion and Training of Rural Women in Income-Raising Group Activities**, Bangalore, 1978: Report. New Delhi, Ministry of Social Welfare, 1978, 65 pp. (ISST).

876. **People's Institute for Development and Training**: Vocational training needs of women in Betul District (Madhya Pradesh). New Delhi, PIDT, n.d., 124 pp. (ISST).
Assesses the training needs in Betul District and suggests a feasible training plan and strategy.

877. **People's Institute for Development and Training**: Vocational training needs of women in Sirmour District of Himachal Pradesh. New Delhi, PIDT, 1981, 116 pp. (ISST).

878. **Seminar on All-India Women's Vocational Training**, New Delhi, 1982: Report. New Delhi, Ministry of Labour (ISST).
Discusses the development of relevant training programmes which can increase economic opportunities for women. The seminar themes concentrated on the dynamics of

designing and implementing innovations which incorporate the socio-economic development of women through vocational training.

879. **Seth** (Mridula) : Educating women through economic activities. *Social Welfare* V 25(8), 1978, pp. 14–15.

Describes the working of some training-cum-production centres.

880. **Shiva Rao** (Kitty) : Bal sevika training programme. *Kurukshetra* V 11(2), 1962, pp. 6, 14.

881. **Shridevi** (S) : Problems of women's education. *Khadi Gramodyog* V 10(1), 1963, pp. 123–27.

882. **Tamil Nadu Conference on New Perspectives on Women's Vocational Training**, Madras, 1983 : Papers. New Delhi, Ministry of Labour, 1983, 104 pp. (ISST).

The objectives of the conference were (a) to introduce new economic perspectives on women's vocational training, (b) to explore new curriculum dimensions in women's vocational training, (c) to promote community awareness regarding the changing role of women in national economic development, (d) to explore potential co-ordination with other programmes, and (e) to explore new opportunities for women in industrial growth centres.

883. **Training Programme for Women Assistant Project Officers for Implementing DWCRA**, Hyderabad, 1984 : Report (NIRD).

884. **Usha** (C) : Widening horizons of vocational training for women—Women's Polytechnic, Delhi. *Social Welfare* V 10(5), 1963, pp. 8–9.

885. **Varalakshmi** (P K) : Bal sevika training scheme. *Kurukshetra* V 12(2), 1963, pp. 6–8.

886. Workers' education—Report of the Seminar on Women Workers Working on the Employment Guarantee Scheme in Maharashtra. *Hind Mazdoor* V 25(1 & 2), 1981, p. 5.

14
Women : Attitudes to Work

887. **Bajaj** (Neelam) : Job involvement in high and low anxious working women. *Journal of Psychological Research* V 22(1), 1978, pp. 33–36.

888. **Baker** (Dorothy) : A study of women students—Values, goals and conflicts regarding studies, career, social life and marriage. Bombay, Nirmala Niketan, 1972. Thesis.

889. **Banerjee** (D) and others : A study on the attitudes of unemployed women. *Indian Journal of Psychology* V 48(20), 1973, pp. 69–72.

890. **Bhatia** (Pratima) : Role conflict among working women. Lucknow, Lucknow University, 1977. Thesis.

891. **Bhatia** (S K) : Job satisfaction of women workers—A survey. *Indian Management* V 21(5), 1982, pp. 37–42.
Survey conducted in a large engineering industrial organisation to find out the extent of job satisfaction among women artisans engaged in micatapes, sheets, electric soldering and varnishing, etc.

892. **Bilmoria Rani** (M) : Work situation and behavioural pattern—An analysis of female criminality. Paper presented at the Workshop on Women and Work, Hyderabad, 1985 (ISST).
Analyses the impact of the work situation of women on their involvement in deviant or criminal activities. The findings are based on interviews with 120 women convicts in AP.

893. **Garza** (Joseph M) and **Rao** (Nandini) : Attitudes towards employment and unemployment—Status of mother

in Hyderabad. *Journal of Marriage and Family* V 34(1), 1972, pp. 153–55.

894. **Jetley** (Surinder) : Cultural variations in women's work and women's organisations. Paper presented at the Second National Conference on Women's Studies—Session on Women and Work, Trivandrum, 1984, 13 pp. (CWDS, ISST).

Examines the empirical data on women's work in Punjab and West Bengal and the response of women to organisations for employment generation against the norms and ideals associated with women's work.

895. **Kapoor** (K D) : Attitudes of would-be career women towards employment — A study of colleges under Kanpur University. Kanpur, P.N. College, n.d., 6 pp. (CWDS).

896. **Khanna** (R M) : A socio-psychological study of middle class working mothers of Uttar Pradesh with special reference to Kaval Town. Agra, Agra University, n.d. Thesis.

897. **Neelam** (J K) : Emotional, social and educational adjustment of children of working mothers vis-a-vis non-working mothers. New Delhi, Indian Institute of Public Administration, 1983. Thesis (IIPA).

898. **Paranjpe** (S D) : Problems of graduate employed women—A socio-psychology and attitude survey. Poona, Poona University, 1972. Thesis.

899. **Pereira** (B F) : Organisational and personal correlates of attitudes towards women as managers. *Indian Journal of Social Work* V 39(3), 1978, pp. 287–96.

900. **Rallia Ram** (Mayavanti) : Kashmiri women—Attitude to professions. *Social Welfare* V 23(2), 1976, pp. 13–14.

Analyses the attitude of Kashmiri women towards different professions.

901. **Rupande** (S) : Job attitudes of female operators. *Indian Journal of Social Work* V 37(3), 1976, pp. 259–65.

902. **Seth** (Madhu) : Motives to work and authoritarianism among

working and non-working women. Paper presented at the National Conference on Women's Studies, Bombay, 1981 (ISST).

903. **Singh** (K P) : A comparative study of the attitudes of working and non-working women towards women's education and employment. *Interdiscipline* V 11(3), 1974, pp. 89–99.

904. **Srivastava** (Vinita) : *Employment of educated married women in India—Its consequences and causes.* New Delhi, National Publishing House, 1978, 192 pp.
A study of educated women in Chandigarh currently employed—observes that educated women seek white-collar jobs only.

905. **Srivastava** (Vinita) : Professional education and attitude to female employment. A case study of married working women in Chandigarh. *Social Action* V 27(1), 1977, pp. 19–30.

906. **Surti** (Kirtida) and **Sarupria** (Dalpat) : Psychological factors affecting women entrepreneurs. *Indian Journal of Social Work* V 44(3), 1983, pp. 287–95.
Makes an attempt to investigate the stresses women entrepreneurs experience and the manner in which they adjust to the stressful situation.

907. **Surti** (Kirtida) : Role-stress, role efficacy and coping styles in working women—Some findings. Paper presented at the National Conference on Women's Studies, Bombay, 1981 (ISST).
Investigates how efficacious working women feel in their roles in different professions, what kind of role stresses they experience in the working situation and the way they cope with the stressful situation.

908. **Vidya Rani** (C) : Morale of women employees in Government. *Administration* V 24(3–4), 1979, pp. 106–21.

15

Women and Multiple Roles

909. **Agarwal** (Anil) : Domestic air pollution—The effect of wood
    smoke on the health of women. *Manushi* No. 28, 1985,
    pp. 13–21.
    Highlights the health problems faced by women because of
    indoor air pollution and reviews the available solutions
    such as choice of tree species, and smokeless chulahs.

910. **Agarwal** (B) : In employment—The status of women.
    Seminar No. 165, 1973, pp. 21–24.
    Gives an account of rural working women and their subor-
    dinate role in society alongwith the conflicting roles inside
    and outside the home of the urban employed woman.

911. **Ahuja-Patel** (Krishna) : Development for women.
    Mainstream V 16(7), 1977, pp. 18–24.
    Discusses the professional and household problems of
    working women.

912. **Asuri** (Padamasini T) : Farm women and home manage-
    ment. *Indian Farming* V 25(8), 1975, p. 55.
    Discusses the dual role of women as agricultural labourers
    and home managers. Being a farm worker does not relieve
    her from housework.

913. **Bahuguna** (Anjali) : Role of rural women in the economy of
    Garhwal region. Paper presented at the Technical
    Seminar on Women's Work and Employment, New
    Delhi, 1982, 10 pp. (ISST).

914. **Baig** (Tara Ali) : *India's woman power.* New Delhi, S. Chand,
    1976, 301 pp. (JNU).

Analyses the careers, professional life and status of working women and gives the statistics of women in employment.

915. **Banerjee** (Nirmala) : Economic development and the sexual division of labour. Paper presented at the Tenth International Congress of Anthropological and Ethnological Sciences, New Delhi, 1978 (ISST).

Emphasises that economic development can only be achieved if there is equality between men and women workers and also argues against the exploitation of women workers.

916. **Basu** (Sreelekha) : Role of women in rural economic development. *Yojana* V 23(21), 1979, pp. 23–27.

917. **Bedekar** (Malati) : Women in man's world. *Yojana* V 19(13 & 14), 1975, pp. 26–28.

918. **Bhasin** (Kamala) and **Malik** (Baljit) : The status of women in a changing rural society. *Indian Farming* V 25(8), 1975, pp. 48–50, 52.

Emphasises that rural women have been actively involved in economic production.

919. **Bhatia** (Pratima) : How they spend their leisure—The working women of Lucknow. *Social Welfare* V 23(10), 1977, pp. 12–13, 16.

Reiterates that women spend most of their spare time in domestic work.

920. **Bhatnagar** (S) : A day in the life of a rural woman. *Science for Villages* No. 62, 1982, pp. 7–8.

921. **Blumberg** (Rhoda Lois) and **Dwarki** (Leela) : *India's educated women—Options and constraints*. Delhi. Hindustan Publication Corporation, 1980, 172 pp. (AIWC).

Discusses the influence of women's education and employment on marital life and outlines the conditions under which married women can work.

922. **Bose** (Maithreyi) : Women in labour force. *Indian Worker* V 17(20), 1969, p. 6.

Discusses why women take up employment even at low wages.

923. **Chako** (T I) : Women and equal employment opportunity—Some unintended effects. *Journal of Applied Psychology* V 67(1), 1983, p. 119.

924. **Chakraborty** (Krishna) : *Conflicting worlds of working mothers—A sociological enquiry.* Calcutta, Progressive, 1978, 305 pp. (LML).

925. **Chakraborty** (Krishna) : Maternal employment and its effect on the mother. *Socialist Perspective* V 3(3), 1975, pp. 22–33.

926. **Chettur** (Usha) : The Indian girls 1966—Her problems of work and marriage. *Yojana* V 10(1), 1966, pp. 14–15, 21.

927. **Chettur** (Usha) : The woman invades man's world. *Yojana* V 11(1), 1967, pp. 32–36.
    Highlights the various occupations where women have taken the place of men such as law, publishing and tourism.

928. **Choudhry** (Sudhir) : Women in employment. Delhi, University of Delhi, 1969. Thesis.

929. **Dabholkar** (V A) : Life and labour of employed women in Poona. *Arth Vignana* V 3(3), 1961, pp. 181–93. Based on the doctoral thesis, Poona University, 1960.

930. **Dandekar** (V M) : Integration of women in economic development. *Economic and Political Weekly* V 17(44), 1982, pp. 1782–86.
    Presents some data regarding women's participation in economic activities in India and against this background discusses the problem of increasing women's participation in economic activity so that they may contribute to and are fully integrated in economic development.

931. **Dange** (Rajani P) : Gainfully employed Maharashtrian brahmin women in Vidharbha and their family pattern. Nagpur, Nagpur University, 1970. Thesis (SSDC).

932. **Dange** (R P) : Working mothers and child rearing. Part I. An unpublished paper based on the lectures delivered during the Parents Education Week organised by the Association of Moral and Social Hygiene, 1966.

933. **Dasgupta** (Biplab) and others : *Village society and labour use.* Delhi, Oxford University Press, 1977, 229 pp. (CED).

934. **Desai** (Neera) and **Anantrama** (Sharyu) : Review of middle class women's entry into the world of work. Bombay, SNDT Women's University, 1982, 17 pp. (RUWS).

935. **D'Souza** (Anthony A) : Should wives work. *Social Action* V 18(1), 1968, pp. 15–24.

Emphasises the importance of technological development and attitudinal changes within the family which play a major role.

936. **Dhillon** (Gurmeet) : The changing role of rural women. *Social Change* V 11(2), 1981, pp. 21–30.

Discusses the changing roles of women. Dairying has essentially been a woman's responsibility, in addition to agricultural operations.

937. **Dixit** (Asha) : Survey of leisure time activities of working women in Jaipur. *Indian Journal of Adult Education* V 37(1), 1976, pp. 11–14.

938. **Dixon** (Ruth B) : *Rural women at work—Strategies for development in South India.* Baltimore, John Hopkins University Press, 1978.

939. **Feminist Resource Centre** : Women's work, part of subsistence production. Bombay, FRC, 1982 (ISST).

Discusses how women's work forms a part of the capitalist development process.

940. **Gadgil** (D R) : *Women in the working force in India.* Bombay, Asia Pub., 1965, 33 pp. (NN).

Analyses the extent of women's participation in economic activity in India and the impact of development on them.

941. **Gauba** (Anand) : Wife-husband participation at home. Paper presented at the Asian Regional Seminar on Women and the Household, New Delhi, 1985 (ISST).

A survey of working and non-working wives to study their time use and work participation.

942. **Gopujkar** (P V) : Working mother and early childhood education. New Delhi, National Institute of Public Co-operation and Child Development, 1978, 120 pp. (NIPCCD).

943. **Grover** (S) : A study of career women. Delhi, University of Delhi, 1962. Thesis (CRL, DU).

944. **Gulati** (Leela) : Images and image makers—Some insight from work with working women. Trivandrum, Centre for Development Studies, 1983, 26 pp. (CDS).

945. **Gulati** (Leela) : Impact of occupational structure on the role and status of women. Paper presented at the Seminar on Women and Development, Anand, 1977, 22 pp. (ISST).

Based on three case studies in Trivandrum District, it examines the roles and status of working women in Kerala, given their occupational structure.

946. **Gupta** (Anupa) : The problems of working women. *Yojana* V 14(4 & 5), 1971, pp. 21–30.

Discusses the problems of working women and the traditional views about women's work.

947. **Gupta** (Jayoti) : Family structure, bondage and status of women in Jaunsar Bawar. Paper presented at the Asian Regional Conference on Women and the Household, New Delhi, 1985.

Discusses the factors leading the wives of bonded labourers to prostitution.

948. **Gupta** (Uma) : Status and role of educated working women—A study of Agra. Agra, Agra University, 1979. Thesis.

949. **Harichandran** (C) : Socio-economic conditions of widows— A study. *Yojana* V 26(10), 1982, pp. 11–12.

Report of a study conducted in the Kanyakumari District of Tamil Nadu to investigate the educational background, work participation, and family income of widows.

950. **Hemalatha** (P) and **Suryanarayana** (M) : Married working women—A study on the role interaction. *Indian Journal of Social Work* V 44(2), 1983, pp. 153–56.

951. **Ikkramullah** (S S) : *From purdah to parliament.* London, Cresent Press, 1963, 168 pp.

952. **Ilaiah** (K) : Women in development. The Andhra situation. Paper presented at the National Conference on

Women's Studies, Bombay, 1981, 9 pp. (ISST).
Opines that the division of labour is artificially imposed by
one sex on the other. It argues that though a woman's work
consumes the same amount of time and energy as a man's
yet she does not get an equal share of food. The increased
production has hardly improved her position.

953. **India,** National Planning Committee : *Women's role in planned
economy.* Bombay, Vora, 1949, 255 pp.

954. **Iyer** (K V) : The increasing role of women in economic and
social development. *Social Welfare* V 14(7), 1967,
pp. 4–7.

955. **Jain** (S P) : Leadership among rural women. *Social Change*
V 13(3), 1983, pp. 8–12.

956. **Jauhari** (Prema) : Status of working women. Lucknow,
Lucknow University, 1970. Thesis.

957. **Jhabvala** (Renana) : Working women—Myth and reality.
How V 4(2 & 3), 1981, pp. 4–10, 16.
A note on the life, problems and struggle of Muslim women
workers in Ahmedabad.

958. **Kabra** (Vijendra) : Ladened with tradition—Working women
in rural India. Paper presented at the National
Seminar on Unorganised Labour, New Delhi, 1984
(ISST).

959. **Kala Rani** : Performance of job role by working women.
Indian Journal of Social Work V 37(3), 1976, pp. 281–92.

960. **Kala Rani** : *Role conflict of working women.* New Delhi,
Chetana, 1976, 242 pp. (AIWC).

961. **Kapur** (Promilla) : *Changing status of the working woman in
India.* New Delhi, Vikas, 1974, 178 pp. (AIWC).

962. **Kapur** (Promilla) : *Marriage and the working woman in India.*
New Delhi, Vikas, 1970, 528 pp. (AIWC).
A collection of case studies of working women.

963. **Kapur** (Rama) : Role conflict among employed housewives.
Indian Journal of Industrial Relations V 5(1), 1969, pp.
39–76.

964. **Karlekar** (Malavika) : For women and employment. Paper

presented at the National Conference on Women's
Studies, Bombay, 1981 (ISST).

Highlights the important aspects of the working conditions
of women and their home life.

965. **Karlekar** (Malavika) : Perceptions of the woman as earner.
Paper presented at the Second National Conference
on Women's Studies—Session on Work and Employment, Trivandrum, 1984. 9 pp. (ISST).

Deals with the internationalisation of 'housewife ideology'
where irrespective of their economic role, women—who are
earners—accept this point of view.

966. **Kaur** (Surinder) : Inter-relationship of economic indepen-
dence and status of women in marriage. New Delhi,
Indian Institute of Public Administration, 1981.
Thesis.

967. **Khan** (Mumtaz Ali) and **Noor** (Ayesha) : *Status of rural
women in India—A study of Karnataka.* New Delhi,
Uppal Publishing House, 1982, 244 pp. (AIWC).

Discusses the different economic and household activities
of women and also deals with both paid and unpaid work
done by women.

968. **Khare** (Prabhakar Narayana) : A study of the family life of
women earners of Indore City. Ujjain, Vikram
University, 1964. Thesis.

969. **Kishwar** (Madhu) and **Vanita** (Ruth) : *In search of answers—
Indian women's voices from Manushi.* London, Zed
Press, 1984, 312 pp. (ISST).

970. **Krishnaraj** (Maithreyi) : Approaches to self-reliance for
women—Some urban models. Bombay, Research
Unit on Women's Studies, 1980, 50 pp. (RUWS).

971. **Krishnaraj** (Maithreyi) : Employment pattern of university
educated women and its implication. *Journal of Higher
Education* V 2(3), 1977, pp. 317–27.

Discusses the participation of women in work outside the
home, their economic freedom and conditions of
employment.

972. **Krishnaraj** (Maithreyi) and **Ranadive** (Jyoti) : The rural

female heads of households, hidden from view. Bombay, Research Unit on Women's Studies, n.d., 13 pp. (RUWS).

Report of a survey conducted in Maharashtra—gives the overall characteristics of female-headed households and discusses the reasons for its emergence.

973. **Lalita Devi** (U) : *Status, employment of women in India.* Delhi, B R Publishing Company, 1982, 186 pp. (AIWC, JNU).

974. **Lord** (Mary Pills Bury) : Improving human resources through education and employment of women. *Social Welfare* V 10(7), 1963, pp. 60–62.

975. **Mahajan** (A) : Women's two roles—A study of role conflict. *Indian Journal of Social Work* V 26(4), 1966, pp. 377–80.

976. **Maher** (M R) : Problems of women's employment. *Indian Journal of Social Work* V 32(2), 1971, pp. 129–35.
Discusses the existing discrimination in employment between men and women and suggests occupational guidance for women with an aptitude for specialised skills.

977. **Malik** (Rashila) : The decision-making by farm women regarding improved agricultural practices. *Indian Journal of Extension Education* V 15(3–4), 1979, pp. 64–69.

978. **Mehta** (S P) : World of working women. *Lok Raj* V 26(21), 1971, pp. 17–18.
Observes that though women are entering professions like law, journalism and technology, they are facing many problems.

979. **Menon** (R) : Indian working women they stand alone. *Social Welfare* V 11(5), 1964, pp. 3–4.

980. **Mies** (Maria) : *Indian women and patriarchy—Conflict and dilemmas of students and working women.* New Delhi, Concept, 1980, 311 pp.

981. **Mishra** (Lakshmi Shankar) and **Khanna** (Madhu) : Women and work—A study of hundred working women in Kanpur slums. Paper presented at the National

Conference on Women's Studies, Bombay, 1981 (ISST).

982. **Misra** (Rajendra K) : Working women— A frame of reference. *Indian Journal of Social Research* V 18(2–3), 1977, pp. 152–66.

983. **Mitra** (Asok) : A note on proposed research on women's role in the social organisation of production. Paper presented at the Second National Conference· on Women's Studies—Session on Work and Employment, Trivandrum, 1984 (ISST).

Discusses women's contribution to production in the context of their vital role as home makers, responsible for holding the family and household together.

984. **Mitra** (Asok) : Women's economic contribution in subsistence economy. *Journal of Social and Economic Studies* V 8(2), 1980, pp. 177–90.

985. **Mitra** (Manoshi) : Women and work— From historical data in India. Paper presented at the Golden Jubilee Symposium on Women, Work and Society, New Delhi, 1982 (ISST).

Evaluates critically the major historical sources from Bihar and South India regarding the historical data on women's work and the impact of colonialism on their activities.

986. **Mitra** (S M) and **Maharani of Baroda** : *Position of women in Indian life.* Delhi, Neeraj, 1981, 358 pp. (CRL, DU).

987. **Moorthy** (M V) : Problems and welfare of our women workers. *Indian Journal of Social Work* V 6(2), 1945, pp. 106–16.

988. **Nair** (G Ravindran) : The story of the white blouse—BHEL women explode a myth. *Social Welfare* V 22(6–7), 1975, pp. 29–31, 64.

A study of women working in BHEL, Hyderabad, where women do 'male type' jobs.

989. **Nath** (Kamala) : Women in the new village. *Economic Weekly* V 17(20), 1965, pp. 813–16.

Describes the pattern of work practices and how the technological and economic changes have affected the· women in a village in central Punjab.

990. **National Institute of Public Co-operation and Child Development**: Role of working mothers in early childhood. New Delhi, NIPCCD, 1977, 200 pp. (AIWC).

991. **National Institute of Rural Development**: Course on role of women in economic development. Hyderabad, 1982, 102 pp. (NIRD).

992. **Omvedt** (Gail): *We will smash this prison—Indian women in struggle.* London, Zed Press, 1980, 189 pp. (JNU).

993. **Psathas** (G): Towards a theory of occupational choice for women. *Social Science Research Journal* V 52(2), 1968, pp. 253–68.

994. **Puri** (Shashi): Study on decision-making pattern in rural families, with special reference to role of women. Delhi, University of Delhi, 1968. Thesis (CRL, DU).

995. **Ramanamma** (A) and **Bambawale** (U): Intergenerational conflict, with reference to educated employed women. Paper presented at the National Seminar on Conflict, Hyderabad, 1984 (JL).

996. **Ramanamma** (A) and **Bambawale** (U): Resolution of role conflicts among educated and employed women. A sociological analysis. Paper presented at the 14th Sociological Conference, Jabalpur, 1978 (JL).

997. **Ramanamma** (A) and **Bambawale** (U): Social change in family and marriage among educated employed women in urban setting. 1984 (JL).

998. **Ramanamma** (A) and **Bambawale** (U): Transistory status images of working women in modern India. *M.G.Kulkarni Felicitation Volume,* 1984 (JL).

999. **Rangachari** (Shanta): India's working women—Her problems in an office. *Social Welfare* V 11(5), 1964, pp. 14–15.
Describes the working conditions of women such as the type of work they do in an office including discrimination in wages and harassment at the place of work.

1000. **Rao** (V N) and **Rao** (V V P): Analysis of the employed mother in India. *International Journal of Sociology of*

Family V 3(2), 1973, pp. 179–89.

1001. **Reddy** (A Sudershan) and **Girija Rani** (H): Role of women in rural development. *Social Scientist* V 10(6), 1982, pp. 51–57.

1002. **Rohatagi** (Sushila) : Helping women play a dual role. *Social Welfare* V 27(9), 1980, pp. 4–6.

1003. **Rohatagi** (Sushila) : Women's economic development hinges on their social advancement. *Social Welfare* V 29(2), 1982, pp. 8–10.

Emphasises that it has become imperative for the State to provide the necessary conditions and support to enable women to perform their multiple roles as home makers, mothers and working women.

1004. **Royappa** (Hanumantha) and **Grover** (Deepak) : Modernization and female work participation. *Demography India* V 7(1–2), 1974, pp. 157–74.

1005. **Sachdev** (J) : Working mothers—An interview. *Social Welfare* V 21(2), 1974, pp. 10–12, 27.

Discusses the problems faced by working mothers and the reasons why they take up jobs inspite of these problems.

1006. **Saikia** (P D) and **Borah** (Durgeshwar) : Tribal women of North East India—A study of Dhimasa and Garo women. Jorhat, Agro-Economic Research Centre for North East India, 1979, 74 pp. (PC).

1007. **Sandhu** (N S) and **Renuka** : Changing role of farmers' wives in decision-making. *Indian Journal of Home Science* V 20(48), 1982, pp. 29–31.

1008. **Saradamoni** (K) : Women, work and development—Need for some rethinking. Paper presented at the National Conference on Women's Studies, Bombay, 1981. Also in *Mainstream* V 20(14), 1981, pp. 28–29 (ISST).

1009. **Saradamoni** (K) : The working women's cross. *Mainstream* V 12(22–23), 1974, p. 51.

1010. **Sarin** (Rekha) : Study on the role of factory women in household and family organisation in selected rural areas. Delhi, Lady Irwin College, Department of Rural Community, 1968. Thesis.

Studies the role of factory women in their family and household organisation. Factory women felt an acute shortage of time in doing family work.

1011. **Satya Kumari** : Rural economy and role of women. *Khadi Gramodyog* V 19(8), 1964, pp. 592–95.

1012. **Saxena** (U P) : Women labour in Indian economy. *Southern Economist* V 14(10), 1975, p. 21.

1013. **Seminar on the Position of Women in India**, Srinagar, 1972 : Proceedings. Bombay, Leslie Sawhny Programme of Training for Democracy, 1972, 131 pp. (ISST).

1014. **Sengupta** (Shankar) : *Study of women of Bengal.* Calcutta, Indian Pub., 1970, 349 pp. (JNU).
Discusses the socio-economic role and status of working women from the middle class.

1015. **Sethi** (Raj Mohini) : *Modernization of working women in developing societies.* Jaipur, National Pub., 1976, 168 pp. (AIWC).
Analyses the trends in the cognitive structure which is expected from the modernising process in a particular section of the women population.

1016. **Sharan** (Raka) : Working women as agents of social change. New Delhi, Indian Institute of Technology, 1982.

1017. **Sharda** (A L) : Women and professions. Paper presented at the Workshop on Women and Work, Hyderabad, 1985 (ISST).
Some professions have attained an identity and are known as elite occupations. The paper argues that the process of professionalisation may not be in the interest of women.

1018. **Sharma** (J N) : Impact of changes in occupational structure on women's economic roles and status—Urban sector mines and plantation. Paper presented at the Seminar on Women and Development, Anand, 1982, 13 pp. (ISST).
Discusses the economic status, wage rate, standards of living and the role of women. It observes that women participate in almost all economic activities like agriculture,

industry, etc., however, there is a wide gap between the provisions made in the law and the status of women.

1019. **Sharma** (Ursula): *Women, work and property in North West India.* London, Tavistock, 1980, 226 pp. (AIWC).
A study based on a survey conducted in two villages in Punjab and HP reveals that increased mechanisation, purdah and family prestige restrict women's participation in the production process. It shows how economic change has led to relatively little alteration in the relationship between men and women in the household.

1020. **Singh** (Andrea): Walking the tight rope—Migrant women in Delhi. *Samya Shakti* V 1(2), 1984, pp. 135–48.
Collection of profiles of four migrant women in Delhi and their struggle for survival.

1021. **Singh** (C B) and **Usha Rani**: Work burden of farm women—A study. *Kurukshetra* V 17(16), 1983, pp. 10–12.

1022. **Singh** (K P): Career and family—Women's two roles. *Indian Journal of Social Work* V 33(3), 1972, pp. 277–81.
Data collected from 171 married working women about their dual role and whether all of them experienced a sense of guilt.

1023. **Singh** (Satvir) and **Aurora** (Raminder): Motives, work values and child rearing practices of females with full-time employment and full-time housekeeping. *Indian Journal of Social Work* V 41(2), 1980, pp. 157–62.

1024. **Singhal** (Manju): Socio-economic study of working women in a selected village of Delhi. Delhi, Lady Irwin College, Department of Rural Community Ext., 1968. Thesis.
A study conducted in Mahipalpur village covering 105 women engaged in different occupations reveals that very few women are involved in specialised jobs and almost all women find it difficult to cope with the dual role of housewife and working woman.

1025. **Sonalkar** (Vandana): Problems of working women in urban areas. *Social Scientist* V 4(4 & 5), 1975, pp. 124–33.
Focuses on the problems of discrimination in employment.

1026. **Srinivas** (M N): The changing position of Indian women.

Paper presented at the Seminar on Women and Development, Anand, 1977, 35 pp. (ISST).

1027. **Standing** (Hillary) : Free to feed the family—Adivasi women in Chota Nagpur. *Manushi* No. 6, 1980, pp. 27–29.

The adivasi women are free to perform almost all kinds of manual labour and agricultural labour. They play a major role in the marketing of household products and have control over income from this source but the major economic contribution of women is both economically and ideologically undervalued.

1028. **Standing** (Hillary) and **Bandhopadhyaya** (Bela) : Women's employment and the household—Some findings from Calcutta. *Economic and Political Weekly* V 20(17), 1985, pp. WS 23–27, WS 30–38.

Discusses some aspects of the effects of women's entry into wage employment in the urban Bengali household.

1029. **Subbaiah** (Rekha) : The career women : A sociological analysis of problems and changing roles. Mysore, Mysore University, 1975. Thesis.

1030. **Talwar** (Usha) : *Social profile of working women.* Jodhpur, Jain Brothers, 1984, 252 pp.

A survey of working women in Jodhpur (*a*) to specify the social characteristics of working women, (*b*) to identify the reasons for employment, (*c*) to examine division of labour in the family, (*d*) to analyse the role of working women in decision-making, (*e*) the effects on children, and (*f*) to understand the pattern of marital interaction.

1031. **Tandon** (M L) : Women's employment—A point of view. *Social Welfare* V 10(3), 1963, pp. 2–3.

1032. **Thorner** (Alice) : Women's work in colonial India 1881–1931. Paper presented at the Seventh European Conference on Modern South Asian Studies, London, 1981 (ISST).

Presents women's work participation rates based on the 1881–1931 Census and describes the kind of work women did during the colonial period.

1033. **Vanamala** (M) : Women labour in Telegana village. *Mainstream* V 19(48), 1981, pp. 15–18.

1034. **Verma** (J C): Women in rural economy. *Kurukshetra* V 26(10), 1978, pp. 7–10.
Observes that though women participate in a variety of economic activities, their potential is undervalued.

1035. **Verma** (Malka): The study of the middle class working women in Kanpur. *Indian Journal of Social Work* V 26(4), 1964, pp. 305–13.
Reveals that most of the middle class women prefer to do white-collar jobs.

1036. **Visaria** (Pravin): Indian households with female heads— Incidence characteristics and level of living. Paper presented at the Workshop on Women and Poverty, Calcutta, 1983, 38 pp. (ISST, CSSS).

1037. **Wadhera** (Kiran): *The new bread winners—A study on the situation of young working women.* New Delhi, Vishwa Yuvak Kendra, 1976, 311 pp. (JNU).

1038. Women workers—Many compromises. *Link* V 24(29), 1982, pp. 21–22.
Discusses the compromises that women have to make and describes the working conditions of factory workers in Mathura and Faridabad.

1039. A women's calendar. Bombay, Reaching Out, 1981, 30 pp. (NN).

1040. Working class women of working class families—Report of a survey in Bombay. *Economic and Political Weekly* V 13(29), 1978, pp. 1169–74.
Reveals that the wage rates are very low and they are engaged in least skilled and monotonous jobs. Their labour plays an important role in (*a*) the production of labour power, (*b*) the production in factories, (*c*) maintenance and reproduction of reserve of labour.

1041. Working women earn less than men. *Indian Worker* V 21, 1972, p. 12.

1042. Working women in India—Their problems. *Weekly Round Table* V 1(16), 1972, pp. 26–35.
A debate on working women in India by Promilla Kapur, Razia Ismail and Shanta Sarbjeet Singh.

1043. **Young Women's Christian Association of India** : *Educated women in Indian society today—A study.* Bombay, McGraw Hill, 1981, 287 pp. (AIWC).

1044. **Zubeeda** (Banu) : Housewives in profession, a study of the educated Muslim women in Madras. Madras, Madras University, 1979, Thesis (MUL).

16

Women and the
Household

1045. **Agarwal** (Anil) and **Narain** (Sunita) : Women and natural
      resources. *Social Action* V 35(4), 1985, pp. 301–25.
      Studies the effect of environmental deterioration on women
      and shows how it has resulted in their ill-health, malnutri-
      tion and additional work load.

1046. **Batliwala** (Srilatha) : Women and cooking energy. *Economic
      and Political Weekly* V 18(52–53), 1984, pp. 2227–30.
      Discusses the impact of the cooking energy system on
      women. It also highlights the fuelwood crisis and health
      problems of women.

1047. **Behal** (Monisha) : Within the outside, the courtyard—
      Glimpses into women's perceptions. *Economic and
      Political Weekly* V 19(41), 1984, pp. 1775–77.
      Classifies the work done by women inside and outside the
      home. Inside work includes working on the grindstone, pre-
      paring food, child rearing, plastering house walls, while
      outside work includes fetching water, collecting cowdung,
      agricultural operations, etc.

1048. **Dietrich** (Gabriela) : Women and household labour. *Social
      Scientist* V 11(2), 1983, pp. 55–63.

1049. **Ghosh** (Bahnisikha) and **Mukhopadhyay** (Sudhin) : Work
      income and women—A macro-micro exercise in
      India. Paper presented at the Workshop on Women,
      Technology and Forms of Production, Madras, 1984
      (ISST).

Examines how far traditional economic models and the conventional definition of work, income and employment can judge accurately the contribution of women to national income, and at the micro-level to apply the time allocation methodology in an attempt to understand the rationale underlying the categorisation of work done by women into traditionally defined 'economic and non-economic' activities.

1050. **Jain** (Devaki) and **Banerjee** (Nirmala) : Ed. *Tyranny of the household—Investigative essays on women's work.* New Delhi, Vikas, 1985, 278 pp. (ISST).

A collection of essays on women in poor households emphasises the need to view gender-based inequalities as a harsh reality.

1051. **Jain** (Devaki) and **Chand** (Malini) : Report on a time allocation study—Its methodological implications. Paper presented at the Technical Seminar on Women's Work and Employment, New Delhi, 1982 (ISST).

Report of a survey conducted in Rajasthan and West Bengal to test the hypothesis that female work participation in India was undernumerated because of the nature of female work and wages. Data was collected on the basis of time allocated to housework and non-household tasks.

1052. **Jhabvala** (Renana) : Unpaid family labour. *Social Welfare* V 31(2), 1984 pp. 31–32.

Describes the economic contribution made by women in farms and in the handloom weaving industry.

1053. **Kannabiran** (Kalpana) : On evaluating women's labour. Paper presented at the Workshop on Women and Work, Hyderabad, 1985 (ISST).

Describes the kind of work women do inside and outside the home and the issues involved in revaluation of women's work.

1054. **Khan** (M E) and **Ghosh Dastidar** (S K) : Study on women's time use data—A ground level technology of data collection. Paper presented at the Technical Seminar on Women's Work and Employment, New Delhi, 1982 (ISST).

Study conducted in UP tries to analyse the economic contribution of women and its effect on the family structure, fertility and mortality. The study is based on time use data.

1055. **Kishwar** (Madhu) : Unpaid, unorganised—Women speak about housework. *Manushi* V 1(2), 1979, pp. 38–43.
Interviews with women regarding housework and the drudgery that goes with it.

1056. **Krishnaraj** (Maithreyi) and **Patel** (Vibhuti) : Domestic work—Problems and perspectives. Paper presented at the Technical Seminar on Women's Work and Employment, New Delhi, 1982, 6 pp. (ISST).
An overview of the kind and value of household work done by women in socialist and capitalist societies.

1057. **Krishnaraj** (Maithreyi) : Research on women and work in the seventies—Where do we go from here? Bombay, SNDT University, 1983, 36 pp. (RUWS).
A review of studies on women's work and seeks to answer questions relating to the general directions of the studies. It also discusses evolving a framework of analyses.

1058. **Krishnaraj** (Maithreyi) and **Patel** (Vibhuti) : Women's liberation and the political economy of housework. Paper presented at the National Conference on Women's Studies, Bombay, 1981, 14 pp. (ISST).
The paper seeks to (*i*) isolate the problems of definition, measurement and analysis of housework, and (*ii*) consider housework as an economic category within the production process of society.

1059. **Menon** (Usha) : Household labour and modes of production. Paper presented at the Conference on Women and the Household, New Delhi, 1985 (ISI).

1060. **Menon** (Usha) : Women and household labour. *Social Scientist* V 10(7), 1982, pp. 30–42.

1061. **Mitra** (Asok) and others : *Status of women, household and non-household economic activity.* Bombay, Allied, 1979, 78 pp. (SSDC).
Examines the 1961 Census to see how the female participation rate in the major group of household and non-

household industries in the rural and urban areas in India fared in comparison to male participation.

1062. **Mukherjee** (Moni) : Contribution to and use of social product by women. Paper presented at the Workshop on Women and Poverty, Calcutta, 1983, 16 pp. (ISST).
Gives an estimate of the value of the housewife's services in India and women's contribution to the net domestic product.

1063. **Mukhopadhyay** (Swapna) : The nature of household work. New Delhi, Institute of Economic Growth, 1984, 27 pp. (ISST, IEG).

1064. **Nagabrahman** (D) and **Sambrani** (Srikant) : To keep the home fires burning—Firewood collection. *Economic and Political Weekly* V 18(1 & 2), 1983, pp. 33–38.
Reviews the changing pattern of firewood collection and the impact of scarcity on the problems/drudgery faced by women (in Gujarat) and attempts to identify the specific areas that contribute to women's drudgery.

1065. **National Conference on Women's Studies**, Bombay, 1981, Session on Women at Work : Report (ISST).
The discussion centred on the concept of work and the measurement of non-economic activities.

1066. **Palriwala** (Rajani) : Caste, class and women's work—A case study of village in Sikar, Rajasthan. Paper presented at the Second National Conference on Women's Studies, Trivandrum, 1984, 53 pp. (ISST).
The aim of the paper is to understand the implication of women's work in an economy marked by subsistence and petty commodity production.

1067. **Radha Devi** (D) : Working women and household work. *Social Change* V 15(2), 1985, pp. 21–24.
A survey conducted in Trivandrum of working and non-working women to test the hypothesis that working women manage to do their household work in lesser time by increasing their efficiency or lessen their burden by taking help from others.

1068. **Saradamoni** (K) : Work at home—What it means ? *Mainstream* V 20(48), 1982, pp. 29–31.

Discusses the work women do at home, how it is under-estimated and the need for serious thought.

1069. **Seminar on Women's Work and Development**, New Delhi, 1982 : Papers. New Delhi, Centre for Women's Development Studies, 1982, 59 pp. (CWDS).

The seminar was organised to discuss issues relating to women's work and development and also to examine critically the existing methodology and concepts.

1070. **Sharma** (Manju) : Science and technology for the betterment of rural women. *Kurukshetra* V 25(12), 1977, pp. 4–5.

Discusses the progress made in science and technology, and how it could be adapted to suit the needs of women. Biogas, smokeless chullah, grinding machines and other time and energy saving equipments are examined.

1071. **Sonalkar** (Vandana) : Labour value of the housewife's work. *Economic and Political Weekly* V 9(37), 1974, pp. 15–17.

1072. **Swaminathan** (Madura) : Eight hours a day for fuel collection, women's survival tasks in Garhwal Hills. *Manushi* No. 21, 1984, pp. 9–12.

1073. **Thorner** (Alice) and **Ranadive** (Jyoti) : Household as a first stage in study of urban working class women. *Economic and Political Weekly* V 29(17),. 1985, pp. WS 9–WS 14.

Explores the lives of working class women in the city of Bombay.

17

Women and Prostitution

1074. **Bandhopadhyaya** (Bela) : A woman's last resort—Prosti-tution in Calcutta. *Manushi* No. 23, 1984, pp. 12–15.
Four case studies of women who came from rural areas to the city in search of work and were forced to take up prostitution as a last resort.

1075. **Gupta** (Robin) : From the hills of Purola to the brothels of Delhi. *Manushi* No. 20, 1984, pp. 28–33.
It is a condensed version of a study conducted in Uttar Kashi region. The study analyses the forces that facilitate the recruitment of women into prostitution such as landlessness and economic problems.

1076. **Kapur** (Promilla) : *Life and world of call girls in India—A socio-psychological study of the aristocratic prostitutes.* New Delhi, Vikas, 1978, 368 pp. (RTL).

1077. **Vikraman Pillai** (T) : Prostitution in India. *Indian Journal of Social Work* V 43(3), 1982, pp. 313–20.
Discusses the reasons for women taking up prostitution as a profession.

SECTION III

Appendix 1

List of Participating Organisations (Institutions/ Individuals Contacted during the Compilation of the Bibliography)

Ahmedabad

Gandhi Labour Institute
Thaltej Road
Ahmedabad 380 054
Contact Person : *Dr. Indira Hiraway*

Gujarat University Library
Ahmedabad 380 009

Indian Institute of Management
Vastrapur
Ahmedabad 380 015

Sardar Patel Institute of Economic Research and Change
Thaltej Road
Ahmedabad 380 054

Self Employed Women's Association
SEWA Reception Centre
Opposite Victoria Garden
Bhadra
Ahmedabad 380 001

Baroda

Shrimati Hansa Mehta Library
University Library
M.S. University
Baroda
Contact Person : *Shri L.M. Radhya*

Bombay

Ambekar Institute for Labour Studies
Mazdoor Manzil
G.D. Ambekar Road
Naigaon Parel
Bombay 400 012

Bombay University Library
Bombay 400 032

Centre of Education and Documentation
3 Suleman Chambers
4 Battery Street (Behind Regal Cinema)
Bombay 400 039

Department of Sociology
Bombay University Campus
Kalina
Bombay 400 098
Contact Person : *Ms. Manorama Savur*

Ms. Malini Sheth
5 Son Marg
67–B Napean Sea Face Road
Bombay 400 006

Research Unit on Women's Studies
SNDT University
Juhu Road
Santa Cruz (West)
Bombay 400 049

SNDT University Library
1 Nathubai Thakersay Road
Bombay 400 020
Contact Person : *Ms. Vidyut Khandwala*

Tata Institute of Social Sciences
Deonar
Bombay 400 088

Calcutta

Centre for Studies in Social Sciences
10 Lake Terrace
Calcutta 700 029

Indian Statistical Institute
203 Barrack Pore Trunk Road
Calcutta 700 035

Mahila Pathagar
57 B Peary Mohan Roy Road
Chetla
Calcutta 700 027

The National Library
Calcutta 700 027

Women's Research Centre
P–593 Purnadas Road
Calcutta 700 029
Contact Person : *Ms. Ariane Loening*

Cochin

Cochin University Library
Cochin 682 022

Coimbatore

Avanashi Lingam Home Science College for Women
Coimbatore 641 043

Chandigarh

Population Research Centre
Department of Sociology

Punjab University
W-1, Sector 14
Chandigarh 160 014
Contact Person : *Dr. K.P. Singh*

Department of Sociology
Punjab University
Chandigarh
Contact Person : *Dr. Vinita Srivastava*

Delhi

All India Women's Conference
Sarojini House
6 Bhagwan Das Road
New Delhi 110 001

Centre for Women's Development Studies
B 43 Panchsheel Enclave
New Delhi 110 017

Centre of Indian Trade Unions
Talkatora Road
New Delhi 110 001

Central Reference Library
University of Delhi
Delhi 110 007

Central Secretariat Library
Shastri Bhavan
New Delhi 110 001

Central Statistical Organisation
Sardar Patel Bhavan
Sansad Marg
New Delhi 110 001

Delhi Public Library
Shyama Prasad Mukherjee Marg
Delhi 110 006

Delhi School of Economics
University of Delhi
Delhi 110 007

Delhi School of Social Work
University of Delhi
Delhi 110 007

Department of Science and Technology
Technology Bhavan
New Mehrauli Road
New Delhi 110 067

Federation of Indian Chambers of Commerce and Industry
Federation House
Tansen Marg
New Delhi 110 001

Indian Institute of Public Administration
Indraprastha Estate
Mahatma Gandhi Marg
New Delhi 110 002

Indian Institute of Technology
Department of Humanities and Social Sciences
Hauz Khas
New Delhi 110 016
Contact Person : *Mrs. Raka Sharan*

Indian Statistical Institute
7 Sansawal Marg
New Mehrauli Road
New Delhi 110 067

Jawaharlal Nehru University
Social Sciences Library
New Mehrauli Road
New Delhi 110 067

Lady Irwin College
1 Sikandara Road
New Delhi 110 001

Ministry of Labour Library
Sharam Shakti Bhavan
Rafi Marg
New Delhi 110 001

Ministry of Rural Development
Krishi Bhavan
Dr. Rajendra Prasad Road
New Delhi 110 001

National Council of Applied Economic Research
Parisila Bhavan
11 Indraprastha Estate
New Delhi 110 002

National Council of Educational Research and Training
NIE Campus
Sri Aurobindo Marg
New Delhi 110 016

National Institute for Educational Planning and Administration
17–B Sri Aurobindo Marg
New Delhi 110 016

National Institute of Public Cooperation and Child Development
5 Siri Industrial Area
Hauz Khas
New Delhi 110 016

National Labour Institute
AB–6 & AB–18 Safdariang Enclave
New Delhi 110 029

Nehru Memorial Library
Teen Murti House
New Delhi 110 021

Planning Commission
Yojna Bhavan
Parliament Street
New Delhi 110 001

University Grants Commission
Bahadur Shah Zafar Marg
New Delhi 110 002

Voluntary Health Association of India
C–14 Community Centre
Safdarjang Development Area
New Delhi 110 016

Promilla Kapur
K–37A Green Park
New Delhi 110 016

Hyderabad

Small Industries Extension Training Institute
Yousafguda
Hyderabad 500 045

National Institute of Rural Development
Rajindranagar
Hyderabad 500 030

Indian Council of Social Science Research
Osmania University Library Second Floor
Osmania University
Hyderabad 500 007

Osmania University Library
Hyderabad 500 007

Rural Development Advisory Services
Tarnaca
Hyderabad 500 017

Kottayam

Indian Institute for Regional Development Studies
Pullarikunnu
Kottayam 686 027

Lucknow

Giri Institute of Development Studies
B–42 Nirala Nagar
Lucknow 226 007

Institute of Social Science Research
5–A Bishop Rocky Street
Faizabad Road
Lucknow 226 007

Madras

Madras Institute of Development Studies
79 II Main Road, Gandhi Nagar
Adyar
Madras 600 020
Contact Person : *Ms. Subba Lakshmi*

Madras School of Social Work
23/24 Casa Major Road
Madras 600 008

University of Madras Library
Chepauk
Madras 600 005

Working Women's Forum
55 Bhima Sena Garden Road
Madras 600 004

Madurai

Miller Memorial Library
Lady Doak College
Madurai

Mujaffarpur

Bihar University Campus
Mujaffarpur 842 001
Contact Person : *Professor S.P. Sinha*

Nagpur

Nagpur Vidyapeeth Sangrahalay
Uttar Ambakshari Marg
Nagpur 440 010

Nainital

College of Home Science
G.B. Pant University of Agriculture and Technology
Nainital 263 145

Patna

A.N. Sinha Institute of Social Studies
Patna 800 001

Pune

Department of Sociology
University of Poona
Pune 411 007

Tirupati

Sri Padmavati Mahila Visva Vidyalayam
Tirupati 517 502
Chittoor Dt.

Trivandrum

Centre for Development Studies
Prasantha Hill
Aakulam Road, Ulloor
Trivandrum 695 011

Waltair

College of Arts, Commerce and Law
Department of Sociology
Andhra University
Waltair 530 003
Contact Person : *Ms. Indira Devi*

Warangal

Department of Public Administration
Kakatiya University
Vidyaranyapuri
Warangal 506 009
Contact Person : *Dr. K. Murali Manohar*

Appendix 2

List of Periodicals
Indexed in the Bibliography

1. Administration
2. Agricultural Situation in India
3. AICC Economic Review
4. Arth Vignana
5. Asian Labour
6. Awards Digest
7. Capital
8. Commerce
9. Commercial Law Gazette
10. Cooperator
11. Current Anthropology
12. Deccan Geographer
13. Demography India
14. Development Digest
15. Economic Affairs
16. Economic and Political Weekly
17. Economic Development and Cultural Change
18. Education Quarterly
19. Economic Review
20. Economic Weekly
21. Financing Agriculture
22. Fisme Review
23. Herald of Library Science
24. Hind Mazdoor
25. How

26. Human Futures
27. Human Organisation
28. Indian Economic and Social History Review
29. Indian Farming
30. Indian Geographical Journal
31. Indian Horizons
32. Indian Journal of Adult Education
33. Indian Journal of Economics
34. Indian Journal of Extension Education
35. Indian Journal of Home Science
36. Indian Journal of Industrial Relations
37. Indian Journal of Labour Economics
38. Indian Journal of Psychology
39. Indian Journal of Social Research
40. Indian Journal of Social Work
41. Indian Labour Journal
42. Indian Librarian
43. Indian Management
44. Indian Railways
45. Indian Worker
46. Industrial and Labour Relations Review
47. Industrial Relations
48. Industrial Times
49. Industry and Labour
50. Institute of Development Studies Bulletin
51. Integrated Management
52. Interdiscipline
53. International Journal of Sociology of Family
54. International Labour Review
55. International Review of Administrative Sciences
56. International Social Science Journal
57. Janata
58. Journal of Anthropological Society of Bombay
59. Journal of Applied Psychology
60. Journal of Family Welfare
61. Journal of Higher Education
62. Journal of Indian Law Institute
63. Journal of Labour Economics
64. Journal of Marriage and Family

65. Journal of National Academy of Administration
66. Journal of Peasant Studies
67. Journal of Psychological Research
68. Journal of Research Society
69. Journal of Social and Economic Studies
70. Journal of the Institute of Economic Research
71. Khadi Gramodyog
72. Kurukshetra
73. Labour, Capital and Society
74. Laghu Udyog Samachar
75. Link
76. Lok Raj
77. Madras Development Seminar Series Bulletin
78. Mainstream
79. Management International Review
80. Manpower Journal
81. Manushi
82. Margin
83. Modern Review
84. Monthly Public Opinion Survey of IIPO
85. Nagarlok
86. National Geographer
87. National Labour Institute Bulletin
88. Office Management
89. Organizer
90. Political Science Review
91. Productivity
92. Prashasnika
93. Professional Geographer
94. Punjab University Research Bulletin AMIS
95. Quest
96. Rural India
97. Samya Shakti
98. Sarvekshana
99. Science for Villages
100. Seminar
101. Signs
102. Social Action
103. Social Change

104. Social Science Research Journal
105. Social Scientist
106. Social Welfare
107. Socialist Perspective
108. The Sociological Abstract
109. Sociological Bulletin
110. Southern Economist
111. State and Society
112. Swarajya
113. The Voice of the Working Woman
114. Voluntary Action
115. Weekly Round Table
116. World Trade Union Movement
117. Yojana

Appendix 3

Select List of Periodicals and Newsletters on Women's Studies Published in India

Anasuya
SEWA (Bharat)
A–3 Professor's Colony
Bhopal 462 002 (Published in Hindi)

CWDS Bulletin
Centre for Women's Development Studies
B 43 Panchsheel Enclave
New Delhi 110 017

Manushi
Manushi Trust
C1/202 Lajpat Nagar I
New Delhi 110 024

N.F.I.W. Bulletin
National Federation of Indian Women
10002 Ansal Bhawan
16 Kasturba Gandhi Marg
New Delhi 110 001

R.C.W.S. Newsletter
The Research Centre on Women's Studies
SNDT Women's University
Vithaldas Vidya Vihar
Juhu Road
Santa Cruz (West)
Bombay 400 049

Roshni
All India Women's Conference
6 Bhagwan Das Road
New Delhi 110 001

Saheli Newsletter
Saheli Women's Resource Centre
Office Above Shop 105–108
Shopping Centre
Under Defence Colony Flyover (South Side)
New Delhi 110 024

Samya Shakti
National Association for Women's Studies
C/o Centre for Women's Development Studies
B 43 Panchsheel Enclave
New Delhi 110 017

Sangharsh
Vimochana
Forum for Women's Rights
P O Box 4605
Bangalore 560 056

We, The Self Employed : Voice of the Self-Employed Workers
Self Employed Women's Association
SEWA Reception Centre
Bhadra
Opposite Victoria Garden
Ahmedabad 380 001

Women's Link
Indian Social Institute
Programme for Women's Development
Lodi Road
New Delhi 110 003

Appendix 4

Feminist Book Publishing Houses in India

Kali for Women
N 84 Panchshila Park
New Delhi 110 024

Shakti Books
Vikas Publishing House Pvt. Ltd.
Vikas House
20/4 Industrial Area
Sahibabad 201 010
Uttar Pradesh

Streelekha
67, Second Floor
Blumoon Complex
Mahatma Gandhi Road
Bangalore 560 001

Appendix 5
An Update

1 Employment Situation

1078. **Chatterji** (Jyotsna) : The women's decade 1975–1985—An
assessment. Delhi, Joint Women's Programme, 1985,
112 pp. (ISST).
Sums up the changes and progress that has been made in
India in the field of employment, education and training,
technology, etc.

1079. **Pokhriyal** (H C) : Woman power planning in Himalayan
region. *Khadi Gramodyog* V 31(5), 1985, pp. 234–42.
Investigates the role of women in the Himalayan region
and analyses the problems related to economic productivity
and suggests a feasible solution for women power planning
in the Seventh Plan.

2 Employment Statistics

1080. **India**, Ministry of Social and Women's Welfare : Statistics
on women, children, aged and disabled. Paper presen-
ted at the Seventh Conference of Central and State
Statistical Organisations, Hyderabad, 1985 (ISST).
Examines the current availability of statistics on women,
children, aged and the disabled vis-a-vis the data requirement of the Ministry. It lists several lacunae and suggests
measures to improve the range and context with a view to

make them more useful and meaningful for the purpose of planning and formulation of policies and in depth monitoring of the welfare schemes.

1081. **Kalpagam** (U) : Women and household—What Indian data sources have to offer. Paper presented at the Asian Regional Conference on Women and the Household, New Delhi, 1985, 38 pp. (ISI).

Takes stock of Indian data sources particularly the decennial census, NSS data and the Rural Labour Enquiries and examines what kind of information on women's life and work are available that would help in bringing out the differences in the status and role of women in different households.

1082. **Rao** (Usha N J) : Gaps in definitions and analysis. Paper presented at the Asian Regional Conference on Women and the Household, New Delhi, 1985, 37 pp. (ISI).

Examines some of the definitions and concepts of the term household commonly used by the Census organisations, NSS, Department of Social Welfare, Rural Development, etc.

1083. **Tamil Nadu**, Department of Statistics, Manpower and Employment Cell : Women's employment in Tamil Nadu 1979 to 1984—Sex composition, literacy, education, employment and unemployment of women. Madras, 1985 (ISST).

Gives a statistical analysis of women in Tamil Nadu. An analysis of live register data has also been done to highlight the trends in unemployment among educated women. The report pinpoints the low participation rate of women labour force.

1084. **Vanamala** (M) : Household as unit of research and data collection—Limitations and distortions. Paper presented at the Asian Regional Conference on Women and the Household, New Delhi, 1985, 12 pp. (ISI).

Examines the different definitions and concepts used for data collection and for other purposes in India and discusses the impact of these concepts on the socio-economic status of Indian women.

4 *Women in Industries : General Studies*

1085. **Baud** (Isa) : Industrial subcontracting—Effects of putting out
system in India. Paper presented at the Asian
Regional Conference on Women and the Household,
New Delhi, 1985, 31 pp. (ISI).

On the basis of studies conducted in the food processing
industry in Bombay, the beedi making industry in Lucknow, South Indian textile industry, and the clothing industry in Delhi, an attempt is made to highlight the following
issues : (*a*) the manner in which the production process
is organised in the background against the way in which
men and women work, (*b*) the manner in which women
participate in the labour process and the manner in which
this change has to be looked into, (*c*) the consciousness of
women workers of their own situation and the manner in
which they can actively organise.

5 *Women in the Informal Sector : General Studies*

1086. **Deolanka** (Vivek) : Status of women entrepreneurs. *Khadi
Gramodyog* V 31(8), 1985, pp. 331–35.

1087. **Friedlander** (Eva) : Women and the household economy—
Some unintended consequences of industrial develop-
ment (India). Paper presented at the Asian Regional
Conference on Women and the Household, New
Delhi, 1985 (ISI).

1088. **Jumani** (Usha) : The future of home-based production.
Paper presented at the Asian Regional Conference on
Women and the Household, New Delhi, 1985, 23 pp.
(ISI).

Examines the role of women as workers in India but is res-
tricted to those who work within the household.

6.2 *Agriculture*

1089. **Saradamoni** (K) : Women, reproduction and work. Paper presented at the Asian Regional Conference on Women and the Household, New Delhi, 1985, 10 pp. (ISI).

Explains how reproduction affects women agricultural labourers' life on the basis of a study conducted on women and rice cultivation in the villages of Tamil Nadu, Kerala and West Bengal.

6.5 Beedi Rolling

1090. **Jhabvala** (Renana) and others : Women who roll bidis—Two studies of Gujarat. Ahmedabad, Self Employed Women's Association, 1985 (ISST).

The first study describes the socio-economic conditions, training, organisation of production and legal rights of bidi workers while the second study relates to various laws pertaining to bidi workers and to what extent these have been effectively implemented.

6.40 Science and Technology

1091. **National Research Development Corporation** : Appropriate technologies for women—A guide book. New Delhi, NRDC, 1984, 71 pp. (ISST).

Presents tabulated information on identified appropriate technologies for women available with NRDC along with charts indicating the appropriateness of these technologies.

8 Welfare Schemes for the Economic Participation of Women

1092. **Hanumappa** (H G) : Employment of women in sericulture of Karnataka—A case study of silkworm rearing. Paper presented at the Asian Regional Conference on Women and the Household, New Delhi, 1985 .(ISI).

1093. **Jumani** (Usha) : Report of the study on poor rural women's economic activities in Ahmedabad district. Ahmedabad, Self Employed Women's Association, 1983, 162 pp. (ISST).

Aims at developing viable income generating schemes on the basis of a study conducted in Ahmedabad District regarding the economic activities of poor rural women, to be implemented under the DWCRA scheme.

1094. **Rajapurohit** (A R): Women's programme in Tamil Nadu sericulture—An evaluation. New Delhi, Ford Foundation, 1985, 56 pp. (ISST).

Evaluates the Sericulture Development Programme undertaken by the Government of Tamil Nadu with a view to assess the economic viability and usefulness of some of the proposed programmes and the absorption of women trainees in such programmes.

1095. **Srivastava** (Ginny): Invisible hands—Towards empowerment. New Delhi, Society for Participatory Research in Asia, 1985, 31 pp. (ISST).

Summary of discussions held during a workshop on various aspects of women's income generating efforts.

9   Women and Labour Welfare

1096. **Savara** (Mira) and **Everett** (Jana M): Institutional credit as a strategy towards self-reliance for female petty commodity producers in India—A critical evaluation. Paper presented at the Asian Regional Conference on Women and the Household, New Delhi, 1985, 30 pp. (ISI).

Analyses the several models developed by women's organisations to replace the existing exploitative relations of production and provide improved productive capacity. Thus, the real issue is not women's organisation making the loan programme work but the loan programme facilitating organisation and development among women petty commodity producers.

10 Women and Labour Legislation

1097. **Jumani** (Usha) and **Joshi** (Bharati) : Legal status of hawkers in India. Ahmedabad, Self Employed Women's Association, 1984, 57 pp. (ISST).

1098. **Owen** (Margaret) : Legal and policy issues relating to home-based producers. Paper presented at the Asian Regional Conference on Women and the Household, New Delhi, 1985, 31 pp. (ISI).

Highlights some of the major legal problems and practices relating to home-based producers and cites examples of some of the steps taken to bring about legislative reforms.

12 Women : Organisation and Unionisation

1099. **Mies** (Maria) : Landless women organise—Case study of an organisation in rural Andhra. *Manushi* No. 15, 1983, pp. 11–19.

1100. **Mishra** (Anupam) and **Tripathi** (Satyendra) : Chipko movement—Uttarkhand women's bid to save forest wealth. New Delhi, Gandhi Peace Foundation, 1978, 37 pp. (ISST).

Describes the role of Dashauli Gram Swarajya Sangh in organising women in the Gopeshwar region of UP for the Chipko movement.

14 Women : Attitudes to Work

1101. **Mathur** (Purnima) : New look at the employment potential for women—Attitudinal changes in some women entrepreneurs. Paper presented at the Seminar on New Vistas of Economic Independence for Women, New Delhi, 1985, 5 pp. (ISST).

15 Women and Multiple Roles

1102. **Institute of Social Studies Trust** : India's female-headed

households. New Delhi, ISST, 1985, 91 pp. (ISST).
Studies female-headed households in UP, Rajasthan, West
Bengal and Karnataka with a view to capture the economic
contribution made by women in these households and to
evolve a definition of female-headedness.

1103. **Mishra** (Kiran) : Household as unit of analysis—Case study
of tribal communities of North-East India. Paper presented at the Asian Regional Conference on Women
and the Household, New Delhi, 1985, 13 pp. (ISI).
Focuses on the role and status of tribal women of
Arunachàl Pradesh in the socio-economic, cultural and
domestic spheres of life.

1104. **Singh** (Nalini) : Women today. New Delhi, Ministry of
Social and Women's Welfare, 1985, 24 pp.
Summarises the various roles performed by women and the
occupations they are engaged in.

16 Women and the Household

1105. **Agarwal** (Bina) : *Cold hearths and barren slopes—The woodfuel
crisis in the Third World.* New Delhi, Allied, 1985
(IEG).

1106. **Mazumdar** (D N) : Difficulties in taking the household as
the unit of study in the matrilineal societies of North-
East India. Paper presented at the Asian Regional
Conference on Women and the Household, New
Delhi, 1985, 9 pp. (ISI).
Examines how far it is convenient to take the household as
the unit of observation from the methodological point of
view on the basis of a study covering various households of
Meghalaya.

1107. **Vatuk** (Sylvia) : Issues in the analysis of household data
among South Indian Muslims. Paper presented at the
Asian Regional Conference on Women and the
Household, New Delhi, 1985, 20 pp. (ISI)
An attempt to study South Indian Muslims in Madras and
Hyderabad in terms of domestic group organisation and

how best the data collected can help to unravel the actual dynamic processes that are involved in the development of domestic groups.

Author Index

Abraham, Amrita, 414
Achanta, Lakshmi Devi, 317
Acharji, Nilima, 706, 707, 779, 780
Acharya, Sarathi, 1, 744, 745
Adishesh, K, 369
Adranwala, T K, 554
Advisory Committee on Women's
    Studies, 52
Adyanthnya, N K, 2
Agarwal, Anil, 496, 909, 1045
Agarwal, B, 910
Agarwal, Bina, 122, 318, 319, 320, 708,
    746, 747, 748, 749, 1105
Agarwal, R C, 3
Agarwal, S L, 728
Agnew, Vijay, 642
Agnihotri, V, 242
Ahmad, Karuna, 4, 555
Ahmed, Huma, 433
Ahmed, Zubeida, 656
Ahmedabad Women's Action Group,
    781
Ahuja, Kanta, 5
Ahuja-Patel, Krishna, 840, 911
Aiyer K B, 841
Alaka, 580, 612
Ali, Mohd Iqbal, 782
All India Women's Conference, 275
Amba Rao, Sita C, 543
Ambannavar, Jaipal P, 123
Ambekar Institute of Labour
    Studies, 556
Amrit Kaur, Rajkumari, 657
Anand, P A, 197

Anantrama, Sharyu, 934
Anbarasan, Karuna, 488
Andhra Pradesh, Directorate of
    Employment and Training, 6
Andhra Pradesh, Office of the Chief
    Inspector of Factories and
    Boilers, 729
Andhra University, Department of
    Co-operative and Applied
    Economics, 321
Andiappan, P, 7, 8, 9
Annapurna, P, 455
Annapurna Devi, 643, 644
Anthuvan, V L, 10
Apte, M D, 99
Arora, Gulshan, 392
Arunachalam, Jaya, 322, 783, 784
Assam, Directorate of Employment and
    Craftsman Training, 11
Asuri, Padamasini T, 912
Atchi Reddy, M, 323, 438
Atreya, Gita, 445, 446
Aurora, Raminder, 1023
Avachat, Anil, 415
Awasty, Indira, 514
Azad, Nandini, 528, 613, 614, 785

Baboo, Balgovind, 467
Bahl, Sarojini, 243
Bahuguna, Anjali, 515, 913
Bahuguna, Sunderlal, 786
Baig, Tara Ali, 198, 914
Bajaj, Neelam, 887
Baker, D, 456

Baker, Dorothy, 888
Balachandran, Geeta, 730, 731
Balasubramanyan, Vimal, 709, 787
Baliga, B V S, 658
Bambawale, U, 404, 483, 556, 557, 995, 996, 997, 998
Banaji, Rohini, 582, 583
Bandhopadhyaya, Bela, 1028, 1074
Banerjee, D, 889
Banerjee, G R, 710
Banerjee, Nirmala, 12, 13, 244, 276, 277, 278, 915, 1050
Bardhan, Kalpana, 14
Bardhan, Pranab, 124
Barve, Jayashree, 279
Basu, Sreelekha, 916
Batliwala, Srilatha, 1046
Batra, V P, 15
Baud, Isa, 623, 1085
Baxi, Upendra, 416
Bedekar, Malati, 917
Behal, Monisha, 1047
Bergstrom, Greta, 199
Bezboruah, Rekha, 498
Bhaduri, T, 486
Bhaiya, Abha, 468
Bhan, Jai Kishore, 788
Bhandari, K G, 842
Bhardwaj, Aruna, 393
Bharatiya, L K, 16
Bhasin, Kamala, 200, 918
Bhatia, Pratima, 890, 919
Bhatia, S K, 891
Bhatnagar, S, 920
Bhatnagar, Suman R, 324
Bhatt, Ela R, 280, 281, 282, 283, 428, 487, 789
Bhatt, Kokila P, 325
Bhatt, Ramesh M, 516
Bhattacharya, Sudhir, 125
Bhatty, Zarina, 418
Bhoite, Anuradha, 711
Bhowmik, Shanti Kumar, 584
Bhowmik, Sharit, 585
Bihar, Directorate of Employment and Training, 17
Bihar, Labour Department, Factory

Inspection Department, 732
Billings, Martin H, 750
Billington, Mary Frances, 201
Bilmoria Rani, M, 892
Biswas, Kali, 790
Blumberg, Rhoda Lois, 921
Bombay University, Department of Economics, Business Management Section, 544
Borah, Durgeshwar, 1006
Bose, A, 126
Bose, Maithreyi, 922
Bose, Sukla, 326
Brahme, Sulabhe, 640
Brandtzeez, Brita, 751
Brouwer, J, 517
Buch, A N, 283, 487
Burman, Kumar, 284

Central Institute for Research and Training in Employment Service, 18, 19
Central Institute of Research and Training in Public Co-operation, 202
Central Statistical Organisation, 53
Centre for Rural Development, 845, 846
Centre for Women's Development Studies, 20, 791, 843, 844
Centre of Science for Villages, 752
Chadha, S S, 203
Chako, T I, 923
Chakrabarti, Ashok Kumar, 21
Chakraborty, Krishna, 924, 925
Chakravarthy, Gargi, 792
Chakravarthy, Kumaresh, 22, 23
Chakravarthy, Radha, 601
Chakravarthy, Renu, 24
Chakravarthy, S, 328, 847
Chakravarthy, Shanti, 327
Chakravorti, S, 848
Chambers, Robert, 497
Champalakshmi, R, 245
Chand, Malini, 150, 151, 295, 498, 1051
Chandra, R C, 127
Chari, T V R, 659, 660, 793
Chatterjee, Attreyi, 329

Chatterjee, Kamala, 246
Chatterjee, Margaret, 25
Chatterjee, Mridula, 537
Chatterjee, R, 330
Chatterjee, Renuka, 624
Chatterji, Jyotsna, 1078
Chattopadhyay, Kamala Devi, 645
Chattopadhyay, Manabendu, 331
Chaturvedi, Gita, 394
Chaudhary, P, 533
Chaudhary, Paul P, 794
Chaudhary, Pawan, 795
Chawdhari, T P S, 332
Chawdhry, Pant, 26
Chen, Marty, 446, 447, 661, 662
Chetna, 580, 612
Chettur, Usha, 926, 927
Chopra, Kusum, 333
Chopra, S L, 663
Choudhry, Sudhir, 928
Choudhury, Arun, 610
Chowdhary, R L, 499, 505
Coe, Jane Melevey, 27
Committee for the Advancement of
        Legal Literacy, 733
Cooney, Rosemary, 28
Costa-Pinto, Selena, 664; see also Pinto
Cour, Ajit, 205
Course on Identification and
        Planning of Income Generating
        Activities for Rural Women,
        Hyderabad, 1984, 665

Dabholkar, V A, 929
Dalaya, C K, 285, 666
Dandekar, Kumudini, 667, 668
Dandekar, V M, 930
Dang, R P, 932
Dang, Satyapal, 595
Dange, Rajani P, 931
Dantwala M L, 128
Das, Arvind Narayan, 334
Dasgupta, A, 849
Dasgupta, Arunava, 335
Dasgupta, Biplab, 933
Dasgupta, Krishna, 29, 850
Dasgupta, S, 573

Dass, Usha, 796
Datt Sharma, Krishna, 336
Dayal, P D, 247
De, Rama, 30
Deb Roy, Rama, 129
Deepti, 641
Deolanka, Vivek, 1086
Department of Science and
        Technology, 603
Department of Social Welfare—
        Women's Welfare and
        Development Bureau, 43
Desai, Anita, 540
Desai, Armaity S, 31
Desai, M M, 32
Desai, Neera, 753, 934
Desai, Rajani, 626
Desai, S F, 248
Deshmukh, Durgabai, 851
Deshpande, Anjali, 337, 491, 754, 797
Deshpande, Ragini Shankar, 335
Despande, R, 798
Despande, S R, 206
D'Lima, Hazel, 646
D'Souza, Anthony A, 935
D'Souza, C, 712
D'Souza, Victor S, 131
D'Souza, V S, 130
Deulkar, Durga, 852
Devadas, R P, 249
Devadas, Rajammal P, 338, 339, 853
Devadas, P R Muthu, 340
Dewan, Ritu, 90
Dhamija, Jasleen, 518
Dhanagare, D N, 833
Dharampal, 395
Dhillon, Gurmeet, 936
Dholakia, Anila R, 341, 342, 447,
        448, 799
Dholakia, Bakul, 132
Dholakia, R, 170
Dholakia, Ravindra H, 133
Dholakia, Ravindra R, 132
Dietrich, Gabriela, 1048
Dighe, Anita, 286, 713
Directorate of Employment,
        Training and Technical

Education, 44
District Level Conference on Dakshina
    Kannada, Mangalore, 1983, 669
Dixit, Asha, 937
Dixit, D K, 714
Dixon, R B, 670
Dixon, Ruth B, 938
Drewes, Edelstrand, 489
Dwarki, Leela, 921
Dwivedi, Sudha, 800

Eapen, Mridul, 287
Elenjimitiam, A, 469
Eleventh Congress of the National
    Federation of Indian Women,
    Calcutta, 1984, 854
Everett, Jana Matson, 715, 1096

Feminist Resource Centre, 939
Foundation to Aid Industrial Recovery,
    671
Friedlander, Eva, 1087

Gadgil, D R, 940
Gambhir, G D, 288
Gandhi, Indira, 602
Gandhi Madhu, M, 207
Gangrade, K D, 289
Ganguli, H C, 526
Garg, Sadhana, 801
Garg, Saila, 34
Garza, Joseph M, 893
Gathia, Joseph A, 289
Gathia, Joseph M, 893
Gauba, Anand, 941
Gawankar, Rohini, 802
Gharpure, Prabha Mahadev, 470
Ghosh, Anjan, 574
Ghosh, Bahnisikha, 134, 135, 1049
Ghosh, S K, 396
Ghosh Dastidar, S K, 1054
Girija Rani, 343
Girija Rani, H, 1001
Gogoi, Kala, 375
Gokhale, Godavari, 208
Golden Jubilee Symposium on Women,
    Work and Society, New Delhi,

1982, 209
Gopalan, Prema, 753
Gopalan, Sarala, 35, 210, 211, 212, 500,
    672
Gopujkar, P V, 942
Goswami, T D, 519
Gothaskar, Sujata, 582, 583, 803
Goyal, Santosh, 36
Grover, Deepak, 1004
Grover, I, 755
Grover, S, 943
Guha, P, 37, 804
Guha, Sunil, 805
Gulati, J S, 38
Gulati, Leela, 39, 136, 137, 213, 250,
    251, 290, 291, 344, 345, 346, 430,
    756, 757, 758, 759, 944, 945
Gupta, Anupa, 946
Gupta, B N, 40
Gupta, Jayoti, 947
Gupta, Manju, 41
Gupta, R N, 138
Gupta, Rajeshwar Nath, 139
Gupta, Robin, 1075
Gupta, Uma, 948
Gupta, Vimala, 586
Gurucharan Prasad, 507

Halge, Molly Juan, 252
Hamsa, N, 647
Hanumappa, H G, 806, 1092
Haq, Luqmanual L, 760
Haragopal, G, 347
Harichandran, C, 949
Hariharan, V, 457
Hasalkar, J B, 140
Hegde, Pandurang, 501
Heggade, O D, 292
Hemalatha, P, 950
Hiraway, Indira, 42, 673, 761
Horowitz, B, 348
Howarth, Mary, 458
Hussain, Sahiba, 253, 508, 513
Hussain, Saliha Abid, 541

Ikkramullah, S S, 951
Ilaiah, K, 952

Indian Cooperative Union,
294, 675
Indian Council for Social Science
Research, 52, 53
Indian Institute of Public
Administration, 858
Indian Institute of Rural Workers, 859
Indira Devi, M, 143
Institute of Applied Manpower
Research, 218, 676, 860, 861, 862
Institute of Cultural Affairs, 863
Institute of Social Studies Trust, New
Delhi, 492, 677, 678, 679, 680,
762, 864, 1102
International Labour Office, 54, 557
International Labour Organisation, 55,
219, 350, 736
Iyengar, Ashok K, 716
Iyer, K V, 954
Iyer, V J, 144

Jacob, Paul, 145, 146
Jagannathan, M, 147
Jai Prakash, 256
Jain, Devaki, 56, 57, 148, 149, 150, 151,
158, 159, 220, 295, 364, 681, 682,
763, 764, 808, 1050, 1051
Jain, H L, 144
Jain, L C, 520
Jain, Shobita, 810
Jain, S P, 809, 955
Jaiswal, R P, 604, 605
James, R C, 627
Janaki Ammal, E K, 351
Jauhari, Prema, 956
Jayakar, Samuel, 597
Jayalakshmi, L, 58, 811
Jayasingh, J Visuthas, 419, 588
Jeffers, Hilde, 812
Jetley, Surinder, 493, 894
Jha, Sadananda, 737
Jha, Satyavathi, 257
Jhabvala, Renana, 628, 813, 814, 957,
1052, 1090
Jhurani, Kamlesh, 815
Jorapur, P B, 221, 222
Joshi, Bharati, 1097

Joshi, Dina Nath, 717
Joshi, Gopa, 816
Joshi, Heather. 59
Jumani, Usha, 1088, 1093, 1097
Juneja, Harpal, 558
Jyothi Rani, T, 509

Kabra, Vijendra, 958
Kala, C V, 352
Kala Rani, 959, 960
Kalpagam, U, 152, 258, 510, 1081
Kalra, Krishan Kumar, 259
Kamala, V, 865
Kamalanathan, Godavari, 866
Kamat, A R, 867
Kanhare, Sujata, 817
Kanji, Dwarkadas, 260
Kannabiran, Kalpana, 1053
Kanthi Mathi, A B, 818
Kapoor, K D, 895
Kapoor, Ranga, 60
Kapur, Mohinder, 819
Kapur, Promilla, 961, 962, 1076
Kapur, Rama, 963
Kar, Indrani, 296
Kara, M, 261
Karlekar, Malavika, 61, 598, 964, 965
Karnataka, Conference on New Perspec-
tives on Women's Vocational
Training, Bangalore, 1983, 868
Karnataka, District Rural Development
Society, 683
Karnataka, Planning Department, Man-
power and Planning Unit, 62
Kasturi, Leela, 471
Kaur, Surinder, 966
Kelkar, Govind, 411, 765
Keskai, S A, 559
Khan, M E, 521, 1054
Khan, Mumtaz Ali, 967
Khan, Praveen, 560
Khan, Q U, 869
Khanna, Madhu, 981
Khanna, R M, 896
Khanderia, J G, 472
Khare, Prabhakar Narayana, 968
Kishwar, Madhu, 348, 969, 1055

Krishnan, Prabha, 684
Krishnaraj, Maithreyi, 511, 512, 606, 970, 971, 972, 1056, 1057, 1058
Krishnaswami, Lalita, 429
Kumar, Dinesh, 353
Kumar, G, 297
Kumar, K, 870
Kumar, P S G, 538
Kumar, Radha, 629
Kumar, R S, 153
Kumaraswamy, Jacintha, 685

Lahiri, R K, 354
Lakshmanan, Leela, 63
Lakshmi, C S, 542
Lakshmi Devi, V, 64
Lakshmi Raghuramaiah, K, 65
Lalitha, K, 529
Lalita Devi, U, 973
Law, Preeta, 686
Lebra, Joyce, 298
Lessinger, Joanna, 615
Lila, Kanchana, 616
Loening, Ariane, 494
Lok Sabha, Joint Committee on the Maternity Benefit Bill, 1960, 734
Lord, Mary Pills Bury, 974

Madras, School of Social Work, 223
Mago, Snehlata, 870
Mahajan, A, 397, 975
Mahajan, Amarjit, 399
Mahajan, Amrit, 398
Mahajan, O P, 738
Mahanty, B K, 179
Maharani of Baroda, 986
Maharashtra, Committee to Examine the Problems Facing Women Employees in Government Services, 400
Maher, M R, 976
Maheshwari, Prakash Chandra, 420
Malhans, Nirlep, 355, 766
Malik, Baljit, 918
Malik, Rashila, 977
Malti, M, 617
Mandavat, S L, 66

Mankekar, Kamala, 224
Manipur, Directorate of Women and Children's Programme, 225
Manohar, Mukta, 820
Mathew, Molly, 435, 436
Mathur, Anju, 439
Mathur, Madhu, 608
Mathur, Purnima, 1101
Mathur, R N, 439
Mathur, R S, 154
Mattan, Ann, 575
Mazumdar, D N, 1106
Mazumdar, Vina, 67, 299, 356, 357, 648
Mehra, Rekha, 687
Mehrotra, Deepti, 401, 579
Mehta, A B, 473
Mehta, Pratibha, 440
Mehta, Prayag, 421, 871
Mehta, Pushpa, 641
Mehta, Sushila, 226
Mehta, S P, 978
Mehta, Swaranjit, 363
Mehta, Usha, 649
Mehta, V J, 262
Mencher, John P, 358, 359
Menon, L D, 68
Menon, R, 979
Menon, Usha, 1059, 1060
Mies, Maria, 530, 531, 980, 1099
Miller, Barbara D, 155
Minault, Gail, 650
Ministry of, Agriculture, 349; Agriculture and Irrigation, 807; Education and Social Welfare, Department of Social Welfare, 214; Industries, Small-Scale Industries, Development Commissioner, 674; Labour, 215; Labour, Directorate General of Employment and Training, 45, 46, 293, 855, 856, 857; Labour, Labour Bureau, 141, 216, 254, 255, 315, 587; Law and Justice, 735; Social Welfare, 48; Social and Women's Welfare, 47, 1080; Social Welfare, Working Group on Women and Development:

Seventh Five-Year Plan, 49
Mir, Ghulam Qadir, 739
Mishra, A, 1100
Mishra, K, 1103
Mishra, Lakshmi Shankar, 981
Misra, Rajendra K, 982
Misra, Sridhar, 360
Mitra, Aruna, 402
Mitra, Asok, 69, 70, 156, 983, 984, 1061
Mitra, Manoshi, 449, 450, 451, 452, 688, 821, 985
Mitra, S M, 986
Mohandas, M, 422
Moorthy, M V, 987
Morris, Berjye, 539
Mukherjee, B N, 157
Mukherjee, Moni, 1062
Mukherjee, Mukul, 364, 767
Mukherji, A B, 361, 362, 363
Mukherji, Tapati, 534
Mukhopadhyay, Sudhin, 134, 135, 1049
Mukhopadhyay, Sudhir Kumar, 158
Mukhopadhyay, Swapna, 159, 160, 1063
Mulay, Sumati, 365
Murali Dhar, B, 71
Murali Manohar, K, 300, 423, 441, 474, 599

Nadkarni, Nalini, 630
Nadkarni, Sulochana A, 301
Nagabrahman, D, 1064
Nair, Aravindakshan K, 431
Nair, Devaki K, 631
Nair, G R, 302
Nair, G Ravindran, 366, 412, 988
Namjoshi, Virodini, 561
Nandkeolyar, Subhalakshmi, 459, 466
Naponen, Helzi, 822
Narain, Sunita, 1045
Nath, Kamala, 161, 162, 163, 164, 989
National Conference of Women Entrepreneurs, 303
National Conference on Women Doctors in India, New Delhi, 1975, 562
National Conference on Women's Studies, Bombay, 1981, 1065

National Conference on Women's Studies, Trivandrum, 1984— Session on Work and Employment, 72
National Federation of Indian Women, 73
National Institute of Public Co-operation and Child Development, 718, 990
National Institute of Rural Development, Hyderabad, 872, 873, 991
National Labour Institute, 874
National Planning Committee, 953
National Research Development Corporation, 1091
National Sample Survey, 165
National Sample Survey Organisation, 166
National Seminar on a Fair Deal to the Self-Employed and the Seventh Plan, Ahmedabad, 1983, 689
National Seminar on Women in Dairying, Tirupati, 1985, 453
National Workshop for the Promotion and Training of Rural Women in Income Raising Activities, Bangalore, 1978, 690
National Workshop of the ESCAP/FAO Inter-Country Project for Promotion and Training of Rural Women in Income Raising Group Activities, Bangalore, 1978, 875
National Workshop on Organising Self-Employed Women in India, Ahmedabad, 1981, 823
Nayak, Debendra Kumar, 167
Nayak, Sharada, 227
Neelam, J K, 897
Neruakar, Amaraju, 168
Nigar, Fatima Abidi, 522
Nimbakar, Krishna Bai, 460, 461
Ninan, Sevanti, 304, 532
Noor, Ayesha, 967

Odeyar, D Meggade, 462
Omvedt, Gail, 367, 424, 824, 992

Oommen, T K, 563
Orissa, Planning and Co-ordination
    Department, 825
Owen, Margaret, 1098
Oza, Ghanshyambhai, 263

Padmavalli Bharathi, R, 74
Padmavati, S, 564
Pais, H, 719
Palriwala, Rajani, 368, 1066
Pallegar, D N, 651
Pandey, R N, 75
Pant, M M, 502
Panwar, Laxmi, 467
Papanek, Hanna, 463
Papola, T S, 76, 77
Parameswaran, T S, 593
Paranjape, Lata S, 618
Paranjpe, S D, 898
Parliwala, Palwin, 632
Parthasarathy, G, 78, 169, 369
Patel, B B, 170, 229, 264
Patel, Manibhai T, 523
Patel, Tara, 230
Patel, Vibhuti, 768, 1056, 1058
Pathankar, Indumati, 652
Pati, N M, 643
Patkar, Pravin, 745
Patna University, Department of
    Labour and Social Welfare. 442
Paul, Jacob, 171
Pawar, Amarja, 475
Paz, Skoldolsson, 199
Pearson, Gail Olina, 653
People's Institute for Development and
    Training, 876, 877
Pereira, B F, 899
Perlee, Diana Ashley, 79
Pethe, Vasanth P, 619
Phukan, U, 589
Pillai, Indira Ramakrishna, 482
Pillai, Lakshmi Devi, 80
Pillai. Lakshmi Devi K R. 425
Pinchholiya, K R, 231
Pinto, Selena Costa, 691, 701
Planning Commission, 50, 51, 142, 217
Pokhriyal, H C, 1079

Pore, Kumud, 81
Prabhakar, Raj, 611
Prakash, Padma, 565
Prasad, Aruna, 692
Psathas, G, 993
Pujari, Gobardhan, 426
Punekar, S D, 172
Punjabi University, Centre for Research
    in Economic Changes, 228
Puri, Shashi, 994
Purohit, Manju, 720

Radha Devi, D, 305, 693, 1067
Raghuvanshi, Kalpana, 769, 770
Rai, Prabha, 306, 771
Rai, Ratna Prabha, 232
Rai, Usha, 547
Rajalakshmi, N, 620
Rajapurohit, A R, 1094
Rajaraman, Indira, 173
Raju, Saraswati, 174
Rajula Devi, A K, 265, 307
Rallia Ram, Mayavanti, 233, 900
Ram, Kalpana, 490
Ram Prakash, 82
Ramachandran, P, 84, 185, 476
Ramachandran, Saroja, 175
Ramanamma, A, 234, 404, 483, 566, 567,
    995, 996, 997, 998
Ramanathan, 836
Rama Rao, Rajalakshmi, 83
Ranade, S N, 84, 443
Ranadive, Jyoti, 972, 1073
Ranadive, Vimal, 235, 266, 432, 495,
    721, 722
Rangachari, Shanta, 999
Rao, G Dasaradharama, 169
Rao, G R S, 826
Rao, M N, 526
Rao, Nandini, 893
Rao, N T U, 176
Rao, Usha N J, 85, 1082
Rao, V N, 1000
Rao, V R, 253
Rao, V Rukmani. 508, 513
Rao, V V P, 1000
Rathod, C S. 827

Ravindran, 305
Reddy, A Sudershan, 1001
Reddy, Narasimha D, 177, 178, 370
Reddy, V Krishnamurthy, 809
Regional Workshop on Women and
        Technology, Surat, 1983, 772
Renuka, 236, 1007
Richards, M D, 405
Rocco, C, 477
Rohatagi, Rekha K, 267
Rohatagi, Sushila, 1002, 1003
Round Table on Women in Agriculture,
        New Delhi, 1984, 371
Roy, Burman, 372
Roy, Burman B K, 503
Royappa, Hanumantha, 1004
Ruikar, Malathi, 828
Rupande, S, 901

Sachdev, J, 1005
Sadasivam, Bharati, 594
Sahay, T, 268
Sahoo, B, 179
Saibaba, G, 86
Saikia, Anuva, 373, 374
Saikia, P D, 375, 589, 1006
Sambaiah, P, 599
Sambrani, Srikant, 1064
Sandhu, H K, 773
Sandhu, N S, 1007
Sanghera, Jyoti, 766
Sankaran, Laxman, 548
Saradamoni, K, 87, 359, 376, 377, 621,
        687, 1008, 1009, 1068, 1089
Sarin, Madhu, 694
Sarin, Rekha, 1010
Sarkar, Lotika, 535
Sarojinibai, K J, 88
Sarupria, Dalpat, 906
Satya Kumari, 1011
Savara, Mira, 633, 634, 635, 715, 817,
        829, 1096
Savithri, T S, 89
Sawant, S D, 90
Saxena, U P, 1012
Schenk-Sandbergen, Loes, 478
School of Social Work, Research

Department, 479
Seal, K C, 180
Searle-Chatterjee, Mary, 600
Sebstad, Jennefer, 308
Second International Conference of
        Women Entrepreneurs, New
        Delhi, 1981, 309
Seetalakshmi, S, 866
Seetharam, Mukkavalli, 464
Sekaran, Uma, 413
Self Employed Women's Association,
        427, 830
Selvam, V Solomon, 831
Seminar of All-India Women's Vocational
        Training, New Delhi, 1982,
        878
Seminar on Appropriate Technologies
        for Rural Women, Hyderabad,
        1985, 774
Seminar on Role of Women in
        Community Forestry, Dehradun,
        1980, 504
Seminar on Sex Discrimination in
        Gainful Employment, Pune,
        1981, 93
Seminar on the Careers for Women,
        Indore, 1956, 91
Seminar on the Optimum Utilisation of
        Women Power for Development,
        New Delhi, 1975, 92
Seminar on the Position of Women in
        India, Srinagar, 1972, 1013
Seminar on Women in Industry, New
        Delhi, 1968, 269
Seminar on Women—The Untapped
        Potential of Rajasthan, Jaipur,
        1975, 94
Seminar on Women's Work and
        Development, New Delhi, 1982,
        1069
Sen, Amartya, 775
Sen, Chiranjib, 183
Sen, Gita, 181, 182, 183, 378, 379, 380
Sen, S, 654
Sen, Shipra, 655
Sengupta, B, 607
Sengupta, Chandan, 484

Sengupta, P, 95, 96, 237, 270, 271, 272, 480, 527, 576, 590, 636, 723, 740
Sengupta, Padmini, 97, 444, 724
Sengupta, Shankar, 1014
Seth, Madhu, 902
Seth, Mridula, 879
Seth, Padma, 381
Sethi, Manju, 668
Sethi, Raj Mohini, 382, 1015
Shah, M S, 98
Shah, Nandita, 592
Shah, Radhika, 832
Shaheen, 465
Shamala Devi, L N, 695
Shanta Mohan, N, 569
Sharan, Raka, 273, 741, 833, 1016
Sharda, A L, 1017
Shareen, Begum, 184
Sharma, B M, 332
Sharma, G D, 99
Sharma, J C, 172
Sharma, J N, 1018
Sharma, Kanta, 406
Sharma, Kanta Devi, 238
Sharma, Krishan Datt, 383
Sharma, Kumud, 591, 696, 697, 834
Sharma, Manju, 1070
Sharma, Mohan, 523
Sharma, R N, 484
Sharma, S, 755
Sharma, Ursula M, 384, 1019
Shastree, Tara, 725
Shastri, P P, 185
Sherwani, Madeeha, 100, 101
Shinde, P R, 553
Shiva Rao, Kitty, 880
Shobha, V, 310, 385, 474
Shri Balram, 742
Shridevi, S, 881
Shukla, Sheela, 622
Singh, A, 481
Singh, A K, 353
Singh, Andrea, 1020
Singh, Arjun, 750
Singh, Ashbindu, 505
Singh, C B, 1021
Singh, D R, 549

Singh, Jagdish, 365
Singh, K P, 186, 434, 903, 1022
Singh, Kamal, 102
Singh, Nalini, 295, 1104
Singh, Preeti, 525
Singh, R P, 386, 459, 466
Singh, Satvir, 1023
Singh, Shyama, 570
Singh, Sunila, 594
Singh, T R, 102, 387
Singh, Vijay Pal, 637
Singhal, Manju, 1024
Sinha, Frances, 698
Sinha, G P, 443
Sinha, J N, 187
Sinha, M N, 865
Sinha, N N, 743
Sinha, S P, 776
Sinha, Sanjay, 698
Small Industries Service Institute, 699
Sonalkar, Vandana, 1025, 1071
Sonarikar, Sunanda, 103
Sridharan, Sumi, 388
Srikantan, K S, 188
Srinivas, M N, 1026
Srinivasan, K N, 189
Srinivasan, Viji, 311, 682, 835
Srivastava, Ginny, 239, 1095
Srivastava, J C, 777
Srivastava, K C, 506
Srivastava, Vinita, 904, 905
Standing, Hillary, 1027, 1028
Strobel, M, 240
Subbaiah, Rekha, 1029
Subramaniam, K, 726, 836
Sujata, T M, 806
Sundar, Pushpa, 104, 105, 312, 454, 727
Sundaresan, P N, 609
Surin, V, 486
Surti, Kirtida, 906, 907
Suryamani, E, 571
Suryanarayana, M, 950
Swaminathan, Madura, 1072
Swarnalatha, 407
Symposium on Women, Work and Society, New Delhi, 1982, 106

Talpallikar, M B, 577
Talwar, Usha, 1030
Tamil Nadu, Conference on New Perspectives on Women's Vocational Training, Madras, 1983, 882
Tamil Nadu, Department of Statistics, Manpower and Employment Cell, 1083
Tandon, M L, 1031
Technical Seminar on Women's Work and Employment, New Delhi, 1982, 107
Tellis-Nayak, Jessie B, 700, 701, 837
Tewari, Harish C, 550
Thamarajakshi, R, 190, 389
Thangamani, K, 340
Third International Conference of Women Entrepreneurs, New Delhi, 1984, 313
Thorner, Alice, 1032, 1073
Tilak, Jandhyala B G, 108, 109
Titus, Aruna, 408
Tiwari, G C, 23
Training Programme for Women Assistant Project Officers for Implementing DWCRA, Hyderabad, 1984, 883
Tripathi, B L, 191
Tripathi, Satyendra, 1100

United Nations Children's Fund, 702
Unwalla, Jeroo Maneck, 551
Usha, C, 884
Usha, P, 152, 536
Usha, S, 110
Usha Rani, 1021
Usha Rani, C, 111

Vanamala, M, 112, 390, 1033, 1084
Vanita, Ruth, 969
Varadappan, Sarojini, 314
Varalakshmi, P K, 885
Vasantha, M, 113
Vasudevan, Jayshree, 572
Vatuk, S, 1107
Ved, R G, 638
Velayudhan, Meera, 437
Venkat, Dasappa, 194
Venkateswaran, K, 114

Verma, J C, 1034
Verma, Malka, 1035
Vidya Rani, C, 908
Vidyarthi, G S, 842
Vijayalakshmi, K, 274
Vikraman Pillai, T, 1077
Virdi, Jyotika, 401
Visaria, P M, 193
Visaria, Pravin, 192, 1036
Vishwanath, Vasantha, 115
Vithayathil, Teresa, 409

Wadhera, Kiran, 1037
Wadia, Avabai B, 116
Wahan, P, 194
Wasi, M, 195
West Bengal, Directorate of National Employment Service, 117
Women's Research Centre, 639
Working Women's Forum, 703
Workshop for Identifying Occupational Skill Requirements of Electronics Industry, Bombay, 1982, 485
Workshop for Organisers of Income Generating Projects for Women, New Delhi, 1977, 704
Workshop on Promotion of Self-Employment in Rural Areas, Allahabad, 1982, 120
Workshop on the Integration of Women in Agriculture and Rural Development, Hyderabad, 1980, 705
Workshop on the Unorganised Sector, Ahmedabad, 1983, 839
Workshop on Women and Poverty, Calcutta, 1983, 121
Workshop on Women in Indian Labour Force, Trivandrum, 1980, 241
Workshop on Women, Technology and Forms of Production, Madras, 1984, 778

Yadav, M S, 726
Young Women's Christian Association of India, 1043

Zubeeda, Banu, 1044

Subject Index

adivasi women see tribal women

administrators, 407; Rajasthan, 394

agarbatti makers, 315, 316

age, 192, 193

agrarian women, 337, 341, 368, 376

agricultural development, 317, 319

agricultural labour, 182, 201, 331, 350, 356, 357, 378, 381, 385; Andhra Pradesh, 369; Assam, 375; Bihar, 776; case studies, 344, 367, 370, 388; Kerala, 1089; landless, 329; Maharashtra, 823; Medak, 347; Nellore, 323; organisations, 824; Punjab, 348, 382, 765; scheduled caste women, 370; statistics, 329, 364; Tamil Nadu, 358, 389, 1089; Uttar Pradesh, 360; West Bengal, 326; West Godavary, 321, 347, 1089

agriculture, technological change, 745, 746, 747, 748, 749, 750, 768, 776

Ahmedabad Women's Action Group, 781

air pollution, 909

All India Radio, 392

AMUL, 670

anganwadi worker, 465

animal husbandry, 325

Annapurna Mahila Mandal, 671, 802, 829

anxious women, 887

Appiko movement, 501

appropriate technology, 684, 766, 769, 770, 774, 1070, 1091

armed forces, 397

artisans, 275; Bolpur, 284

attitudes, 894; education, 903; employment, 893, 895, 898, 903, 905; managers, 899; professions, 900; unemployment, 893; work, 944

Bal Sevika Training Programme, 880, 885

banks, 411, 412, 413, 714

beedi workers, 288, 306; Ahmedabad, 427; Allahabad, 418; Andhra Pradesh, 416, 423; Bombay, 414; Central India, 420; Gujarat, 1090; Kerala, 422, 425; legislation, 1090; Lucknow, 1085; Nipani, 415, 424; organisation, 813; Orissa, 426; Sinnar, 417; Vellore, 419, 421

beef exporting factories, 489

behaviour, 892

Bhotiya women, 515

biscuit factories, 582

blind women, 841

block printers, 428, 429; unemployment, 520

blue-collar jobs, 229, 264, 789

bonded labour, 334, 388, 947

brahmin women, 931

brick kiln worker, 430

careers, 18, 19, 29, 38, 46, 60, 63, 91, 116, 914, 943, 1022
cardamom plantation worker, 590, 591
case studies, 344, 367, 370, 388
cashew nut industry, 272, 431; Kerala, 432
caste, 143
cattle breeding, 351
Central Social Welfare Board, 659, 660, 672, 793
census, 126, 130, 152, 181, 182
chemical industry, 254, 272
chikan workers, 236, 306; Lucknow, 433
child rearing, 897, 932, 942, 1023
Chipko movement, 786, 810, 816, 834, 1100
cigarette industry, 259
coffee plantation worker, 590, 591
coir industry, Kerala, 435, 436; wages, 437
colonial period, 985, 1032
community, development, 455, 462; forestry, 486; projects, 657
Congress Party, 642
construction workers, 202, 440, 444; Bihar, 443; Delhi, 439, 443; Hyderabad, 438; Patna, 442; tribal women, 443; Warangal, 441
contract labour, 433
cooking energy, 1046
co-operatives, 788, 793, 800, 818, 819, 826, 827; credit, 832; directory, 791; Gujarat, 801; industrial, 804, 838; Jammu & Kashmir, 801; Lucknow, 796; Maharashtra, 801; Punjab, 801; rural women, 805, 812
cotton ginning, 288
creches, 721, 722
credit, 716, 727, 1096; bank, 715; informal sector, 715, 727, 785; rural women, 716
criminals, 892

dairy co-operatives, 448, 799; Andhra Pradesh, 446, 449, 450; case studies, 445, 446, 447, 449, 450, 454; Tamil Nadu, 445
dairying, 451, 452, 453, 688, 865, 936
data collection, 148, 122; economic activities, 144, 241, 1054
decision-making, 847, 977, 994, 1007
demographic characteristics, 221
development functionaries, 462, 464
Development of Women and Children in Rural Areas, 683, 883, 1093
development projects, 661, 669, 671, 688, 693; appropriate technology, 766; Karnataka, 692; rural, 686, 702, 703, 938; sericulture, 677, 679, 682
development scheme see development projects
directories, 546, 791
displacement, 133, 134, 135, 270; technological change, 750, 751, 753, 762, 763, 768
doctors, 233, 555, 562, 563, 572
domestic servants, 285, 469, 473, 474, 477, 480; Bombay, 472; Delhi, 471, 481; Haryana, 467; Kerala, 478; Madras, 479; Poona, 468, 470, 475; wages, 476
domestic work, 183; definition, 1058; statistics, 151; value, 1062, 1071
dual roles, 912, 923, 1002, 1022

earners, 965, 968, 1037
economic activities, 5, 123, 145, 171, 183, 242; collection of statistics, 144, 150, 1081; rural women, 125, 166, 167
economic, contribution, 175, 296, 884; development, 158, 161, 186, 370, 915, 954, 966, 1003, 1026; integration of women, 930, 953, 991, 1011, 1012, 1034; productivity, 662, 918, 983, 1019
educated women, 108, 921, 1043; employed, 4, 234, 948, 971, 995, 997, 1044; employment, 26, 68,

70; studies, 4

education, 193, 312, 700, 853, 854, 862, 867, 869, 879, 881, 903, 905, 974; medical, 564; rural women, 852

electronics industry, 254, 483, 484; skill development, 485; training, 857

elite women, 642

embroidery workers, 434

Employee's State Insurance Act, 731

employers, 707, 708, 717

employment, agriculture, 321, 380; Andhra Pradesh, 6; Bihar, 17; Bombay, 84; cities, 59; Civil Services, 407; Delhi, 27, 44, 84, 207; historical review, 1, 323; industries, 34; Karnataka, 62, 85; Kerala, 80, 211; Lucknow, 77; myths, 66; National Plan, 676; non-agricultural sector, 89; part-time, 17, 31, 55; Patna, 17; Rajasthan, 79, 94; rural, 128, 711; South India, 89; statistics, 142, 189, 190, 1083; technological planning, 764; trends, 47, 73, 95, 101, 217, 271, 1078; United States, 207; urban, 234; West Bengal, 30

employment exchanges, 51; Assam, 11

Employment Guarantee Scheme, 667, 668, 678, 886

engineers, 602, 605, 607; Kerala, 404

entrepreneurs, 292, 302, 303, 307, 308, 312, 313, 314, 1086; attitudes, 1101; development, 297, 301; psychology, 906

environment, 1045

Equal Remuneration Act, 730

executives, 545, 547, 548, 549, 552; Bombay, 544, 551; directory, 546

exploitation, 708

extension workers, 694, 866

extremists, 642

Factories Act, 731

factory worker see industrial worker

family labour in agriculture, 386, 390

farm women, 332, 340, 365, 912, 977, 1007, 1021, 1052; decision-making, 387; Delhi, 365; Haryana, 876; Vidharba, 78; wages, 345

field workers, 463

female-headed households, 972, 1036, 1102

fertility, 158

fine arts, 198

firewood collection, 1064, 1074; pickers, 283

fish processing industry, 492, 495; Gujarat, 492, 495; West Bengal, 494

fisherwomen, in Kerala, 757, 758, 759; in Tamil Nadu, 488, 489, 490

fishing technology, 756, 757, 758, 759

Food for Work Programme, 668

food processing industry, 583; Bombay, 1085; Delhi, 493; technological change, 751, 753; Uttar Pradesh, 493

forestry, employment opportunities, 498, 502, 505; industries, 500; Maharashtra, 499; Manipur, 503; projects, 497

freedom movement, 642, 645, 650, 655

fuelwood crisis, 1046, 1105

gainful employment, 982, 1061

garment industry, 281, 283, 510; Bombay, 511, 512; Delhi, 508, 511, 513; Punjab, 507; unionisation, 510, 513

gobar gas, 766

government employees, 400, 908; Delhi, 405

graduates, employment, 45; unemployment, 99

grass industry, 506, 675

gram sevikas, Haryana, 466; job satisfaction, 459, 466; training, 842

Green Revolution, 765

hand-cart pullers, 281

handicrafts industry, 294, 518;
employment, 519; South India,
517; unemployment, 520
handloom industry, 1052; employment,
516; Gujarat, 524; Kashmir, 675,
762; Tamil Nadu, 675;
technological change, 762, 763;
Uttar Pradesh, 521. 522
head loaders, 283; Mount Girnar, 487;
Ranchi, 486
health, 909, 1045, 1046; workers, 458
hired labour, agriculture, 390
home-based workers, 814, 822, 1088;
legislation, 1097
hospital, ayahs, 558; Government, 559
hostels, 710, 725, 726
hotel industry, 525
household, 139, 1081, 1082, 1084, 1106,
1107; economy, 1087; poor, 319,
326, 1050; survey, 149
housework, 912, 1047, 1048, 1055, 1056,
1058, 1059, 1060, 1063, 1067,
1068
housing, 713

idli sellers, Madras, 613
illiteracy, 391
impact of technology see technological
change
income, 22, 172, 1049; generation, 27,
664, 665, 700, 701, 1095
income generating projects, 658, 675,
685, 690, 691, 704, 875
Indian Administrative Service, 407, 409
industrial growth, 247
industrial workers, 1010; Faridabad,
1038; Mathura, 1038; welfare,
723
industrialisation, impact on women, 261,
1087
industries, export, 244; Gujarat, 264;
Madhya Pradesh, 243; rural, 15,
263; statistics, 261, 265;
technological change, 760; West
Bengal, 244
informal sector, Calcutta, 277, 287;
employment, 286, 299; Kerala,

129, 175; women workers, 287,
289, 291, 388
International Women's Year, 202
inter-state tasar project, 679
inter-state variation in work
participation, 137, 140, 175, 178

job opportunities, 18, 28, 32, 103
job satisfaction, 41, 891; gram sevikas,
459, 466; industrial workers, 273
journalists, 233
junksmith, 281
jute industry, 527; Bengal, 526

Khadi & Village Industries, 523;
Gujarat, 761

labour force, 922, 940, 1079; agriculture,
328; Bengal, 12; educational
composition, 862, 869; Haryana,
210; industrial, 247, 250, 252,
258; Punjab, 127, 750; rural, 673;
statistics, 141, 1080; Tamil Nadu,
152; Telangana, 1033
labour laws, 728, 733, 738, 739, 740,
741, 742, 743; market, 77, 143,
1028
lace makers, 528, 532; Narsapur, 528,
529, 530, 531, 532
law, 96
lawyers, 533, 534
leadership, 955
leather industry, 536
legal literacy, 733
legislation, 700
legislatures, 643, 654
leisure, 853, 919, 937
librarians, 233, 537, 538, 539
lifafa makers, 276, 579
literacy, 133; Karnataka, 85
Lijjat pappad, 670, 675
live register, 11, 51
local government, Maharashtra, 646;
women, 646

mahila mandals see women's
organisations

malnutrition, 1045
management education, 849
managers, 543; personality, 550
marital status, 192
married women, 888, 904, 950, 962, 966, 1022
market segmentation, 159, 168, 258
marketing, 311
match factory, 553
Maternity Benefit Act, 731, 734, 735, 736, 737; Andhra Pradesh, 729; Bihar, 732
maternity benefits, 721, 722
matrilineal societies, 1106
mechanisation see technological change
medieval period, 201
middle class women, 55, 934, 1014, 1035
migrant women, 79, 1020
migration, 158
milk producers, Kaira, 295
mine workers, 237, 573, 578, 1018; Andhra Pradesh, 577; coal, 574, 576, 577; Eastern India, 574; iron ore, 575, 576; mica, 576
mines, mechanisation, 754
mobility, labour, 262
modernisation, 1015
mother, 223
motive to work, 902
mukhya sevika, 455
Muslim women, 233, 1044, 1107; Ahmedabad, 957

National Sample Survey Data, 124, 125, 144, 146, 173, 183, 189; concepts and definition, 241, 1082; Thirty-second Round, 145, 165, 166; Twenty-fifth Round, 354; Twenty-seventh Round, 165
night patrollers, Manipur, 295
night shift, 119
No Birth Bonus Scheme, 680, 934
nurses, 554, 555, 556, 557, 563, 565, 566, 567, 568, 571; Gujarat, 561; Lucknow, 570; personality, 560; Poona, 559
nutrition, poor women, 121

occupation, 199
occupational distribution, 203, 213; Ahmedabad, 230, 231; Haryana, 210; Kerala, 211; Punjab, 228
occupational health hazards, 709; agriculture, 720; cashew industry, 432; jute industry, 526
occupational structure, 1018
optical goods manufacturing industry, 259
organisations see voluntary and women's organisations
organising women workers, Ahmedabad, 280, 295, 579
OXFAM America, 661

paddy production see rice cultivation
painters of Madhubani, 295
papad rollers, 276, 295, 580, 581
peasant movement, 831
piece rate workers, 282
panchayat, 65; elections, 652
personnel policies, 48
pharmaceutical industry, 582, 583
phulkari work, 514
patriarchy, 980
planning, 270, 1079
plantation workers, 237, 1018; welfare, 722
police women, 396, 398; Chandigarh, 399; Delhi, 393, 408; Himachal Pradesh, 399; Punjab, 399
policies, 177; employment, 56, 681, 697
political participation, 647, 648, 649, 650, 655
politics, 198, 642; Orissa, 644; women, 643, 644
poor women, 121, 204, 220, 317, 1040; Kerala, 290
Post and Telegraph workers, 403; Delhi, 395
poverty, 121
primitive women, 351
private sector, 14, 203
problems, at work, 911, 923, 926, 946, 964, 978, 998, 999, 1029, 1042; at home, 911, 926, 964, 998, 1042

professions, 237; Delhi, 240; statistics, 195
prostitution, 947, 1076, 1077; Calcutta, 1074; Delhi, 1075
public life, 653
public policy, 7
public sector, 14, 86, 253; Haryana, 203; Hyderabad, 112

radio parts manufacture, 259, 482
rag pickers, 592
railway employees, 410
Rajasthani women, 79
research, employment, 27, 57, 104
researchers, 603
reservation, jobs, 33, 64
rice cultivation, 322, 359, 377, 379, 748
rice mills, 272; Bengal, 767; Madhya Pradesh, 288; technological change, 767
role conflict, 890, 910, 924, 959, 960, 961, 962, 963, 975, 978, 980, 996, 1009
role stress, 906, 907
rope makers, 695
rubber plantation workers, 590, 591
rural areas, job opportunities, 114
rural development, 355, 357, 809; projects, 686: role of women, 916, 933, 999
rural economy, 353
rural women, 147, 366, 656, 658, 662, 684, 703, 748, 799, 910, 918, 920, 936, 938, 955, 958, 992; agriculture, 317, 318, 319, 339, 355, 371, 389, 705, 776; appropriate technology, 770, 774; co-operatives, 811; development projects, 686, 696; development work, 457, 460, 461; education, 852; employment, 42, 124, 670, 673; Garhwal, 913; income generation, 665, 690, 704; Karnataka, 967; Punjab, 773, 989; self-employment, 102; technology, 755, 777; water, 320; women's organisations, 806, 807

sales girls, 259; Delhi, 593; Madras, 594
scheduled caste women, agriculture, 370; employment, 102, 120; Karnataka, 176; stone, 611
scientists, 601, 602, 605, 606
seclusion, 153
self-employed women, 279, 304; credit, 715, 727; Bombay, 715; Delhi, 293; Gujarat, 308
Self Employed Women's Association, 280, 283, 308, 789, 799, 808, 813, 823, 830, 837
self-employment, 102, 120, 659, 689; handicapped, 659, 660
self-esteem, 944
self-reliance, 970
sericulture, 335; extension workers, 694; Karnataka, 677, 682, 1092; Maharashtra, 679; projects, 677, 679, 694, 1094; Tamil Nadu, 682, 1094
sex bias, data collection, 122
sex discrimination, employment, 7, 8, 9, 10, 65, 80, 87, 93, 98, 718, 976, 1025; India, 8, 9; labour market, 13, 76, 108, 109, 110, 121, 1071; USA, 8, 9; wages, 39, 108, 109, 345, 999, 1041; work, 39
sex ratio, 391
sexual division of labour, 775, 915, 952
sexual harassment, 491, 492
shellac industries, 288
silk waste utilisation, 335
skill, 193
slum women, 981; Bombay, 285
small-scale industries, 248, 675, 699; Goa, 274; Madhya Pradesh, 288
smokeless chulahs, 909, 1070
social action, 27
social development, 951, 954, 1016
social work, 456
socialisation, 312, 647
socio-economic condition, 973, 986, 1018, 1024, 1030; Bengal, 1014; Bhopal, 238; Bombay, 1073; industries, 257, 305; Jabalpur, 197; Karnataka, 669; Lucknow,

956; Manipur, 225; Poona, 929;
Vidharbha, 931; widows, 949;
women workers, 173, 208, 216,
1014
sports women, 198, 608, 609
statistical sources, 148, 1081, 1082, 1084
stone crushers, 610; Delhi, 611
street vendors, 612; Ahmedabad, 295
suffragette movement, 642
supari cutters, 276
sweepers, 596, 597; Andhra Pradesh,
599; Benaras, 600; Delhi, 598;
municipalities, 344; Punjab, 595
Syndicate Bank, 412

tailors, Warangal, 509
tea plantation workers, 587, 588, 589,
581; Eastern India, 58; Nilgiri,
680; Uttar Pradesh, 586; West
Bengal, 584, 585
teachers, 572, 620, 621, 622; government
schools, 617; Poona, 618, 619;
primary schools, 616; private
schools, 617
technological change, 241, 666;
agriculture, 745, 746, 747, 748,
749, 750, 765, 768, 776; fishing,
756, 757, 758, 759; food
processing, 753; handloom
industry, 762, 763; industries,
760; Punjab, 773; rice mills, 767;
women, 772, 775, 778, 1019
technologists, 605
technology, employment generation,
752; employment of women, 744;
planning, 764; women, 840
technical education, 840
telephone operators, 404; Delhi, 401,
406
textile industrial workers, 148, 254, 626,
630, 632, 634, 636, 638;
Ahmedabad, 625, 628, 637;
Bombay, 264, 627, 629, 633;
Delhi, 1085; Gujarat, 264;
Madhya Pradesh, 631; South
India, 623, 1085; Vidharbha, 624;
West Bengal, 639

Third World women, 747, 751
tobacco industries, 272
toy makers, 276
time allocation, 933, 934, 1049, 1051,1054
trade unions, 241, 792; participation,
779, 780; women, 787, 795, 820,
828, 833
traders, 237, 615, 822, 1096
training, 253, 851, 854; bal sevikas, 880;
dairying, 865; DWCRA, 883;
electronics industry, 857;
extension work, 866; farm
women, 847, 876; gram sevikas,
842; income generation, 875;
rural women, 848; village level
workers, 842; women's
organisations, 850
tribal women, 232, 279, 679; Arunachal
Pradesh, 1103; Bihar, 821; Chota
Nagpur, 1027; Maharashtra,
817; North East India, 1006;
organisations, 817, 821;
Rajasthan, 324; West Bengal, 326

uneducated women, employment, 37
unemployment, 889; agricultural
labourers, 346; Andhra Pradesh,
6; graduate, 99; Madras, 113;
statistics, 142, 189, 190; West
Bengal, 118
United Nations Decade for Women,
1078; changes in employment,
47, 73, 1104; India, 21, 196;
statistics, 196
unorganised sector see informal sector
unpaid work, 967, 1052, 1055, 1061
urban women, 647, 971, 1025, 1028

vegetable vendors, 281, 285; Madras,
614
village level workers, 842
voluntary organisations, 67
vocational training, 868, 878, 882, 884;
Andhra Pradesh, 872; Bihar, 874;
Gujarat, 846; Haryana, 845;
Himachal Pradesh, 877;
institutes, 856, 864; Jammu &

Kashmir, 860; Kerala, 858;
Madhya Pradesh, 876;
Maharashtra, 863; Orissa, 874;
Punjab, 843; rural women, 843,
844, 845, 846, 855, 858, 859, 860,
861, 863, 871, 872, 873, 874, 876,
877; Tamil Nadu, 873; Uttar
Pradesh, 861; West Bengal, 844
wages, agricultural, 369, 378; disparity,
75; Andhra Pradesh, 108; labour,
330
welfare measures, 717, 719, 724, 797,
987
wheat cultivation, 750
white-collar jobs, 212, 223, 988
woollen textile industry, Kumaon Hills,
698
women power see labour force
women's organisations, 794, 809, 836;
Andhra Pradesh, 1099; Bombay,
666; credit facilities, 716;
economic activities, 666; Gujarat,
809; Jammu & Kashmir, 809;
Maharashtra, 817; members, 782;
organising tribal women, 817;
organising women workers, 781,
783, 784, 803, 812, 813, 815, 822,
823, 839, 1099; Orissa, 809, 825;
Punjab, 809, 825; rural women,
806, 807, 815; Tamil Nadu, 809;
training, 850
Women's Polytechnic, 884
women's work, 125, 939, 952, 1066;
colonial period, 985, 1032;
definition, 181, 377, 1008, 1049,

1057, 1069; evaluation, 1053,
1057, 1069; historical sources,
985; measurement, 153, 160, 175,
1065
wool production, Garhwal, 515
work output, 74
work participation, 83, 85, 131, 132, 136,
137, 138, 146, 154, 156, 161, 170,
172, 177, 184, 186, 188, 192,[1]1004:
agriculture, 305, 333, 336, 344,
355, 361, 363, 383, 384; Andhra
Pradesh, 362; census, 130; farm
work, 352, 373; industries, 267,
305; Karnataka, 194, 669;
married women, 157; Northern
India, 383; Orissa, 179;
plantation, 305; Punjab, 127;
rural areas, 122, 155, 167, 185,
191; scheduled caste women, 176;
trends, 193; urban areas, 140,
174; Uttar Pradesh, 361
workers, 219, 204, 379; Dharwar, 222;
enumeration, 151; Haryana, 203;
urban, 162
worker's education, 886
working conditions, Madhya Pradesh,
243; Rajasthan, 239
working mothers, 710, 712, 819, 897,
924, 925, 932, 942; attitude, 896
Working Women's Forum, 322, 613,
703, 783, 784, 785, 812, 822, 835,
837
writers, 540, 542; Urdu literature, 541

zardosi workers, 641

Geographical Index

India, agriculture, 343, 357, 384, 389; agricultural labour, 363, 370, 378, 379, 385; dairy workers, 688; development projects, 661, 662, 670, 688; employment, 1, 4, 7, 8, 9, 47, 54, 82, 97, 98, 142, 158, 165, 214, 217, 719; entrepreneurs, 292; forestry, 497; hostels, 726; industrial workers, 242; labour force, 135, 141, 159, 164, 168, 169, 174, 180, 250, 940; legislation, 739, 742, 743; Maternity Benefit Act, 735, 736, 737; nurses, 556, 557, 566, 569; occupations, 199, 207; part-time employment, 55, 59; piece rate workers, 282; political participation, 648, 650; professional women, 195; prostitution, 1076, 1077; scientists, 601; statistics, 139, 141, 142, 165, 364; technological change, 748, 751; textile industry, 633; unemployment, 99, 142, 165; unorganised sector, 139; wages, 98; women workers, 198, 206, 208, 219, 235, 237, 391; women's organisations, 836; women's work, 160, 985, 1032; work participation, 132, 134, 154, 155, 158, 167, 172, 174, 177, 343, 363, 384

Central India, beedi workers, 420

Eastern India, coal miners, 575; tea plantations, 584, 585

Himalayan region, labour force, 1079

North East India, agriculture, 375; matrilineal society, 1106; tribal women, 1006, 1103

North India, agriculture, 383; agricultural labour, 336; rice production, 379; work participation rate, 336, 383

South India, development projects, 938; employment, 89; handicrafts, 517; historical sources, 985; household, 1107; Muslim women, 1107; rice production, 379; textile industry, 1085

States

Andhra Pradesh, agricultural labour, 362, 369; beedi workers, 416; criminals, 892; dairy co-operatives, 446; employment, 6; Maternity Benefit Act, 729; wages, 369; women's organisations, 1099; women's work, 952; work participation, 362
Anantpur District, vocational training, 872

Bellampalli, mine workers, 577
Chittoor District, dairy co-operatives, 449, 450
East Godavary District, agricultural labour, 347
Hyderabad, attitudes of mothers, 893; construction workers, 438; employment, 112; household, 1107; Muslim women, 1107; public sector, 112
Hanumakonda Block, women's organisation, 782
Krishna District, dairy co-operatives, 449, 450
Medak District, agricultural labour, 347
Nagaram, sweepers, 599
Nalgonda District, dairy co-operatives, 449, 450
Narasapur, lace makers, 528, 529, 530, 531, 532
Nellore, agricultural labour, 323
Nizamabad District, beedi workers, 423
Telangana (villages), labour force, 1033
Warangal City, construction workers, 441; tailors, 509
Warangal District, beedi workers, 423
West Godavary District, agricultural labour, 321, 347; labour market discrimination, 108; mukhya sevikas, 455

Arunachal Pradesh, tribal women, 1103

Assam, agricultural labour, 374; employment exchange, 11; tea plantations, 589

Bihar, agricultural mechanisation, 776; grass industry, 675; historical sources, 985; Maternity Benefit Act, 732; tribal movement, 821
Chota Nagpur, Adivasi women, 1027; construction workers, 443
Keonjhar, coal miners, 575
Meghatuburu, coal miners, 575
Patna, construction workers, 442, 443; part-time employment, 17

Ranchi, coal miners, 575; head loaders, 486
Santhal Paraganas, vocational training, 874
Tata Nagar, women workers, 232

Gujarat, agrarian reforms, 341; agriculture, 342; beedi workers, 1090; co-operatives, 801; credit co-operatives, 832; dairy co-operatives, 447, 448; employment, 42; food processing, 492, 495; Khadi and Village Industries, 761; women workers, 264; women's organisations, 809
Ahmedabad, beedi workers, 427; block printers, 428, 429; employment, 229; firewood collection, 1064; nurses, 561; occupational pattern, 229; professional women, 230; textile industry, 625, 628, 637; unorganised workers, 280; wages, 229; women workers, 231
Ahmedabad District, DWCRA, 1093
Bharuch, vocational training, 846
Bhav Nagar, nurses, 561
Mahesana District, handloom industry, 516, 524
Mount Girnar, firewood pickers, 487
Valod, pappad rollers, 580, 581

Haryana, employment, 203; labour force, 210; training, 670
Ambala, vocational training, 845
Rohtak, domestic servants, 467
Sukhomojri, development project, 695

Himachal Pradesh, police women, 399; women's work, 1019
Sirmour District, vocational training, 877

Jammu & Kashmir, co-operatives, 801; handloom industry, 762; vocational training, 860; women's organisations, 809

Karnataka, agarbathi industry, 315;
Appiko, 501; development project,
677, 682, 692; employment, 62,
85; female-headed household,
1102; rural women, 967;
sericulture, 677, 682, 1092; work
participation, 176, 194
Bangalore, sericulture, 335; women's
organisation, 806
Chikamagalur District, DWCRA, 683
Dakshina Kannada, development
projects, 669
Dharwar Taluka, women workers, 222
Kanakpura District, sericulture, 684
Kolar District, sericulture, 335
Mandya District, sericulture, 335
Mysore District, sericulture, 335
Nipani, beedi workers, 415, 424

Kerala, agricultural labour, 377, 1089;
beedi workers, 422, 425; cashew
industry, 432; coir industry, 435,
436, 437; engineers, 604;
fisherwomen, 758; fishing
technology, 756, 757; industrial
workers, 251; occupational
distribution, 211; poor women,
290; sex discrimination, 80;
unorganised women workers,
287, 291; vocational training,
858; women workers, 945
Allepey, domestic workers, 478
Central Kerala, farm work, 352
Mannar, tea plantations, 588
Trivandrum, electronics industry, 482;
housework, 1067; women
workers, 945

Madhya Pradesh, industrial workers, 243;
small-scale industries, 288; textile
industries, 631
Bhopal, women workers, 238
Betul District, forestry, 498; vocational
training, 876
Indore, women earners, 968
Jabalpur, women workers, 197
Maharashtra, agricultural labour, 367;

elections, 652; Employment
Guarantee Scheme, 667, 668,
678; female-headed households,
972; organising women, 817;
political participation, 646; rural
revolt, 824; women in banks, 411
Aurangabad, vocational training needs,
859
Bombay, bank credit, 715; beedi
workers, 414; cooperatives, 801;
domestic workers, 472;
electronics industry, 484;
employment, 84; executives, 544;
food processing, 580, 1085;
garment makers, 511, 512;
household, 1073; industrial
institute, 841; job reservations,
33; pharmaceutical industry, 580;
political participation, 653; poor
women, 1040; street vendors,
612; textile industry, 627, 629,
633; unorganised workers, 285;
women's organisations, 666
Chandrapur District, forestry, 499;
inter-state tassar project, 679
Indoli, elections, 652
Khadgodhra, dairy co-operatives, 454
Kolaba District, vocational training, 863
Nagpur, banks, 714
Poona, domestic servants, 468, 475;
match factory, 553; nurses, 559;
teachers, 618; transporters, 640;
women workers, 929
Raipur, agarbatti industry, 316
Shahada, organising women, 803
Sholapur, teachers, 619
Vidharbha, employed Brahmin women,
931; employment, 78; farm, 78;
textile industry, 624

Manipur, forestry, 503, 505; women
workers, 225
Meghalaya, matrilineal societies, 1106

Orissa, beedi workers, 426; women's
organisations, 809, 825; work
participation, 179

Sundergarh, vocational training, 874

Punjab, agricultural labour, 348; agricultural mechanisation, 750, 773; attitude to women's work, 894, co-operatives, 801; labour force, 127; occupational pattern, 228; police women, 399; sweepers, 595; technological change, 989; women's organisations, 809; women's work, 1019; work participation, 186
Jullunder District, vocational training facilities, 843
Patiala, garment makers, 507
Tejpur, women's organisations, 815

Rajasthan, administrators, 394; bureaucrats, 394; employment, 94; female-headed households, 1106; time allocation, 1051; tribal women, 394; women workers, 239
Jaipur, leisure time, 937
Jodhpur, women workers, 1030
Sikar Village, women's work, 1066

Tamil Nadu, agriculture, 358; agricultural labour, 359, 1089; development projects, 682; employment, 1083; fisherwomen, 489; labour force, 152; leather industry, 536; sericulture, 682, 1094; women's organisations, 809
Chingleput District, agriculture, 358; fisherwomen, 488
Coimbatore, textile industry, 623
Kanyakumari, fisherwomen, 490; vocational training, 873; widows, 949
Madras, credit, 785; household, 1107; idli sellers, 613; Muslim women, 1044, 1107; sales girls, 594; street vendors, 615; unemployment, 113; vegetable vendors, 614

Uttar Pradesh, agricultural labour, 360,

361; Chipko movement, 810; economic contribution of women, 1054; female-headed households, 1102; food processing, 493; grass industry, 506; handloom industry, 521, 522; industrial employment, 34; industrial workers, 257; tea plantations, 586; vocational training, 861
Allahabad, beedi workers, 418
Benaras, sweepers, 600
Faridabad, factory workers, 1038
Jaunsar Bawar, bonded labour, 947
Garhwal, fuel collection, 1072; garment industry, 515
Kanpur, attitudes towards employment, 895; industrial laws, 741; industrial workers, 267; slum women, 981; work participation, 267
Kaval Town, attitudes of working mothers, 896
Kumaon Hills, woollen textile production, 698
Lucknow, beedi workers, 1085; chikan workers, 433; co-operatives, 796; discrimination, 77, 919; employment, 77; leisure, 990; nurses, 570
Mathura, factory workers, 1038
Uttarkhand, Chipko movement, 1100

West Bengal, agricultural labour, 1089; attitudes to employment, 894; employment, 30, 124; export industries, 244; female-headed households, 1102; jute industry, 525, 526; labour force, 12; rice mill technology, 767; tea plantations, 584, 585; textile industry, 639; time allocation of women, 1054; unemployment, 117; women's work, 1014
Bankura District, vocational training, 844

Bholpur Block, artisans, 284
Calcutta, employment, 1028; lifafa
    makers, 276; papad rollers, 276;
    prostitution, 1074; supari cutters,
    276; toy makers, 276; unorganised
    women workers, 277
Haroa, fish head cutters, 495
Malda District, sericulture, 335
Raniganj, coal miners, 574

Union Territories

Chandigarh, attitudes to female
    employment, 905; police women,
    399

Delhi, construction workers, 439, 440,
    443; domestic workers, 471, 481;
employment, 27, 44, 79, 84, 685;
food processing industry, 491,
493; garment makers, 511, 513;
hotel industry, 525; hospital
ayahs, 558; lawyers, 533; lifafa
makers, 579; migrant women,
1020; police women, 408; Post
and Telegraph workers, 395;
professional women, 240;
prostitution, 1075; sales girls,
593; self-employed women, 293;
stone crushers, 611; sweepers,
598; telephone operators, 401,
406; textile industry, 1085;
women workers, 1024; zari
workers, 641

Goa, industrial workers, 274